Signs Are All Around Us

In his latest book, former President Nixon suggests that World War III may have already begun.

English soldier-scholar General Sir John Hackett argues persuasively that World War III is destined for August, 1985.

Current international turmoil, particularly in the Middle East, seems to resonate with biblical prophecies of the end times.

Dire economic forecasts intensify the instability of our times.

What is God's strategy for the end times?

ARMAGEDDON 198?

by
Stephen D. Swihart

aven books
A division of Logos International
Plainfield, N.J. 07060

All Scripture verses are taken from the New American Standard Bible unless otherwise noted as KJV (King James Version).

ARMAGEDDON 198?
Copyright © 1980 by Logos International
All rights reserved
Printed in the United States of America
Library of Congress Catalog Card Number: 80-81381
International Standard Book Number: 0-88270-435-4
Logos International, Plainfield, New Jersey 07060

Dedicated to

The Church of the Living Word,
Who Gave Me the Time, Prayers and
Encouragement for This Work!

TABLE OF CONTENTS

Publisher's Preface ix
Introduction xi

PART I: THE FUTURE—EVERYONE'S CONCERN
1. The Road to Armageddon 3

PART II: EVENTS IN THE NEWS AND IN BIBLE PROPHECY
2. Knowledge in the Last Days 13
3. Mockers in the Last Days 19
4. Crime in the Last Days 29
5. War in the Last Days 33
6. Famine and Pestilence in the Last Days 37
7. Earthquakes in the Last Days 41
8. Christianity in the Last Days 43

PART III: NATIONS IN THE NEWS AND IN BIBLE PROPHECY
9. The World in Biblical Perspective 53
10. Israel 65
11. The Middle East 91
12. Russia 101
13. China 117
14. America 123

PART IV: BEYOND THE NEWS MEDIA
15. The Antichrist 129
16. The Second Coming of Jesus Christ 149
17. Hell 165
18. Heaven 177
19. Getting Ready for the Last Days 185

APPENDIXES
1. Blueprints for the Last Days 193
2. "Last Day" Terminology in the Bible 205
3. Israel's Seventy Weeks 209
4. The Great Holocaust 229
5. The Rapture 245
6. The Kingdom of God 257

PUBLISHER'S PREFACE

The word "Armageddon" is rapidly becoming a household word. Even politicians, statesmen, military leaders, scientists and others employ it to describe the probable cataclysmic events of this decade.

According to Webster, "Armageddon" is defined as being "the place where the last, decisive battle between the forces of good and evil is to be fought. . . ." The Bible refers to this confrontation in the last book of the New Testament, "And he gathered them together into a place called in the Hebrew tongue Armageddon" (Rev. 16:16). More precisely, this ultimate battle will take place on the Plain of Megiddo in northern Israel.

Current events have fixed world attention on the Middle East. People are beginning to wonder, "Are today's developments giving credence to ancient prophecies?" Some even go so far as to suggest that World War III has already begun.

The International Peace Research Committee of Sweden has printed a prediction of atomic war in 1985. The *Chicago Tribune* reported on the committee's prediction in a caption that reads, "Experts See Atomic War by 1985."

A recently published book by General Sir John Hackett is boldly entitled, *The Third World War:*

ARMAGEDDON 198?

August 1985. The author is considered by many to be the foremost soldier-scholar of his time.

These predictions and other signs of the times raise many questions. Has the ominous possibility of a nuclear war become a probability—even a predictable certainty? What is God's plan for the planet Earth? Is there any hope for the future?

Because these questions trouble many of us, I looked for an author who could prepare a comprehensive book on the end times. I discovered some material Steve Swihart had written and was impressed with the depth of his scholarship and the directness and simplicity of his style. I learned he has spent more than six years compiling research on this important topic. Steve is an accomplished author and researcher and I am certain you will find his insightful coverage of the chronology of the last days helpful and challenging. He is the author of *Angels in Heaven and Earth*.

Armageddon 198? will enable you to draw your own conclusions about the nearness of prophetic events. You will learn how to prepare for the crucial days ahead—but more importantly, you will find hope and strength to carry you through.

Dan Malachuk

INTRODUCTION

God Is Speaking

Some people do not believe God exists at all. Therefore, they do not "waste their time" listening for any word from Him. Such persons are called atheists.

Other people do not think it is humanly possible to really know if there is a God. They deem dialogue with any sort of deity a "waste of time." These persons are known as agnostics (from the Greek language, meaning unknowable).

Christians, on the other hand, hold tightly to the conviction that God does exist, that He can be known, and that we are even capable of communicating with Him. This is the bold assertion of the Bible. God is alive, well and speaking with those who will listen.

What Is God Saying?

The first book of the Bible, Genesis, records the dawn of God's plans. This is the great book of beginnings. Here we discover historical firsts such as the creation of the heavens and earth, the beginning of the human race in the Middle East, satanic deception and sin, and the start of the nation of Israel.

The final book of the Bible, the Revelation, records the dusk of God's plans. This is the great book of completions. Here we find historical lasts such as the completion of all hunger, thirst, perspiration, tears, satanic deception, sin, and war.

Between the dawn and the dusk of the Bible there is a progressively detailed saga of God's plans for the people of the planet called earth. Reduced to its simplest form, the everlasting message of the Bible can be stated in this fourfold manner:

    1. *Creation:* God (Father, Son and Spirit) made all that exists.
    2. *Communion:* God created people for fellowship.
    3. *Crisis:* People reject communion with God and choose His wrath.
    4. *Christ:* God offers restoration to communion through Jesus Christ.

This everlasting message is repeated again and again, from start to finish, throughout the Bible. (For example, read Gen. 1-3; Acts 7 and Acts 17:22-28.)

The pivotal thrust of prophecy, therefore, must not centralize on the antichrist, or the great tribulation, or the rapture, or any other man-centered event. The impetus behind predictions is not what is going to happen to planet earth, or when it will occur or how it will transpire. Rather, the momentum of prophecy is the Lord Jesus Christ himself. He is the foundation upon which all is built, and the capstone under which all things have been directed.

The principal intent of this study is to unveil the majesty of God and His Son, Jesus Christ. I trust that the overall context will bring honor and glory to Him alone who is worthy of our study and devotion.

ARMAGEDDON 198?

PART I

THE FUTURE—EVERYONE'S CONCERN

1

The Road to Armageddon

Jeane Dixon Speaks Out

When Jeane Dixon was fourteen years old, she began predicting the future of Hollywood stars. Her success ratio (that is the number of correct foresights against the number of incorrect foresights) soon made her one of the world's most acclaimed prognosticators. Here is a partial itemization of her more famous accurate predictions.

1. She foretold the soon-to-occur deaths of Franklin Delano Roosevelt, Joseph Stalin, Mahatma Gandhi and Martin Luther King. In predicting John F. Kennedy's death she even came up with the number of letters, including the first letter in the name of Kennedy's assassin—"Oswald." Prior to their deaths, she also foresaw the fire that would consume three astronauts in a space capsule on the ground. The assassination of Senator Robert Kennedy was also included in her death list.

2. She predicted that the Korean War would end in a stalemate.

3. She told the world in 1949 that Richard Nixon would someday be elected president. In 1968 she also announced that a wiretapping scandal would hit Washington—three years later it occurred.

ARMAGEDDON 198?

4. She announced that U.S.-China relations would greatly improve.

Jeane Dixon's predictions for the future (the 1980s and beyond) seem to embrace a combination of personal psychic insights with biblical prophecy for the last days. She envisions an aggressive China, the appearance of the antichrist (whom she says was born in the Middle East in 1962), and the Battle of Armageddon, which will involve millions of people.

Parenthetically, it should be noted that although Jeane Dixon's prediction list is not always accurate, it is impressive. What accounts for these phenomenal insights? Is she a prophetess? Does she have a direct line with God himself?

The Bible answers each of these inquiries for us in an astonishing manner. First, according to the Bible, a true prophet or prophetess of God will never err in a prediction—not even one (Deut. 18:21-22). Dixon has been mistaken numerous times. Second, a true spokesperson of God will both believe and declare His Word (Deut. 13:1-11; Gal. 1:6-9). Dixon's views of the Scriptures are far, far removed from acceptable Christian beliefs. (For instance, she thinks she might be the reincarnation of a Tibetan llama!) Third, when the two above points are not in evidence, then the inevitable conclusion, based on what the Bible teaches, is that the psychic party is actually receiving messages from non-biblical sources. There can be little doubt that this is the case with many psychics today. It is certain that God is not the power behind such phenomena as ESP, psychics, clairvoyants, astrologers, mediums, occult seers and fortunetellers (Deut. 18:9).

George Orwell—1984
'George Orwell" is the pseudonym of Eric Arthur

The Road to Armageddon

Blair who wrote a most intriguing and pessimistic book about the future. It is called *1984*. Although the book was published in 1949 (the year before Blair's death), it possesses rare insight into the political structure of many countries today. Some people are seriously convinced that the statements in Orwell's book will actually come true by the year suggested in his title. Here is a list of Orwell's leading descriptions of the world as he imagined it would be in 1984.[1]

1. The world will be divided between three superpowers: Oceania (the Americas, Great Britain, Australia and South Africa); Eurasia (Russia, Europe and Siberia); and Eastasia (China, Japan and Southeast Asia). It is clear that today's world is in fact dominated by three powers—the United States, Russia and China.

2. The three superpowers will be involved in unending warfare, but the arms will be conventional (non-atomic), and the sites of the conflicts will be north and central Africa, the Near East and India. The results will be continued stalemates. The situation described by Orwell is classic. None of the "Big Three" have touched each other, though the lands discussed in *1984* are the object of constant attention and aid from each of these three powers.

3. The actual differences between the "Big Three" are to progressively melt away. That is, government will assume an ever larger degree of control in the private sector. It will become the employer and the provider for the poor. This means, according to Orwell's figures, that 85 percent of the masses will be middle

---

[1] This analysis is adapted from an article entitled, "George Orwell's 1984—How Close Are We?" by Robert Reginald and James Natal in *The People's Almanac #2* (Bantam Books, 1978).

ARMAGEDDON 198?

class workers; 2 percent will be the rich governmental controllers; and 13 percent will enforce the laws of the government.

In Russia today only a very few reside on the upper crust of society, and these are largely government officials. The only road to success in Russia is a strict adherence to the party line. (Interestingly, only a small percentage of the Russian people are actually members of the Communist Party.) In China, which is a little less rigid in its party line requirements, only 20-30 percent of the people live outside Orwell's "mindless, middle class" category. In America, which is the least rigid, there is still a trend in this direction. Presently, 20 percent of the American population earns over 50 percent of the country's income and exercises control over 75 percent of the nation's goods.

4. The method for controlling the people in Oceania by 1984, says Orwell, is through constant surveillance through two-way telescreens. Today, through the rapid spread of the cable television system, it is actually possible to reproduce this effect with remarkable ease. Exterior monitoring devices are also being suggested and experimented with in connection with police and security officials. Computer-controlled videotape cameras and alarms can be installed atop buildings in order to survey masses of people. Suspicious activities can be zoomed in on for close-up pictures.

5. Educational literature, especially history, will be rewritten in order to achieve the desired effects of the government. The aim, declares Orwell, is to generate a dependency upon and a love for "Big Brother," the symbolic head of the nation. Russia has rewritten history with this aim in mind. She claims unsupported credit for numerous inventions (including the airplane

and television). She also asserts that Russia was the victor in World War II, leaving the United States out of the picture almost altogether. In China, many literary works have been rewritten in order to appeal to the current leader's ambitions. In America the press is much freer, though history books do reveal changes in attitudes and approaches (for instance, see past and present articles on the American Indian and Japan).

There are other parallels between Orwell's *1984* and the present world, but this listing is sufficient. Whether *1984* represents some bitterness from the author's diverse—and sometimes negative—experiences in life (he was a policeman in Burma, a soldier in the Spanish Republican Army, an editor of a Socialist newspaper, and a lifelong victim of tormenting tuberculosis), or whether Orwell actually envisioned these events as inevitable, is uncertain. But this one thing is clear—the threats suggested in *1984* are not altogether fiction. Some of the conditions he described are more factual and prophetic than we might desire to admit.

Biblical Signs for the Last Days

Whatever fantasies may reside in the predictions of a popular psychic or in the latest science fiction thriller, there is a sudden and solemn shift in attitude when we pick up the Bible and read how it foretells the end of the present world.

When you want to know where you are or where you are going, you look at a map. But if you want to know where the world is or where it is going, then you must look at the prophetic signs in the Bible.

Prophetic signs from the Bible have been used and abused by prophetic teachers. Here are some safeguards that ought to be observed in understanding the nature of these last day indicators.

1. *Some of the signs are general in nature.* These particular signs show forth the intensification of natural types of phenomena (such as famines, crimes, earthquakes, etc.). Since the crucifixion of Christ, each generation has asserted that its particular era marked the fulfillment of these natural signs, so we must guard against any date-setting techniques based solely upon these markers.

A primary example of how *not* to interpret these signs comes to us from the episodes surrounding the teachings of William Miller. Mr. Miller had studied prophecy carefully for several years when he came to the conclusion, based upon prophetic signs (various ones of the *general* variety), that the world would come to an end on April 3, 1843. His followers, numbering in the thousands, followed him up some hills in New England in order to await Christ's return in the clouds. According to Miller, the world would be destroyed by fire. But nothing happened. Miller wisely concluded that his calculations were a little off, but he unwisely set a new date for the same event. This time it was to be March 22, 1844, but, again, he was wrong. Undaunted, however, Miller set another date; this one would be for the Battle of Armageddon. He set the time for October 22, 1844. It fizzled out too. Miller then refrained from setting specific dates, though his convictions were still persuasive enough to start a religious body that is with us today: Seventh-Day Adventists.

2. *Some signs are specific in nature.* These signs are unique because they go beyond the natural order of events and into an elaborately detailed and sequential

arrangement of precise activities (the regathering of the Jews to Israel, the uniting of ten nations into an alliance and so forth). As such, their appearance (or occurrence) and nonappearance (or nonoccurrence) are much more easily discerned. It is from these signs that the nearness of the "last days" is better ascertained.

PART II

EVENTS IN THE NEWS AND IN BIBLE PROPHECY

2

Knowledge in the Last Days

The Increase of Knowledge

Between 1900 and 1950, accumulated knowledge doubled. Between 1950 and 1965, knowledge doubled again. And between 1965 and 1975, it doubled once more! How can an individual keep abreast of the developments in every field?

The Bible predicts that near *"the time of the end [just prior to the return of Jesus Christ to this earth] . . . knowledge shall be increased"* (Dan. 12:4 KJV).[1] The truth of these words could be no more real than they are today.

Seventy-five percent of all the scientists who ever lived are alive today. Presently, 35,000 scientific journals are published annually.

According to Dr. Malcolm Todd, President of the American Medical Association in 1975, about 50 per-

---

[1] Commentators have offered varying interpretations for this passage. Some contend that the "knowledge" referred to here is only of a religious or prophetic nature. They understand the running "to and fro" (KJV) to be an act of the eyes, which sweep God's Word for insights about the last days. Other scholars follow the approach used above. Neither interpretation, however, needs to be held in such a way that it will exclude the other. Both answers will be evidenced in the last days.

ARMAGEDDON 198?

cent of all our medical knowledge is outdated every ten years. Of all the medicines in use today, 75 percent of them have been created since World War II.

Perhaps the most astonishing creation in recent years has been the invention and development of the computer. These electronic machines are absolutely incredible. Sophisticated models can store 70 million units of information on a square inch. They can perform 60 billion transactions per second!

In the very near future minicomputers will be as available to the common buyer as the calculator is today. Virtually every home is expected to have them. Models are now available that perform a number of household duties in response to either a programed schedule or an audible command. These computers are also capable of responding with a simulated voice.

In 1948 a scholarly scientific journal stated that placing a person on the moon would require so much new knowledge that it might be another 200 years before any attempt would ever be made. But on July 20, 1969, just twenty-one years later, the so-called impossible feat was accomplished. Today's advancements in science and technology are practically incalculable.

Someone has estimated that there are so many new facts discovered and developed each year that it would take a full lifetime for a person to read them all, even if he devoted forty hours per week to the project. That is incredible.

Today, more than 50 percent of high school graduates enter college. Twenty years ago the figure was less than 25 percent. Also, in the past twenty years the number of total institutions of higher education has increased from 1,850 to nearly 3,100. Additionally, the average enrollment has doubled. About 50,000 students are declined entrance to colleges annually.

Knowledge is one of the top priorities in almost every nation of the world. You cannot deal competently in our complex and technological world without a high-rated education. Belgium takes this note so seriously that children start school there at the age of three. Most countries require schooling of their citizens, starting usually no later than at age six. Also, the majority of the countries of the world require their children to remain in school for at least nine years. No nation in the world today can afford to neglect this most vital asset.

The old League of Nations building in Geneva, Switzerland, is now the house of the International Bureau of Education. It works chiefly as a statistical and advisory board. Also in Geneva is the International School, where over 1,600 students from more than sixty countries make up the student body. Stress is placed here upon an international understanding of people and events. In 1970 the United Nations designated its twenty-fifth year of existence as the International Education Year—with an aim of promoting higher ethics in teaching and in advancing the cause of international peace.

China has set a goal of becoming a fully modern nation by the year 2000. In order to reach this target she has made new educational policies. China wants 30 percent of its young students to enter universities and to learn the latest knowledge (which, by the way, will be supplied by the United States).

Russia has no desire to be behind in the field of knowledge. According to statistics for the period near the close of the seventies, Russia had 45,000,000 elementary and secondary school students (the U.S. had

ARMAGEDDON 198?

49,000,000), and 5,000,000 university and technical school students (the U.S. had 11,000,000). Nearly 19 percent of this initial number stay in school through high school (36 percent do so in America). There are 861 institutions of higher learning in Russia (3,047 in the U.S.). They spend nearly $30 billion annually on education (the U.S. spends $144 billion). Russia has a literacy rate of 99.7 percent (the U.S. rate is 99 percent).

The Inadequacy of Knowledge
Apparently, in the last days the quest for and discovery of new knowledge will not find full satisfaction. The high degree of intensive and extensive research will not culminate in answers to the age-old inquiries of mankind: "Where did I come from?" "Why am I here?" "Where am I going?"

Nearly 2,000 years ago the apostle Paul wrote, "*Realize this, that in the last days difficult times will come. For men will be . . . always learning and never able to come to the knowledge of the truth*" (2 Tim. 3:1-2, 7).

Truth is everybody's business. It is the bond that unites and liberates, the light that discovers and challenges, the sword that separates and judges. You cannot live a meaningful or secure life around anything else.

Jesus said, "*I am the truth*" (John 14:6). No one can live a full life until he comes to Jesus. The world is full of hypothetical truths, partial truths and total lies. Only in knowing Jesus can anyone draw a line between the spurious and the known, the fallacious and the facts.

During the final days of modern civilization these

Knowledge in the Last Days

statements will be pressed into us more and more. Science and technology do not hold the keys to the questions that probe our deepest sense of being. These answers can only come through a personal and penetrating devotion to the source of all truth, Jesus Christ.

The "god of this world" (2 Cor. 4:4), the god who instills within people the desire to begin a pursuit for incomplete truths and temporal fulfillments, is none other than Satan. It is he who distorts the picture of creation, cause and effect, and the consummation of life as we know it. He is behind the humanistic thrust of education. He is the author of godless (or semi-godless) evolution. These are his lies, and he desires that you believe them until you die. But truth is to be found by resisting his hold, and by reading the Bible, God's own story of what is really the truth—the truth about people, life, purpose, fulfillment and eternal existence. May I suggest the book of Romans and the Gospel of John for openers. You just might be surprised at what you find!

3

Mockers in the Last Days

There is an Arabian Proverb that goes like this:

> He who knows, and knows he knows—
> He is wise—follow him.
> He who knows, and knows not he knows—
> He is asleep—wake him.
> He who knows not, and knows not he knows not—
> He is a fool—shun him.
> He who knows not, and knows he knows not—
> He is a child—teach him.

In the last days there will be many people who know not, and do not know that they know not. In fact, according to the Scriptures, they will even further display their ignorance by scoffing and mocking the truth.

The Contemporary Scene

The Bible declares, *"In the last days mockers will come with their mocking, following after their own lust"* (2 Pet. 3:3; cf. Jude 18).

The key point this Scripture makes is that people, in general, will be consumed with their own appetites and interests in the last days. There will be little sympathy toward the Bible's message because people's

ARMAGEDDON 198?

desires will be going in another direction. The result of this misguided affair with personal lusts (or strong desires for the world's possessions and pleasures) is a scornful attitude for the purity of Christian doctrines and holy living. Here are but a few contemporary signs that display the widespread influence of this attitude in our own hour.

1. *The Influence of Television:* Television is on for forty-five hours a week in the average American home. Mom watches it for thirty-one hours, dad for twenty-five hours and the kids for twenty-six hours. The average American child spends more time in front of television than in the schoolroom. Studies reveal that these massive dosages of television viewing are creating passive audiences who want everything in life to be easy, a push-button existence.

The first television was invented by John L. Baird in London, England. The date was October 30, 1925. Baird used piano wire, darning needles, hatboxes, glue, string, an electric motor, lenses, and whatever else seemed appropriate, in order to make the initial set. The first person to be televised was a fifteen-year-old named William Taynton—Baird had to pay the boy to sit in front of the bright lights and transmitter. We have come a long way since these unusual origins.

Some people contend that television has done more to change our life styles and beliefs than anything else in the world. In North America alone there are more than 570 television sets for every 1,000 people (that means many families own two or three sets). If you placed all of these televisions end to end, it has been estimated that they would circle the earth at least

Mockers in the Last Days

twice. That is a lot of sets. And there are millions more in the rest of the world too.

With increasingly liberal sex presentations and gross violence on the tube, it is not difficult to measure the negative effects caused by television. This advice from the Bible seems to be the best overall guideline for what our eyes should be permitted to see: *whatever is true . . . honorable . . . right . . . pure . . . lovely . . . of good repute . . . let your mind dwell on these things* (Phil. 4:8).

2. *The Smoking Habit:* On September 28, 1904, the first woman was arrested in New York City for smoking in public. In a few short years the tide of public opinion was to reverse itself. Every day 4,000 more teen-agers join the smoking habit—that is 1.4 million annually. The American Cancer Society has spent over $5 million on campaigns to reduce the rise in this habit. An estimated 55,000,000 Americans smoke daily. According to medical statistics some 300,000 people die prematurely each year because of smoking-related illnesses. The number of female smokers is now equal to the number of male smokers.

The habit is by no means restricted to youth or to the United States. In fact, America, as a whole, ranks a little below the average number of smokers in other countries. Here the percentage of smokers is approximately 37 percent; in the Netherlands it is almost 60 percent. (Holland has the worst record in the world.) Most other countries average between 30 percent and 45 percent.

An alien from outer space is said to have returned to his planet with this report: "The earth people have an odd practice. They light a fire at the end of a poisonous

ARMAGEDDON 198?

substance and then suck the smoke into their bodies. This results in sickness and death. The habit is also expensive. Strange, those earth people!"

3. *The Alcoholic Syndrome:* Alcohol is another major problem. According to the National Clearinghouse for Alcohol Information, 70 percent of all schoolchildren in the junior high and high school ages drink—10 percent are literal alcoholics. Little wonder, with adults heavily engaged in drinking, that this is called the nation's number-one problem.

Since 1945 each state has passed laws to create agencies that will deal exclusively with the problems caused by alcohol. Over 9,000,000 Americans have problems "holding their liquor." The growth rate for alcoholics among women is now greater than it is among men.

According to international statistics, the drinking of alcoholic beverages is a common practice and problem nearly everywhere. The West Germans drink most heavily, consuming nearly 400 pints of alcohol (including beer, wine and spirits) per person, per year. (The statistics are based upon the total population, over and against the total consumption; which means that the consumption by those actually drinking will represent a much higher figure, possibly as much as three times higher!) Elsewhere in the world, the figures are staggeringly high. The country with the lowest figures is Japan, with an average of about eighty pints per person, per year. In America that figure is about 220 pints.

Laws are odd sometimes. Someone has made this observation: we license a tavern to teach vice and then tax people for schools to teach virtue. We license a man

Mockers in the Last Days

to make drunken paupers and then tax sober men to take care of them. We license a bartender to sell that which will make a man drunk and then punish the man for being drunk!

4. *Drug Addiction:* The dependency of many persons on the use of drugs may indicate our problem of pleasure-seeking too. The use of marijuana is now widely accepted. Some 43 million Americans have tried the drug, while 16 million are regular users. Nine percent of all high school seniors use the drug daily—this is higher than the percentage who use alcohol. About 15 percent of all auto accidents are attributed to marijuana intoxication. Finally, on the national scene, America is officially the largest user of hard drugs—over half a million people are narcotic addicts (and this includes only the known addicts).

Fifteen to twenty years ago you would rarely hear or read about drug abuse. Today it is one of society's ugliest and most difficult-to-solve dilemmas. On May 1, 1971, the Comprehensive Drug Abuse Prevention and Control Act went into effect. Subsequent to this decision a number of other federal and state laws were enacted in order to research, prevent, treat and rehabilitate the drug habit and the drug user. Today, the drug dilemma is a billion-dollar annual project. And with the relative ease in securing drugs, coupled with the weakness in the laws against drug abuse, it seems destined to become a still greater threat in the days ahead.

Drugs are also an international problem. In England nearly 500,000 people are drug addicts. The figures for West Germany are 400,000; Australia has nearly 200,000; and France, with incomplete records, shows

ARMAGEDDON 198?

100,000 on drugs. There are very few nations that can claim immunity from the drug problem. Elaborate plans and millions of dollars have been utilized in order to stop the flow of drugs to reach the American homeland. But thus far these efforts are estimated at being only 10-15 percent successful. And if this statistic is not deplorable enough, this one is—only 2 percent of those treated in special hospitals designed to help people on hard drugs are actually delivered. It must be noted, however, that an organization known as Teen Challenge, with a number of centers around the United States, has an 80 percent success ratio! This is a Christian organization under the leadership of David Wilkerson, and it has an amazing story worth far more publicity than it receives. The bottom line is this: science, as good as it is, cannot usually cure a drug addict; the answer is a personal relationship with Jesus Christ. These kinds of statistics compel this sort of conclusion!

Art Linkletter has been asked why he condemns drugs when he has not tried them himself. His answer is classic: "The greatest obstetricians in the world have never been pregnant."

5. *Teen-age Pregnancies, Abortions and Prostitution:* Teen-age pregnancies are increasing at a record-breaking rate (about one million annually), especially among girls between the ages of nine and fifteen. One out of five births today involves teen-age parents. One out of three abortions is performed on teen-age girls. According to surveys, 60 percent of all teen-agers favor premarital sex. Such facts should not alarm us then that over 600,000 teen-age boys become unwed fathers **annually.**

Mockers in the Last Days

Iceland, on June 28, 1935, became the first nation in the world to legalize abortion for pregnancies that jeopardize the mother's mental or physical health. Today, in America, there are an estimated 1.5 million "legal" abortions annually. (Of the women having abortions, 75 percent are unmarried; 67 percent are white; and 66 percent are under the age of twenty-five.) In 1976, in Washington D.C., there were more abortions than live births!

Just recently U.S. Judge John F. Dooling, Jr. handed down a 329-page ruling that will require the federal government, through its Medicaid program, to pay for "medically necessary" abortions. This ruling will affect potentially 3 million women each year. The case will now go to the Supreme Court for a final ruling. Pro-abortionists are naturally optimistic. Anti-abortionists are angry.

The focus of the debate, incredible as it seems, is largely placed upon the "rights" of the one seeking the abortion, the mother. But what about the "rights" of the infant baby? Some contend that "life" does not actually begin at conception, but at some unknown later time (as if to say at the start you only have busy little, multiplying cells, which at some point in time—presto—turn into a real-life baby). This argument should be rejected as being first class dumbness. The Scriptures are plain in stating that life starts at the moment of conception; common sense confirms this as well. (Read Psalm 139 especially verses 13-16 for details.)

Some 15 million sex magazines are sold monthly, while 100,000 girls become prostitutes. Rome had the same problem, and it fell from within.

ARMAGEDDON 198?

In England the attitude toward sex is much the same as in America—so are its sex statistics. There can be no doubt about the fact that sex attitudes have gone liberal, and that much of the world is tasting the effects of this change. Actually, the so-called "new morality" is nothing more than the "old immorality"!

6. *Common Law Marriages and Divorce:* Originally, brides wore veils in order to protect themselves from the evil eye of a jealous man; rice was thrown so that the couple might be blessed with sexual and financial prosperity; and a ring was worn on the third finger because it was believed that in this finger was a vein that ran directly to the heart. These are familiar customs with unfamiliar meanings. Today, many are finding the whole wedding package to be a waste of time, money and meaning. According to Census Bureau figures, more than 1.3 million unmarried people are living together. It seems that a morality of pleasure-before-ethics has taken over our life styles.

The divorce rate is also staggering. The ratio of marriage to divorce in the United States is 2.3 to 1—the second worst record in the world. The most horrible record is Sweden's ratio of 1.7 to 1. Denmark is not far behind with a 2.5 to 1 ratio. In Canada, Austria, Switzerland and West Germany the ratio is 4 to 1. Only in Italy is there a longer lived marital bond (probably due to the strong Catholic view against divorce) where the ratio is 26 to 1.

The Russians are so alarmed at their divorce rate that they are now adding sex education courses in school for students aged fifteen through seventeen. Their aim is to make the sexual drive appear as late in the individual's life as possible. In the divorce scene, one out of three Russians are breaking the marital bond—one-sixth end their marriage during the first ninety days of marriage. One out of ten children born in Russia is born to an unwed parent. Adultery is seen as being a major problem in this communistic state.

7. *The Homosexual/Lesbian Snare:* America is a nation with twenty million homosexuals/lesbians (or gays). At one time in our not-too-far past this act was considered a crime punishable by law. Today, however, it is generally accepted as a new life style. Across the land are bathhouses for homosexuals, where they can meet and have "relationships." In San Francisco, with a population of 680,000, some 120,000 are gays. Approximately 28 percent of all voters in the city are believed to be homosexuals.

A few years ago no one would have even discussed this subject. Today, however, the gays are even publishing their own newspapers and magazines. They are also actively involved in passing laws in order to protect their sexual rights. But American trends are not as bad as some countries. In the Netherlands, for instance, nearly 60 percent of the people there see nothing wrong with this practice. American and Canadian figures are closer to fourteen percent on this subject. In England, one out of forty-five women are, supposedly, lesbian.

If you want God's view regarding homosexuality/lesbianism, here is an easily understood declaration: *"If there is a man who lies with a male as those who lie with a woman, both of them have committed a detestable act; they shall surely be put to death"* (Lev. 20:13). It might be argued that this is an outdated quotation from the Old Testament; God has changed His mind now. No.

ARMAGEDDON 198?

The New Testament says essentially the same thing. Read it yourself—Romans 1.

The Eternal Solution

There is pleasure in sin—the Bible agrees with this fact (Heb. 11:25). But the Bible also says, *"the wages of sin is death"* (Rom. 6:23). That is a pretty high price for having "fun."

There is a peculiar notion adrift that in the world there is *fun*, but in the church there is *faith*. What a contrast—as if to say that the dullest spot around is in God's presence or among His straight and narrow people! No greater lie could be concocted by men or demons. That is not to say that life is always a bowl of cherries for every Christian. It is not—everyone's cherries have pits in them. But at least the Christian anticipates the pits, knows how they got there, and understands how to remove them without a lot of fuss.

There *is* joy in being a Christian. In fact, the people who know the greatest depths of sustained joy are sincere Christians. And they will *not* lose it in the "last days"!

4

Crime in the Last Days

The Visible Fruit

Every country in the world has a prisoner population. What you may not realize is that the United States has nearly twice as many apprehended criminals as any other country in the world. There are some 400,000 inmates in jails around America—that is a ratio of 189 "bad" guys for every 100,000 supposedly "good" guys. The prison growth rate has grown so rapidly that building jails has become one of America's fastest growing industries. In the 1970s some 524 prisons, at a cost of $4 billion, were constructed.[1]

The highest number of police officers for any country

---

[1] Until fairly recently (about the last half of the nineteenth century) jails were *not* used for holding prisoners *after* being convicted. Instead, they were used to confine the accused party *prior* to his or her trial. At the conclusion of the trial a financial or physical sentence was rendered. No one returned to a jail cell. Today, however, this process has been largely reversed—physical retribution is gone, fines are small, and jail terms are prolonged.

The present aim of many penal administrations is rehabilitation. The very name "penitentiary" is derived from the belief or hope that confinement, plus contemplation, will result in "penitence." Thus far the idea has proven to be more ideal than real. Nevertheless, numerous reforms have been (and are being) inaugurated to protect the "rights" of prisoners, and to enable them to receive more personalized help.

ARMAGEDDON 198?

(in proportion to its population) is France. She employs over 450 policemen per 100,000 inhabitants. Next in line is Austria, with nearly 330 police per 100,000 citizens. Then comes Italy with 323, Canada with 280, Belgium with 263 and America with 250.

Presently over 300 crimes are committed each hour in America, despite a fairly high number of policemen. In France there about 275 offenses hourly. Apparently the presence of added police does little to actually curb criminal acts.

In our nation's capital some appalling facts of so-called justice have now been made public. In a study of more than 7,000 felony arrests, 64 percent of the cases were dropped, and only 7 percent ended up with convictions. Of those convicted of murder, 50 percent went free; those convicted of rape, 71 percent were set free; for robbery, 66 percent were released; and for burglary, 53 percent were let go. These kinds of statistics are not unique. Is it any wonder that criminals are practically encouraged to continue their illegal practices?

The Bible says, *"In the last days difficult times will come. Evil men and impostors will proceed from bad to worse"* (2 Tim. 3:1, 13; cf. Matt. 24:10, 12).

In America the rise in crime is 11 percent greater than the rise in population. Street crime costs U.S. citizens between $50-75 billion annually.

Lawlessness can take the form of activities other than street crimes, of course. Possibly the most noticeable are crimes of the executive variety. Taxpayers pay between $50-200 billion annually on "white-collar" crimes alone. Corruption is so rampant that articles in national magazines routinely reveal the deplorable state of affairs.

One study reveals that of nearly 600 major U.S.

Crime in the Last Days

corporations, some 60 percent of them have been charged with violations of at least five laws. In other words, breaking the law is more common than keeping it! And with the advent of the computer, it is becoming harder and harder to detect white-collar crimes. Further, very, very few executives, if convicted, actually end up going to jail. The usual result is a relatively insignificant fine. Those who cry "injustice!" in the courtroom are not altogether without a good case.

Today, America records over 300 serious crimes every hour of the day and night. Italy, with a population that is one-half that of the United States, reports nearly 150 serious offenses hourly. These are the leaders in daily violations of the laws, but no country can show off its criminal record with any justifiable degree of pride. Wherever there are people, there are crimes. Perhaps the safest place to live is Norway. There are less than ten murders or attempted murders reported there each year. In the United States that number exceeds 18,000!

The Invisible Root

Dr. James Q. Wilson, a Harvard University political scientist, states that after tracing crime statistics back to 1830, he has found there is always a rise in crime when spiritual and family ties falter.

Let us permit these words to sink deeply inside each one of us. They are worth pondering. The direct link between the depths of crime and the shallowness of spirituality is a certainty. Without Jesus Christ living His life in the spirits of numerous occupants of this planet, the human race would probably have annihilated itself long ago.

Prisons reform virtually no one. They cannot. Only

ARMAGEDDON 198?

Jesus Christ can truly reform a person and give him a new life. A jail cell cannot transform a hardened heart into a pure and gentle one. This act belongs to God alone. The need is not more and better prisons, but instead the need is more and better chaplains of the gospel of Jesus Christ.

If you want to solve the visible problem of crime, then you must strike at the root of the moral problem—sin. The need is not education—smart folks can be crooked too. The need is not finances—rich people are often corrupt. The need is a spiritual rebirth. Unless a person surrenders to Jesus Christ, he or she will always be a ripe candidate for temptation to break the laws.

Examine the jail population for a moment. How many entered these institutions being devout Christians? (Notice, I did *not* say, "How many went there with a faith in God," but how many went through the doorway being a *devout follower of Christ*?) You probably won't find a handful in the entire nation. Why? Because Jesus Christ makes people into better people, and into better citizens. It is just that simple!

5

War in the Last Days

Wars in the World

"Peace is rare. Less than 8 percent of the time since the beginning of recorded time has the world been entirely at peace. In a total of 3,530 years, 286 have been warless. Eight thousand treaties have been broken in this time" (*Personal Journal*).

Jesus predicted that right up until the final hour there would be *"wars and rumors of wars"* (Matt. 24:6-7; cf. Rev. 6:1-8). The eternal optimists who believe that people will eventually evolve into creatures of peace had better look at the nature of the human species more closely. As long as people are people, there will always be the real threat of war.

The Soviet Union spends over $110 billion on "defense" programs. The same amount is spent by the United States for the same purpose. Each year the costs are soaring upwards.

According to Rear Admiral Gene R. LaRocque, of the American Center for Defense Information in Washington, America possesses 30,000 nuclear weapons. Some 15,000 are located in the United States and ready for launching. Another 7,000 are placed in strategic areas around Europe. The remainder are scattered throughout the Pacific.

ARMAGEDDON 198?

A panel of nuclear arms experts from Harvard and MIT recently published these grim conclusions. They feel that by the year 1999 the world will either have seen nuclear war or it will have submitted to an authoritarian international government in order to avert such a possible holocaust.

It is doubtful that the world's superpowers (the United States, Russia and China) will start a nuclear war. But with the rapid production and spread of nuclear weapons, it is not hard to imagine that a small nation like Israel, Egypt, Syria, Pakistan, Iran, Iraq, or some other small and frustrated nation, might be seriously tempted to perform such an attack.

Within a short time—by 1985—it is estimated that fifty countries will be able to produce their own nuclear hardware! At this incredible rate of development, the threat of nuclear war is no idle notion.

By 1999, some 1,000 large nuclear reactors will be operative around our tiny globe. This means the possible production of over 50,000 nuclear bombs by the end of our century.

A "small" nuclear war could immediately obliterate 1,000,000 lives. A "large" nuclear war could as easily destroy the entire population of several continents!

Professor George Wald, Nobel Prize winner and Harvard biologist, estimates that there are presently enough nuclear and thermonuclear warheads to equal ten tons of TNT for every man, woman and child in the world today.

Physicist Alan Munn believes that there is sufficient power in the world to entirely obliterate the human race in two to three minutes!

According to many military experts, the Cruise Missile is the most feared weapon of modern history. Skim-

War in the Last Days

ming along the ground at 30 feet, rising and falling according to the nature of the terrain, this missile can accomplish as much or more than the B-1 bomber.

As if this wasn't enough, recently the "death ray" has been created. By mounting this device to an aircraft, it is able to actually melt anything on the surface of the ground within a seventy-five-mile range.

Supposedly the United States is spending $2 billion annually to advance its "kill" technology. Presently developed is a laser-beam gun that can track down fighter planes and cut them in two.

Some of the irony in all this mess of weapons, war and peace is to be found in our negotiations with foreign countries. Take for instance the prolonged talks of the United States with Israel and Egypt. At first we might ask the cause for the U.S. involvement at all. But when you look beneath the surface it becomes quite clear. The United States is currently supporting Israel and Egypt with over $3 billion in annual foreign aid! Sadat and Begin want the flow to stay open. It should also be noted that at the heart of these peace negotiations are war weapons—over $3 billion worth. These countries want massive aid to beef up their defenses—in case of war!

From a Chicago UPI source we learn that the government has recently filmed a series of five fifteen-minute video tapes telling you what to do in the event of a nuclear holocaust. If it must ever be shown, it may well be the last movie you will see.

Wars in the Heart

Let us turn for a moment from the telescopic, the universal, and the general. Let us pursue a more specific and individualistic look at the source of all wars.

ARMAGEDDON 198?

Nations do not go to war; people do. Countries do not fight; people do. The most fundamental element, often overlooked in the study of wars, is the primary factor—people. More specifically, the hearts of people contain the root causes for killings.

The ideology of a nation has never hurt anyone, no matter how different it was from any other nation's beliefs. It is the attitude of individual people who decide the fate of a nation's people. Individuals can either make war or peace. It is a matter of the heart.

James, the half brother of Jesus Christ, gives to us this truth. He writes, *"From whence come wars and fightings among you? come they not hence, even of your lusts"* (James 4:1 KJV).

Wars are not international; instead, they are interpersonal. It is one person's lust in conflict with another person's. This is the source of each war. We quarrel, fight, and kill because our hearts are greedy! We want more!

The extent to which our hearts will mislead us can be frightening. Our lust for things—whether tangible or intangible—can be extremely strong. We must see this snare of ours. Our problem is within us.

Before we can expect nations to calm down, we must see their people (that is, the hearts of people) respond in a nonlustful manner. The Bible tells us that this state is achievable, but that it is only reached through a personal surrender to the lordship of Jesus Christ. Peace in the world is possible because the peace that comes from knowing Christ is personal. But until people genuinely receive Jesus Christ, there will be wars and rumors of wars.

People (and nations) usually find what they are looking for in life. If you go looking for trouble, you will surely discover it. But if you will go seeking peace, you can find it, too!

6

Famine and Pestilence in the Last Days

The planet called earth has been hit by innumerable natural disasters, but the two most sweeping and fatal attacks upon the human species have come through famines and pestilences.

These two common foes have been traced as far back as written records exist. The tremendous advance of technology has not caused their march to cease. The current situation is practically critical in these areas, and the future looks less than optimistic.

Jesus said that in the last days there would be "plagues [or pestilences] and famines" (Luke 21:11; cf. Rev. 6:5-8). Few prophetic words from Jesus have a greater visible impact for us who live in the last generation of the twentieth century.

The Reality of Famines

When Jesus lived on this earth there was a worldwide population of about 500 million. In the next 2,000 years the population doubled. Twenty years later it doubled again. Today the earth is the residence of 4½ billion people, with 9,200 being added every hour! By the year 2,000 the earth's population will be 7 billion!

Lester Brown, a food and population expert, believes

ARMAGEDDON 198?

that our overpopulated planet may be on the verge of overburdening its natural resources. The lack of food is our number-one immediate problem in the world.

During the entire eighteenth century an estimated 10 million people died of hunger. In the nineteenth century that figure rose to 25 million. In 1970 alone, 10 million persons starved to death! Five years later the count was at 30 million. Today the number is closer to 60 million, or 157,000 each day! One-fourth of the world's population is always hungry, and one-tenth is on the brink of starvation.

One eminent scientist feels that the food-versus-population situation is so critical that unless something is done immediately, there will be no modern civilization in another thirty to fifty years! When the population doubles in the next twenty-five years, our food production must also double. Otherwise, news about massive famines will be a daily occurrence.

The Reality of Pestilence

With famine comes pestilence or disease. And more people have died from these two enemies of the human race than from any other cause!

The terrible bubonic plague/Black Death (A.D. 1347-1351) swept Asia and Europe like a tidal wave, leaving the stench of death nearly everywhere. It is believed this plague originated in China, and then was spread to Europe by rodents. Rats spread the disease to fleas. The fleas bit people, depositing the germ into the bloodstream. The result was a painful inflammation of the lymph glands, accompanied by large lumps and black welts. An estimated 4,000,000 people died from this pestilence. That is between one-fourth and one-third of the existing population for the entire world during that era!

Famine and Pestilence in the Last Days

When an epidemic of influenza struck the United States at the close of World War I, some 500,000 people died as a result. This number is nearly ten times higher than the fatalities caused by direct combat with German soldiers during that war. The total loss in lives around the world from this "bug" has been set at between 25 and 50 million people!

Through research, a number of our worst pestilences of the past have been practically eliminated (for instance, polio and smallpox). Still, new and unexplained diseases are almost constantly arising. The Asian flu of 1957, for example, though it took relatively few lives, spread faster and farther than any disease known in previous history. Today, the United Nations is concerned about the fact that a deadly poison could be carried from animals in one nation across the globe, through jet transportation, and deposited in another continent in just a matter of hours.

Another Angle

Lest someone become overly weary from this gloomy forecast and resign themselves to a state of despair, let us also hear these positive comments:

1. While the severity of famine and pestilence to individuals cannot be overstated, its global dimensions can be somewhat exaggerated. Jesus did *not* predict worldwide calamity through these diseases. Instead, He said they would appear "in various places" (Luke 21:11). This scope must be kept in its proper perspective.

2. There are a number of agencies, including Christian organizations, that are specifically devoted to helping people who suffer from these natural ailments.

ARMAGEDDON 198?

While their efforts are not adequate to meet the enormous needs, their labors do benefit millions of otherwise helpless people. The Church of Jesus Christ can (and should!) be partners with those groups directly involved in aiding people who are less fortunate than ourselves. Several of these organizations and groups are active in presenting the gospel of salvation, while at the same time ministering to the physical needs of the people. This is sound evangelism, deserving of our prayerful and financial support. Ask your pastor about agencies that reach out to meet both the physical and spiritual needs of such persons.

3. While the threats of famine and pestilence evoke a penetrating fear, this adverse emotion need never dominate the Christian's mind or heart. The sincere believer recognizes that God's promises are always greater than earth's perils! For the Christian, then, it is faith (and not fear) that controls his emotions. God guarantees He will work all things together for good to them who love Him. This potent promise from God surpasses the problems of this world. Read these passages for some rich and practical insights: Romans 8:28-39; Philippians 4:11-13, 19; and Hebrews 11:1-40.

7

Earthquakes in the Last Days

Earthquakes have been called the most frightening of all natural disasters. Jesus predicted the occurrence of "great earthquakes" near the end (Luke 21:11). Seismologists are in accord that today massive earthquakes happen with a greater degree of frequency than ever before.

It has been estimated that 1,000,000 earthquakes occur somewhere in the world every year (an average of more than 2,500 per day). Out of this number, about 6,000 can be felt by humans. Annually, 800 quakes cause some damage, while twenty are violent enough to destroy an entire city. (Fortunately most of the larger earthquakes occur either in the oceans or on remote land sites.)

The power generated by an earthquake is awesome. The severest quakes release an amount of energy equivalent to nearly three times the most devastating thermonuclear bomb.

It is interesting to study theories on the causes of earthquakes. Aristotle believed pockets of gas beneath the earth's surface explode, thus creating earthquakes. Modern-day scientists, however, attribute the source of earthquakes to the movement of the approximately twelve rock plates (sixty to ninety miles thick) which

ARMAGEDDON 198?

make up the earth's crust. These plates float on the earth's semi-molten mantle. Wherever they come together there is a fault line. The most famous one in America is the San Andreas Fault, which runs 650 miles through California. The friction created by the contact between two of these plates often becomes so intense that earthquakes develop. There is usually a warning of stress in this friction that precedes actual earthquake activity. Scientists, therefore, can often predict the likelihood of an earthquake. Fortunately, only those who reside along a fault line are actually in any danger. Still, many have died from these disasters.

The death toll from earthquakes is surprisingly high. Since the beginning of written history (around 3100 B.C.) approximately 13,000,000 deaths have been caused by earthquakes. Currently, 15,000 people die annually from these quakes.

A national magazine recently stated that there have been more severe and destructive earthquakes in the past twenty years than in the previous one hundred years. They are on the increase everywhere.

The year 1976 has been designated as the worst year of earthquakes. First came the Guatemala quake which killed 22,000, injured 50,000 and left 1,000,000 homeless. Next came a quake that killed 1,000 in northern Italy. Following this stronger quakes rocked Russia, China, Peru, Indonesia and Mexico.

Could we be experiencing the fulfillment of Jesus' prediction about earthquakes? Many scholars think so.

8

Christianity in the Last Days

The picture of Christianity in the last days is situated in a frame that is both roughly beaten and glorious. One side is bleak and the other side is bright. The final hours of Christianity on the earth seem to be mixed with opposite extremes. Below is a threefold sketch of this unique picture.

A Departure From the Faith

Data for this category can be quite deceptive, for being religious and being Christian are *not* the same thing. For instance, 95 percent of American women state that they believe themselves to be religious, though only 26 percent accept the Bible as being God's Word, according to a survey by *Redbook* magazine.

In other polls it has been revealed that 94 percent of all Americans believe in God, while an amazing 44 percent of this number feel their faith is not really important. In fact, only 20 percent said they believe in life after death—80 percent say when you die, that's it, period. When the bottom line has been drawn, the facts reveal that most persons who profess a belief in "God" do not see Him as operative in daily affairs. In other words, this "God" (or more correctly, god) of far too many is but a mental concoction!

ARMAGEDDON 198?

Statistical studies in other countries reveal that Americans are, by far, the most religious people on earth. In the United States, for instance, only 3 percent profess to be atheists, while in Canada this number is doubled to 6 percent; in England the number is more than fourfold to 14 percent; in France the number is 23 percent and in Japan it is a staggering 30 percent!

Not long ago a leading magazine polled students attending several divinity schools. In the matter of Christ's Second Coming, only 1 percent (one student out of 100!) believed this teaching. In many seminaries today, it is easy to graduate without a single course in the books of the Bible. The extent to which this fundamental departure from biblical roots will manifest itself can be seen in a recent service at a liberal church where thirteen dogs, four cats, and a rabbit were sprinkled and "blessed" by the pastor!

These trends are keenly disappointing, but they are not alarming, especially when you know Bible prophecy for the last days. Here are a couple of passages to remember:

> The Spirit explicitly says that in later times some will fall away from the faith, paying attention to deceitful spirits and doctrines of [or from] demons. (1 Tim. 4:1)

> The time will come when they will not endure sound doctrine; but wanting to have their ears tickled, they will accumulate for themselves teachers in accordance to their own desires; and will turn away their ears from the truth, and will turn aside to myths. (2 Tim. 4:3-4)

Christianity in the Last Days

For decades now liberal theologians have attempted to find the "historical Jesus" (as if he were not to be found in the simple study of the Scriptures). The thoughts of biblical inspiration and miracles have often been soundly rejected by scores and scores of "Christian" teachers and pastors. Their quest has frequently led them to find a so-called deeper and mystical meaning than that provided by the plain sense of the text itself. This line of interpretation is not at all uncommon.

It is not popular, especially in certain academic circles and among numerous mainline churches, to accept the Bible as it stands. While there is a superb level of fundamental scholarship available to the Christian community at large, there is also a finely trained body of teachers who are deceived, and who propagate their distorted views of God, man and the Bible. Here is a fair test for everyone. Ask your pastor if he accepts the Scriptures (both Old and New Testaments) as inspired by God, and as the *sole* standard for all faith and practice. How do *you* answer this inquiry? See Matthew 5:17-19 and 2 Timothy 3:16-17 for the Bible's own answer to this test.

Outside the Christian church there is also quite a flurry of activity. The cults are growing with great swiftness. In the past decade the Mormon enrollment has gone from 1.8 million to 2.7 million. Another group, Jehovah's Witnesses, has printed 17 million books and distributed 73 million magazines (annually) to enlarge its membership.

Scores of religious and pseudo-religious cults and occultic groups have emerged in recent years. Some 30,000,000 Americans are involved in these offbeat organizations. For instance, the Unification Church,

ARMAGEDDON 198?

headed by Rev. Sun Myung Moon, has 7,000 "core" members in the United States and a treasury of over $20 million.

While anti-Christian Marxism was practically ousted from college campuses a decade ago, it has now become quite popular once again. The essential principles of communism are commonly taught in many schools of higher education.

Popularity toward the devil has not wavered, but actually increased in recent years. Some bookstores have turned their stock over exclusively to satanic and occult subjects. The motion picture industry has been tapping this public interest with a gross income of more than $50 million annually on devil-based films.

A Persecution of the Faith

Christian Life recently conducted a survey of various prominent Christian leaders, asking them what three issues concerned them as they faced the decade of the eighties. Interestingly, twelve of these persons envisioned political/religious freedom as one of the key issues now before us. (Those citing this problem were Ben Armstrong, Robert A. Cook, Jerry Falwell, Charles Lee Feinberg, John Haggai, Carl F.H. Henry, Harold Lindsell, Billy A. Melvin, Bob Mumford, Stephen F. Olford, Warren Wiersbe and Jack Wyrtzen.)

Terrorist groups and anti-Christian governments have very little interest (or more probably, no interest) in protecting missionaries, pastors or church members. While most governments profess a bill of human rights, in many instances it is only a front cover, not a reality.

Christians in Asia are preparing for suffering. It is no hidden fact that Russia, China, Vietnam, Laos and

Christianity in the Last Days

Cambodia are largely atheistic and anti-Christian. Numerous Christians, in China for instance, have spent many years in prison and in work camps with no ray of hope for release.

The Moslem countries of Saudi Arabia, Afghanistan, and Mauritania have never permitted a missionary to enter their lands. Additional countries who do not presently allow entrance to missionaries include the following: Burma, Libya, Iraq and Syria. In other Moslem countries where these laws do not exist, there are other laws that prohibit all forms of witnessing. Should a Moslem become a Christian in any of these countries, he is considered to be an infidel worthy of death. Disbarment from the family is immediate.

It has been documented that in eastern European countries Christians are denied higher education opportunities and professional positions because of Communistic controls.

Russia, in her recent history, has slaughtered more than sixty million of her dissidents. China has done the same to nearly 100 million persons. Numerous ones in these figures have been Christians.

In various African countries tribal wars have been launched specifically against Christians. In other instances missionaries and Christians are merely the slaughtered subjects in political upheaval. Literally thousands of Christians have been needlessly killed in Uganda alone.

According to Roger S. Greenway, writing for the Christian Reformed Church, there is more torture, violence and oppression today than in any other period in history. He goes so far as to consider the situation a primary issue facing the universal church.

It may be that we are beginning to see the fulfillment

ARMAGEDDON 198?

of prophesied persecution for the last days. Jesus, speaking of the time near the end, said, *"They will deliver you up to tribulation, and will kill you, and you will be hated by all nations on account of My name"* (Matt. 24:9; cf. Rev. 6:9-11; 12:17; and 13:7).

A Flocking to the Faith

Despite the fact that many will be persecuted and will depart from the faith, in the last days many will also turn to Jesus Christ and find Him as their personal Savior. In fact, we are on the brink of one of the world's greatest periods of evangelization.

When the apostle John was imprisoned because of his faith (around the year A.D. 95), he was given this vision of Christianity in the last days. He writes this account:

> After this I beheld . . . a great multitude, which no man could number, of all nations and kindreds and people . . . These are they which came out of great tribulation, and have washed their robes, and made them white in the blood of the Lamb. (Rev. 7:9-17 KJV)

The world population is approximately 4.25 billion. Over one-half of these persons (2.7 billion) do not know of Christ at all! More than 1.3 billion people are ensnared and blinded by Communism. But through the use of satellites, this situation may soon change.

Today (1979) there are 1,200 religious radio stations in America, twice the number of 1972. Television is also being utilized with great effects by numerous Christian leaders. In addition to these national projects, much effort is being spent on radio and television broadcasts around the world. Trans-World Radio, for instance, has six new towers that transmit the gospel of Christ into Mainland China, Eastern Russia and Southeast Asia.

Real Christians are always interested in winning the lost to Christ. Proof for this statement is abundant. The Protestant Church has 55,000 people engaged in worldwide missions (28 percent of this number are directly engaged in the task of evangelism).

News regarding God's worldwide work today is superbly documented in two fine magazines—*Logos Journal* and *Evangelical Review*. There are sections in both of these that deal with world evangelism, global missions and Christian education. The research these periodicals report inspires believers with the realization that the gospel is actually being presented to all the nations of the world. And this, too, is one of the signs to be fulfilled prior to the end (cf. Matt. 24:14).

Without any hesitation, it must be confessed that these are exciting days. God *is* moving throughout the world to enlarge His family of saved people. The future may have its dark spots, but its bright spots far outweigh the gloom of the ugly events to come. Indeed, the best is yet before us!

PART III

NATIONS IN THE NEWS AND IN BIBLE PROPHECY

9

The World in Biblical Perspective

"The Bible is the chart of history. It affords a panoramic view of the whole course of events from the creation and the fall of man, to the final judgment, and the inauguration of the new heaven and the new earth. It gives us not only events, but their moral character, tracing the motives of the various actors in the drama, as well as the results of their actions. Events are shown in relation to their causes and effects. Without the Bible, history woud be a spectacle of unknown rivers flowing from unknown sources to unknown seas; but under its guidance we can trace the complex currents to their spring, and see the end from the beginning" (Dr. H. Gratton Guiness).

A Historical Atlas

If you want a real eye-opening experience, then visit your local public library and ask to see a historical atlas. This is a book of maps, or more specifically, maps of the world as it was outlined by national boundaries during the various centuries. When you pick up your copy, turn to the section that deals with the start of the twentieth century. You might be surprised at what you discover.

Did you know that on January 1, 1900, there was no

ARMAGEDDON 198?

USSR, no Iran, no Iraq, no Israel, no Jordan, no Syria, no Lebanon, no Ethiopia, no Libya, no Vietnam, and many other countries we recognize today? Maps of the world have undergone many changes in our very own century.

It may also surprise you to know that on the first day of the twentieth century there were only 45 states in the American union. The following states were not yet admitted: Oklahoma (1907), Arizona (1912), New Mexico (1912), Alaska (1959) and Hawaii (1959).

The Flow of History

It may be thought, after looking at a historical atlas, that history drifts aimlessly, going wherever the winds blow strongest. But this is not the case at all. Nations do not merely rise and fall according to the whim or wit of political leaders. *Behind every country on this planet are angelic beings who, under either God's or Satan's commands, play a direct role in the outcome of every national affair.*

Behind the country of Israel, for example, is the archangel Michael, along with many lesser-ranking angels who serve under his authority (Dan. 12:1; Jude 9). These angelic beings are directly involved in the political activity of this small nation.

Elsewhere in the Scriptures we discover evil angelic princes who are engaged in the affairs of Persia and Greece (Dan. 10:13, 20). It is equally clear that they will be immediately responsible for the rise in power of the antichrist (Rev. 13:1-7; 16:13-14). The Bible plainly states that many nations have been and are yet to be deceived into political policies that come directly from demons (Rev. 16:13-14; 20:3, 7-10).

We might naively suppose that both men and

The World in Biblical Perspective

nations control their own destinies. But this is only partially true. The establishment, expansion and/or decline of each nation—in all of time—owes its history to God and to the kind of angels who preside over them.

All the nations of the world can be divided into one of two classes: (1) those guarded and directed by God's angels, or (2) those guarded and directed by Satan's angels. Above each nation, wielding their influence, are these different angels. In other words, some nations, because of their desire to follow scriptural principles, receive God's angelic assistance. Other nations, because of their refusal to follow the Bible's pattern, receive Satan's angelic assistance. These points are carefully examined in my book, *Angels in Heaven and Earth* (Logos, 1979).

It is not difficult to discern which nations have either God's or Satan's influence over them. Neither is it hard to detect which nations are either increasing or decreasing in the support offered from these invisible superpowers. The United States, for instance, has most definitely received the aid of God's angels in the past; today, however, this influence is growing weak because so many Americans have abandoned a genuine, Bible-based faith and life style.

God's Hand in National Affairs

There is a passage of Scripture which ought to be read no less than 100 times by every Christian. Its truths need to become settled facts in our hearts and minds. There is no way you can look at the world and have peace until you are intimately familiar with these bold declarations about God's involvement with the nations of the earth:

ARMAGEDDON 198?

And Paul stood in the midst of the Areopagus and said, "Men of Athens, I observe that you are very religious in all respects.

"For while I was passing through and examining the objects of your worship, I also found an altar with this inscription, 'TO AN UNKNOWN GOD.' What therefore you worship in ignorance, this I proclaim to you.

"The God who made the world and all things in it, since He is Lord of heaven and earth, does not dwell in temples made with hands;

Neither is He served by human hands, as though He needed anything, since He Himself gives to all life and breath and all things;

And He made from one, every nation of mankind to live on all the face of the earth, having determined their appointed times, and the boundaries of their habitation,

That they should seek God, if perhaps they might grope for Him and find Him, though He is not far from each one of us;

For in Him we live and move and exist, as even some of your own poets have said, 'For we also are His offspring.'

"Being then the offspring of God, we ought not to think that the Divine Nature is like gold or silver or stone, an image formed by the art and thought of man.

"Therefore having overlooked the times of ignorance, God is now declaring to men that all everywhere should repent,

Because He has fixed a day in which He will judge the world in righteousness through a Man whom He has appointed, having furnished

The World in Biblical Perspective

proof to all men by raising Him from the dead." (Acts 17:22-31)

Let's analyze the major thoughts contained in this fantastic text:

1. God is the "Lord" (or Ruler of all that happens) in *both* heaven *and* earth (v. 24). Some people are content to know that God polishes the stars so that they will twinkle in the night, but they fail to recognize that His sovereign authority extends to the earth as well. There has never been an accident on the planet called earth, not a single one. This does not imply that everything happening on the earth pleases God, but it does mean that nothing can take place without first passing through His all-authoritative hands. God is the Lord of the earth, regardless of what anyone else may wish to believe (see Dan. 4:35).

2. God is complete in himself (v. 25). God has no needs—He never has had any and He never will have any needs. It is a mistaken notion to imagine that God created people because He was lonely or needed some company. It is not God who needs us, but the very opposite—we desperately need Him. For without God we would never exist in the first place. Even after our creation, our life is solely dependent upon Him for its continuance.

3. God makes nations too (v. 26). Behind the need for drawing a new world map every several years is the powerful hand of God. Nations cannot exist without Him. Every nation of earth (past, present or future) owes both its duration and its size to direct, divine interventions. The existence and significance of the United States, of Russia, of China, of Egypt, of Israel, and of every other nation is due solely to God's plans

ARMAGEDDON 198?

and principles. No nation can last any longer or grow any larger than what He has set for its limits.

4. God wants the nations to know Him (vv. 27-31). Making and moving nations across a planet is not a pastime with God. His interest and involvement with nations is intensely serious. His purpose in all of these manipulations is that the people within the borders of any given country might find Him, repent of their sins, and be spared an eternal judgment in hell. God does not want to see a single American, Swede, Irishman, Roman, Nigerian, Arab, Israeli, or anyone else, end up being eternally separated from His presence. So, He works in every country, being as close to people as their very own breaths, in order that they might recognize Him and enjoy Him forever.

The following charts outline world history from a divine perspective. By carefully examining these diagrams, and by reading the scriptural references, you will clearly see God's hand in the development and destiny of each empire on earth.

The World in Biblical Perspective

EMPIRE	STATUE	METAL	DANIEL 2	ANIMAL AND PERSONAGE	DANIEL 7
Babylon	Head	Gold	v. 37, 38	Lion with Eagle's wing	v. 4
Medo-Persia	Breast and Arms	Silver	v. 39	Bear with 3 Ribs	v. 5
Greece	Belly and Thighs	Bronze	v. 39	Leopard with 4 Heads 4 Wings	v. 6
Rome	Legs	Iron	v. 40	Dreadful Beast	v. 7
Revised Rome	Feet and Toes	Iron and Clay	v. 41-43	Ten Horns	v. 7
Kingdom of God		Stone	v. 44-45	Son of Man K. of Saints	v. 13-14, 27

THE RISE AND FALL OF EMPIRES
CONTRASTING DANIEL, CHAPTERS 2 AND 7

THE VISION OF GENTILE POWERS
DANIEL 7 AND 8

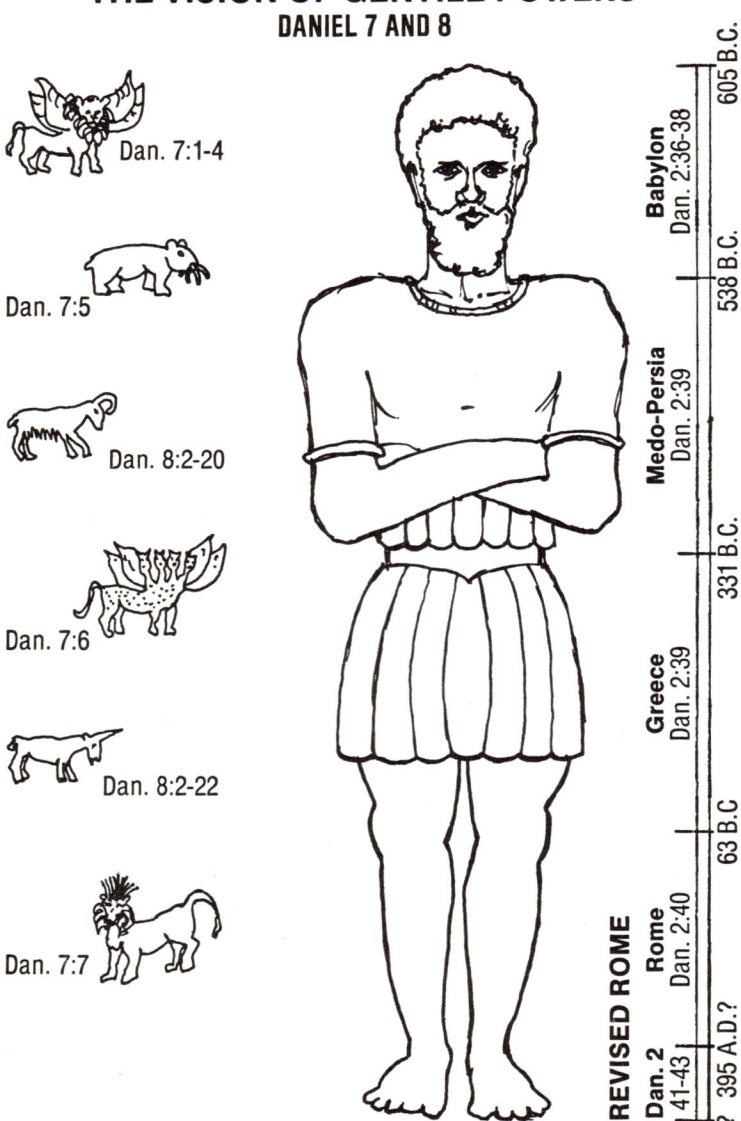

Dan. 7:1-4

Dan. 7:5

Dan. 8:2-20

Dan. 7:6

Dan. 8:2-22

Dan. 7:7

Babylon Dan. 2:36-38 — 605 B.C.

538 B.C.

Medo-Persia Dan. 2:39

331 B.C.

Greece Dan. 2:39

63 B.C.

REVISED ROME | **Rome** Dan. 2:40

395 A.D.?

Dan. 2 41-43 — ?

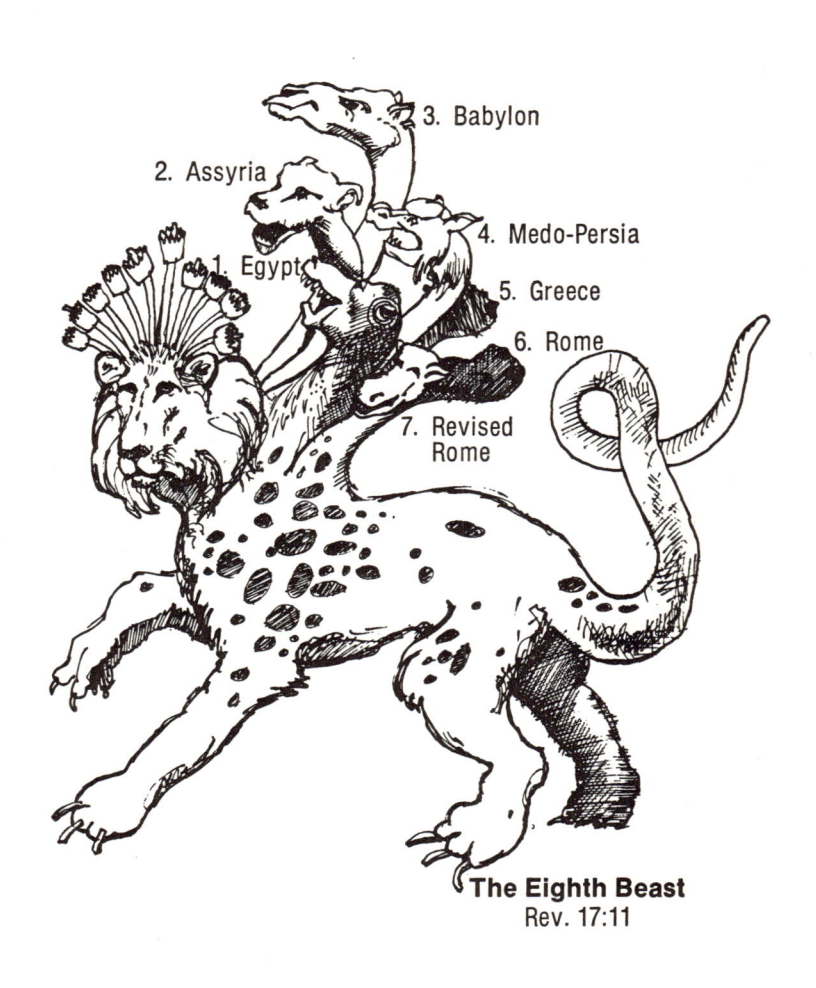

- 1. Egypt
- 2. Assyria
- 3. Babylon
- 4. Medo-Persia
- 5. Greece
- 6. Rome
- 7. Revised Rome

The Eighth Beast
Rev. 17:11

THE KINGDOM OF THE BEAST
Revelation 13 and 17

THE BEAST'S KINGDOM

Revelation 17:9-11

The Seven Heads

1	EGYPT	
2	ASSYRIA	
3	BABYLON	"... the beast WAS (before John's day)
4	MEDO-PERSIA	
5	GREECE	
6	ROME	"... the beast ... IS NOT (in John's day)
7	REVISED ROME (the harlot's kingdom)	
8	REVIVED GREECE (the beast's kingdom)	"... the beast ... is YET TO COME" (after John's day)

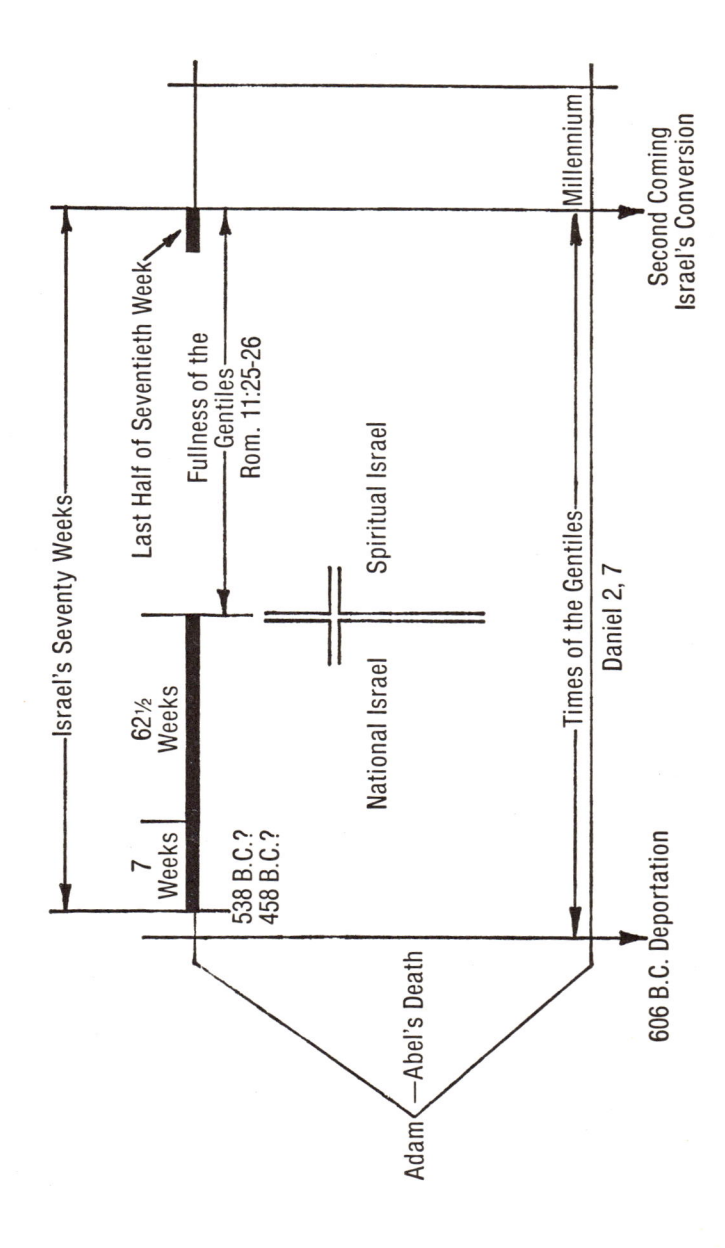

THE TIMES OF THE GENTILES
AND THE FULLNESS OF THE GENTILES IN PERSPECTIVE

10

Israel

Pressed against impossible odds, the Jewish nation has managed to survive. When it would appear that their enemies have engulfed them, the Jewish people come forth even stronger.

Land—God's Gift to the Jew

The Jewish people have a long history of sorrows and joys. It is impossible to understand Israel's present state without first grasping her past.

The land we call Israel today is called "the Lord's land" by the Old Testament prophets (Hos. 9:3; cf. 2 Chron. 7:20; Jer. 2:7, etc.). Literally dozens of times this real estate is proclaimed to be God's gift to the Jews (Gen. 12:1-2, 7; 13:14-17; 15:18, etc.). From the Euphrates River in the North, to the Nile River in the South; from the Mediterranean Sea in the West, to the Jordan River in the East, all of this territory is, by divine arrangement, Jewish soil. Israel's contention is that this land belongs to her.

From Ur of the Chaldees (or possibly modern Tell el-Muqayyar in southern Iraq) God called a man named Abraham (about 2090 B.C.) to leave his family and to settle in a region called Canaan (Gen. 11:28, 31; 15:7; Acts 7:2, 4). This territory derives its name from

ARMAGEDDON 198?

a son of Noah, Canaan, who inhabited and populated the area now called Israel (Gen. 9:18, 22-27). It was this real estate that God promised to Abraham and to his descendants. Although Abraham was not to see himself control the soil vowed to be his, it would be his great grandchildren (ten or so generations later) who would be instructed to take the land by force.

According to Moses, the Canaanites were to be driven off the land because of their gross sins (Gen. 15:12-20; Lev. 18:24; Deut. 18:9-13).[1] They were unworthy of the land rights. So, under the military leadership of Joshua (1405-1390 B.C.), this territory was to become the homeland of the Jews forever (Jer. 7:7; 25:5; Ezek. 37:12, 21, 25, 28, and 39:25-29; Joel 3:20; Amos 9:15; Mic. 4:6-7).

It has not always been easy for the Jews to maintain control of their inheritance. Under the leadership of her first three kings, Saul (1043-1011 B.C.), David (1011-971 B.C.), and Solomon (971-931 B.C.), Israel became a thriving nation, with its capital in Jerusalem. But after Solomon died, the kingdom was divided, resulting in a Northern Kingdom and a Southern Kingdom.

In 722 B.C. Assyrian troops forever destroyed the identity of the Northern Kingdom through war, deportation and intermarriage. About 125 years later (606 and 587 B.C.) a powerful Babylonian army subdued the Southern Kingdom. The Jews were herded away like cattle to the land of Babylon (modern southern Iraq). Fortunately the Jews were permitted to maintain their identity, though outside their homeland. In 537

---

[1] These same rules apply to any nation that claims God's blessing, including America (cf. 2 Chron. 7:14 and Prov. 14:34).

Israel

B.C. the Babylonians were defeated by the combined forces of Media and Persia. It was in this year that the Jews went back home to rebuild their past and face the struggles of the future.

Although the Jews were allowed the freedom to reestablish their nation, Israel, they still remained the subjects of the Medo-Persian rule (537-333 B.C.). When Alexander the Great conquered most of the then known world, Israel's subjection shifted to Greece and its subsequent rulers, namely the Ptolemies of Egypt and the Selucids of Syria (333-166 B.C.). After a revolt in the second century before Jesus, the Jews were again a free nation—though it only lasted approximately one hundred years (166-63 B.C.). In the rise of Rome to worldwide prominence, Israel soon found herself the subject of another Gentile bondage.

It was under the rule of the Roman Empire that Israel faced her darkest hour. The details and consequences of these final years before being scattered to the four points of the compass are very significant and the following section unfolds the developments.

The Scattering of the Jews

It was in the spring (of probably A.D. 29 or 30) when Jesus came to Jerusalem for His final proclamation. It was to be an extremely busy period of six days—Sunday through Friday. But it was also to be the most distressing and difficult week of Jesus' life, for it would conclude with His cruel and sadistic death.

On Sunday, Jesus entered Jerusalem with jubilant shouts (Mark 11:9-10; Luke 19:38). These joyful sounds followed Him to the Temple, where He healed all who were sick. It was an exhilarating day. The air was electrified. When the time had grown late, Jesus

ARMAGEDDON 198?

departed with His twelve companions and went out of the city to Bethany where they lodged.

On the next day the scene radically changed. There were no shouts of glee and no healings. The tone was distinctly different. The atmosphere was tense. It was early in the morning, and Jesus directed himself to the Temple.

By the time He reached the holy center His countenance was flushed with raging jealousy for God's house. The priests, scribes and principal religious leaders had converted the Lord's holy house of prayer into a public house of robbers. With fury Jesus began to scatter the tables that were covered with money, and to drive out the money-changers. Once this was accomplished, He began to teach them God's will (Mark 11:12-18).

Jesus fervently taught many things on Monday and Tuesday, but by Tuesday afternoon it was apparent Jerusalem had become too callous as a result of the sins of man-made religion to receive His divine message. With a broken heart Jesus lamented over the city and finally departed, realizing that her doom was inevitable (Matt. 23:37).

It is against this brief, but crucial, backdrop that Jesus delivered His most severe prophecy against the Jews and Jerusalem. The theme of this judgmental prediction is called "the times of the Gentiles," and a single verse supplies the gist of Jesus' pronouncement:

> And they [the Jews of Jerusalem] will fall by the edge of the sword, and will be led captive into all the nations; and Jerusalem will be trampled underfoot by the Gentiles until the times of the Gentiles be fulfilled. (Luke 21:24)

Israel

According to this prophecy "the times of the Gentiles" will possess three principal marks of identity:
1. the fall of Jerusalem,
2. the scattering of the Jews, and
3. the submission of Jerusalem to Gentile domination.

The record of history dramatically confirms this consuming prediction. In the year A.D. 66 the Jews revolted against Rome and attempted to gain their independence. Vespasian was sent from Rome to put down the rebellion by the use of mass murders. And until the emperor's death in A.D. 69, he slaughtered the occupants of numerous cities. In A.D. 69, Vespasian left for Rome to become its emperor, but he left his son, Titus, to finish the task of squashing the Jewish revolt. While the actual siege against Jerusalem lasted 134 days, the repulsive and numerous details of this dreadful period are staggering.

The military occupants within Jerusalem—a number recorded as being between 23,000 and 24,000—were divided into three self-centered factions, each holding a certain section of the city, and occasionally fighting one another. Under Titus there were 54,000 legionnaires, along with archers and horsemen—an army twice the size of Jerusalem's militia.

Famine within the walled city was inevitable. The stench of dead bodies became so great that 600,000 corpses are said to have been thrown over the walls. In the peak of destitution, children were even eaten for survival. Finally, in A.D. 70, General Titus's men overran the city, slaughtering indiscriminately and burning the city. In total, some 1,100,000 people supposedly died in the siege. Another 97,000 were

ARMAGEDDON 198?

taken captives, while some were allowed to go free.[2]

A.D. 70 is most assuredly a black date in Jewish history, but it is neither her first nor her last such period of horror. Gentile tyranny over the Jews and Jerusalem has occupied much of her history. Below is a small sketch of Jerusalem's dominance by Gentile powers since A.D. 70.

70-131	Desolation
131-312	Jerusalem rebuilt—called Aelia Capitalina
312-395	Jerusalem's name restored under Constantine
395-614	Greek control
614-969	Persian control
969-1077	Egyptian control
1077-1517	Crusader/Arab control mixed
1517-1917	Ottoman Empire (Turkish) control
1917-1948	British control
May 14, 1948	Independence

The Zionist Movement

After the horrible fall of Jerusalem, the Jews (with few exceptions) were scattered in every direction, just as Jesus had prophesied would occur. But they never forgot God's original promise, that the land belonged to them. Despite the years and the miles that separated the Jews from their homeland, there was an ever burning expectation that somehow, someday they

---

[2]These figures from the first-century historian Josephus, are doubtlessly highly exaggerated. It seems more probable to envision, as a maximum, 70,000 people within Jerusalem. For further details consult *Smith's Dictionary of the Bible*, Volume II, pp. 1304-1308, 1320.

Israel

would return.

Israel's years in exile were most difficult. They were treated as second-class citizens, at best. Called "Christ-killers," they were frequently persecuted and thought of as being less than human. Various countries went so far as to even bar them from living within their boundaries. In effect, numerous Jews discovered they were people without a home, without a country they could call their own.

The history of Jewish suffering throughout the world is nearly unbelievable. Here are but a few illustrations. On November 1, 1290, England expelled all Jews from her land (this was the law for 370 years). It has been estimated that in 1298 100,000 Jews were put to death in Franconia, Bavaria and Austria. Eight years later, in 1306, another 100,000 Jews were expelled from France at the threat of death. In 1348 the Jews were accused of causing the Black Plague, resulting in the killings of hundreds of thousands of Jews. From 1648-1658 nearly half a million Jews are said to have been killed in Poland. And on it goes. There seems to be almost no limit to the gross details that can be gathered regarding the mistreatment of the Jews during the course of their long history without a national homeland.

Eventually, there came a popular movement in the late 1800s that sought to relieve this problem of prejudice and to secure a homeland for the Jews. The supporters of this plan were called "Zionists." Originally, the leaders of this body desired to settle anywhere they would be accepted. The lands of Cyprus, Uganda and South Africa were initially discussed as a possible home. The land of Israel did not seem to be a compulsory site as they began their project. But soon the weight of

ARMAGEDDON 198?

opinion favored this area of the Middle East, and here would become the location for Jews who sought a national home.

Below is the resolution passed by the 197 Zionists who met at their first congress in Basel, Switzerland, in 1897.

"Zionism strives to create for the Jewish people a home in Palestine secured by public law. The Congress contemplates the following means to the attainment of this end:

> "1. The promotion on suitable lines of the colonisation of Palestine by Jewish agricultural and industrial workers.
> "2. The organisation and bringing together of the whole of Jewry by means of appropriate institutions, local and international, in accordance with the laws of each country.
> "3. The strengthening and fostering of Jewish national sentiment and consciousness.
> "4. Preparatory steps towards obtaining Government consent where necessary to the attainment of the aim of Zionism."

While many Jews had no interest in the Zionist movement, many others did. Soon scores of Jews returned to their native land (then under the control of the Ottoman Empire) in order to become farmers, start business, and establish new Jewish communities. By 1914 there were 90,000 Jews who lived in forty-three agricultural settlements in Palestine.

Language was a problem at the start. The Jews spoke the language of the land to which they were scattered. Still, they had retained the Hebrew tongue, because it is the language of their Bible (the Old

Israel

Testament). Within a short time Hebrew became the language of the Jews throughout Palestine. Today, this is the primary language of Israel. This event marks the remarkable fulfillment of a 2,500-year-old prophecy (Jer. 31:23). God promised the restoration of this language for all of Israel.

Israel's National Independence
During World War I the region of Palestine fell under the control of the British. It was at this time that the Zionists (represented by Lord Rothschild) were granted the formal favor of the British government in establishing their national home in Palestine. They performed this granting through what is called the Balfour Declaration, dated November 2, 1917. Because of its paramount significance, the 117-word document is now quoted below:

Foreign Office
November 2nd, 1917

Dear Lord Rothschild,
I have much pleasure in conveying to you, on behalf of His Majesty's Government, the following declaration of sympathy with Jewish Zionist aspirations which has been submitted to and approved by the Cabinet:
His Majesty's Government view with favour the establishment in Palestine of a national home for the Jewish people, and will use their best endeavours to facilitate the achievement of this object, it being clearly understood that nothing shall be done which may prejudice the civil and religious rights of existing non-Jewish communities in Palestine, or the rights

ARMAGEDDON 198?

and political status enjoyed by Jews in any other country.

I would be grateful if you would bring this declaration to the knowledge of the Zionist Federation.

Yours sincerely,
Arthur James Balfour

The span of time from A.D. 70 (when Jerusalem was utterly crushed, and the Jews were scattered into all the world) to November 2, 1917, (when the Balfour Declaration gave the Zionists an official home) marks an incredible journey. No other nation has ever lost her nationality and then regained it after so many years of non-existence. For instance, where are these empires today: Babylon, Philistia, Media, Persia and so forth? They are gone—forever. But Israel has returned. Why has she alone succeeded?

The answer to this question is simple, if you believe the message of the prophets and Jesus. Israel's scattering was prophesied to be only temporary. It was God's act of disciplining a disobedient people (Matt. 21:43, 44; Rom. 9-11). But once the punishment was finished—according to Bible prophecy—Israel was to return home (Isa. 11:11, 12; Jer. 24:6; 36:22, 24; 37:21-28).[3] This is precisely what has happened!

On July 24, 1922, the League of Nations accepted the

---

[3] It should be noted that certain scholars, especially amillennialists, do not envision any prophetic future for national Israel. Such prophecies are seen as being fulfilled either in the ancient past or within the Church, God's new spiritual Israel (see *Israel In Prophecy* by William Hendriksen, Baker Book House). This extremely narrow approach to prophecy seems to be an oversimplification of the facts. This line of interpretation makes light of many literal fulfillments, which, because of current events, may prove to be an inaccurate approach to prophecy.

Israel

British declaration. This recognition, however, was not shared by the neighboring Arabs. Two years earlier (June 2, 1919) the General Syrian Congress pointedly renounced the Zionist state. Others joined with them in rejecting the Balfour Declaration. This resistance on the part of the Arabs caused the British officials to reexamine their role in the Zionist homeland. Eventually they were to pass laws that either limited or even suspended Jewish immigration, and prohibited their right to settle in the land east of the Jordan River.

Despite these (and other) guidelines, Arab-Israeli riots were frequent and fatal. The Arabs wanted all immigration of Jews to cease, forever. The Jews wanted a welcome mat to be placed at the doorway of Palestine for every Jew in the world. The bitterness mounted. Ultimately a full-scale confrontation became inevitable.

On November 29, 1947, the United Nations approved a recommendation, at the request of the British, that Palestine be divided into two separate and independent states—one for the Arabs and another for the Zionists. According to this arrangement the British were to leave by August 1, 1948.

On May 14, 1948, the British High Commission for Palestine departed. On that same day the Jewish National Council and the General Zionist Council met and proclaimed the establishment of the nation of Israel. On May 15, 1948, the very next day, Egypt, Jordan, Syria, Lebanon, Iraq, and Saudi Arabia (representing a total of 40,000,000 Arabs) sent troops to destroy the one-day-old nation (numbering around 650,000—1/60 the count of the Arabs). After seven months of fighting, the incredible Israelis had won the

ARMAGEDDON 198?

conflict, and the Arabs signed an agreement with Israel, granting her 23 percent more land than the United Nations had originally specified in their plan a year earlier. It was, indeed, the hour that proved the seriousness of the Jewish purpose to defend their new national status. At last, the Jews had a place they could call their own.

See the map on page 70, which shows how the land was divided by the United Nations in 1947. Also, note the next map, which indicates the additional land gained after Israel's seven-month conflict with the Arab nations.

The Six-Day War

Unfortunately, the state of Israel never gained any genuine peace settlement with the Arabs. Her enemies continued in the years ahead to boycott and to blockade all goods bound for her land. Practically daily there were terrorists who committed acts of violence and destruction. Added to this tension was the massive military support Russia gave to the oil-rich Arabs. Israel's neighbors were becoming very strong. Again the threat of annihilation was real.

It was May 17, 1967 (three days after the anniversary of Israel's nineteenth year of independence), when Egypt formally declared verbal war on Israel; she did not, however, actually start fighting the Jewish state until June 5, 1967. The odds against Israel's success in the face of war were nearly hopeless. The Egyptians boasted of having an army of 50,000 troops, with over 1,000 tanks. Additionally, Syria and Jordan united with Egypt to crush the tiny nation of Israel.

The war started early Monday morning. By Thursday, however, Israel had destroyed two-thirds of

Israel

Egypt's air power and paralyzed her ground forces. Jordan was ousted from the Old City portion of Jerusalem. And Syria was ready to follow both Egypt and Jordan in accepting the cease-fire proposals of the United Nations. The Six-Day War had ended, and Israel, the pathetic underdog, had won!

The statistics of the war reveal that Israel lost 700 men, while the casualties for the Arabs range between 10,000 and 30,000 men. Also through the conflict Israel enlarged her borders from 8,000 to 26,000 square miles—in less than a week. See the map on page 80 which shows the territory Israel held both before and after this war.

The Yom Kippur War

Six years later the Arabs became even more determined than ever before to erase Israel's name from the maps of the Middle East. Under the leadership of Egypt's new president, Anwar Sadat, and with the multi-million-dollar arms support from Russia, the Arabs attacked. The day was October 6, 1973—the most sacred day of the Jewish year, Yom Kippur, the Day of Atonement.

The Arabs were overwhelmingly well armed. Egypt marched one of the world's largest armies—800,000 men, 2,000 tanks, 500 planes and 150 antiaircraft missile batteries. Syria came against tiny Israel with another 1,400 tanks. This was to be the largest tank war ever fought in all of modern history. If the chances of Israel's victory during the Six-Day War were poor, then her odds for success now were absolutely hopeless.

Israel, no larger than the state of Massachusetts, retaliated with a miraculous force. In the South, she managed to get within sixty miles of Cairo, Egypt's

Map

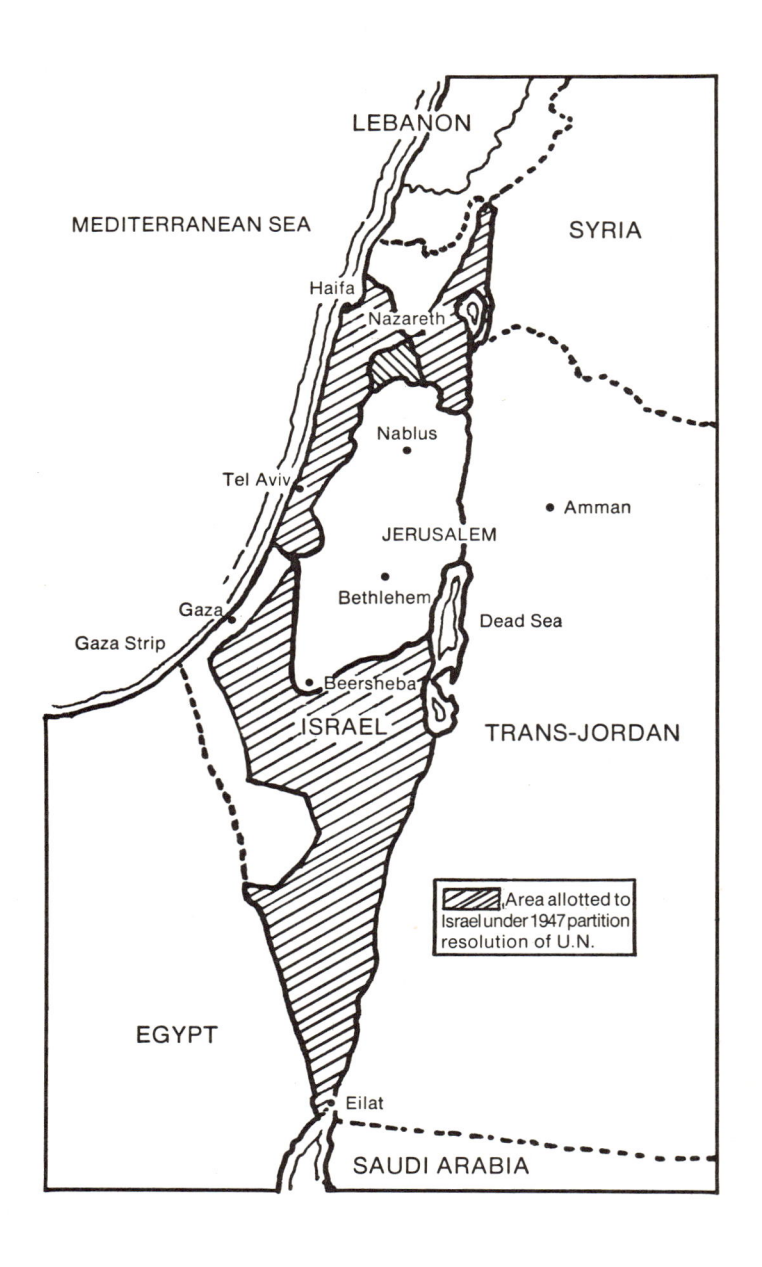

LEBANON

MEDITERRANEAN SEA

SYRIA

Haifa
Nazareth
Nablus
Tel Aviv
JERUSALEM
• Amman
Gaza
Bethlehem
Gaza Strip
Dead Sea
Beersheba
ISRAEL
TRANS-JORDAN

Area allotted to Israel under 1947 partition resolution of U.N.

EGYPT

Eilat

SAUDI ARABIA

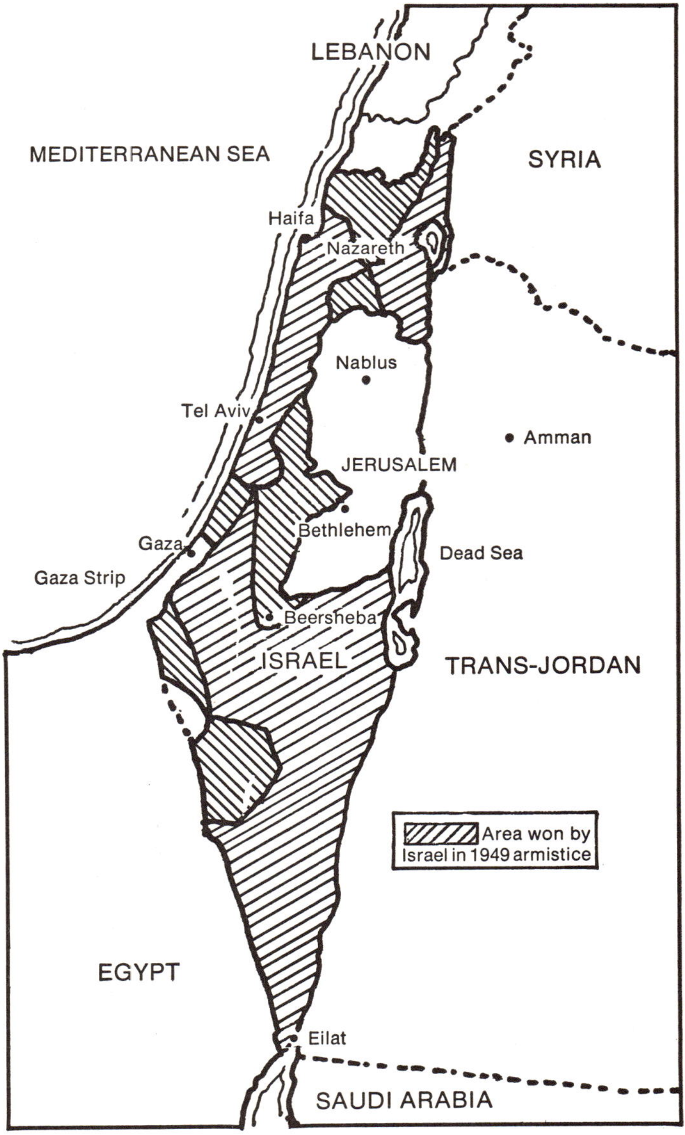
LEBANON
MEDITERRANEAN SEA
SYRIA
Haifa
Nazareth
Nablus
Tel Aviv
Amman
JERUSALEM
Bethlehem
Gaza
Dead Sea
Gaza Strip
Beersheba
ISRAEL
TRANS-JORDAN
Area won by Israel in 1949 armistice
EGYPT
Eilat
SAUDI ARABIA

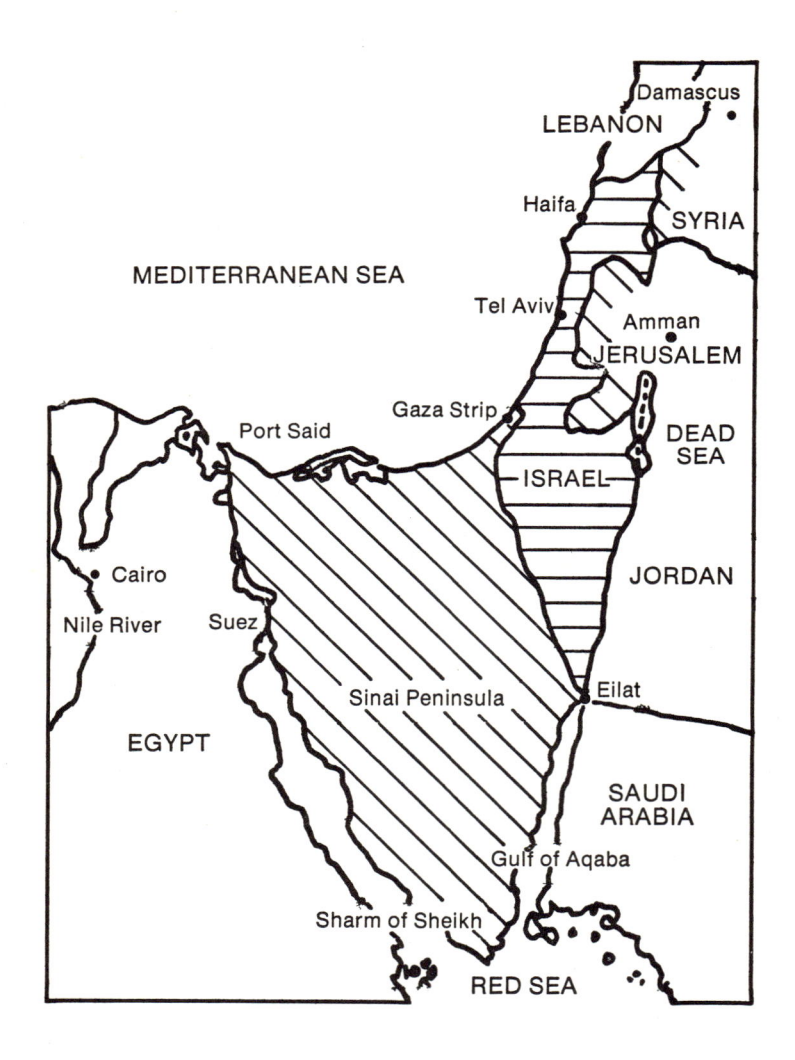

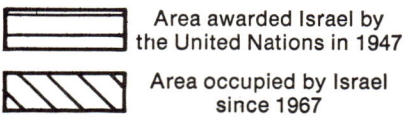

Area awarded Israel by the United Nations in 1947

Area occupied by Israel since 1967

capital, before a cease-fire was passed on October twenty-fourth. In the North, she got within twenty miles of Damascus, Syria's capital, before the cease-fire took effect. Israel had won again, and in less than three weeks!

Can anyone deny the miraculous nature of these victories for Israel? Can anyone doubt that God, who gave them this land in the first place, and who promised to return them to this territory to live there forever, was intimately involved in these military campaigns? The Jews gave God the credit for their triumphs. Who would dare deny it in the face of such startling proofs?

Peace With Egypt

In 1978, Israel's prime minister, Menachem Begin, and Egypt's president, Anwar Sadat, were awarded the Nobel Peace Prize for their negotiations of peace. The Arab world was shocked, and the Communistic nations were outraged, but the rest of humanity was delighted in seeing these two former enemies embrace in the bonds of peace.

The negotiations were prolonged and taxing. When everything seemed to spell disaster, there came a breakthrough at Camp David that brought agreement to both parties. On September 17, 1978, at the White House, President Carter, along with Begin and Sadat, signed the documents of hope.

Will these documents bring to Israel the long-awaited tranquility she desires? Or, is Israel yet to see further turmoil and war?

On the surface we are naturally inclined to take great delight in the peace pact between Israel and Egypt; below the surface, however, there are some

ARMAGEDDON 198?

unsettling eye-openers. We discover that America's involvement in the negotiations may have been more out of desperation on the part of these two nations than out of seeing us as a friendly big brother.

Both Israel and Egypt are economically unstable, running and annual deficit of multi-billions of dollars. The United States is expected to pay Israel $4.5 billion to finance her withdrawal from the Sinai. Additionally, we are to pay for the construction of two new air bases in the Negev, as a replacement for the ones Israel loses in giving up her southern territories. Also, Israel is expecting an annual rise in American military loans, amounting to $1.5 billion for each of the next ten years. Finally, the tiny state wants $2.4 billion worth of economic assistance for use in 1980.

Egypt, finding the United States to be a better financial friend than her Arab and Communist neighbors, is also to receive billions of dollars in both economic and military support.

When the final line has been drawn, one point stands out above everything else: the United States recognizes the importance of the Middle East in global affairs and wants her hand to be secure in this segment of the world, should anything happen to threaten her security. Apparently this hold is worth multiplied billions of American dollars.

The Dark Side of Israel's Future

Israel's future is both bleak and bright—in that order. There are numerous prophecies yet to be fulfilled for these harassed people. Many of these predictions are filled with eternal glory, but many others spell out yet another holocaust for Israel. As marred as Israel's history has become, there is yet at

Israel

least one more moment of utter distress before them. The prophet Daniel describes this period in these general terms: "There will be a time of distress such as never occurred since there was a nation until that time" (Dan. 12:1). Here are several key features prophesied for this bleak period in Israel's future.

1. *The Principal Figures:* At the heart of this period will be the return of Jerusalem to foreign control. Although Israel gained her independence on May 14, 1948, she will lose it to an empire yet to arise, called the kingdom of the antichrist. A full analysis of this figure, along with his kingdom, is located in Chapter 15. Suffice it to say that this person will dominate Jerusalem in every imaginable manner. His rule will be utterly godless (Rev. 13:1-10).

In addition to the antichrist will be three other key figures: Satan, the false prophet, and the image (clone?) of the antichrist. Let's consider each one briefly.

Satan will be cast out of heaven and unto the earth for the full duration of the tribulation period (Rev. 12:7-12). His primary attention will focus on persecuting the Jews, especially Christian Jews. Additionally, he will be granted permission to unleash a terrible mass of demons who have been confined for thousands of years in the abyss (Rev. 9:1-11). As a result, many people (who are not Christians) will be bitterly tormented. Finally, Satan will join the antichrist, apparently in bodily form (presumably by indwelling someone's body), and require all within his jurisdiction to worship him. (See the notes in Chapter 15 on the actual extent of his rule.)

The false prophet will attempt to persuade people

ARMAGEDDON 198?

(particularily Jews) that the antichrist is just what they have been looking for (Rev. 13:11-15). His ambition is not to sell the antichrist as being the long-awaited Messiah, but a deliverer nonetheless. It seems, however, that the following he is able to attract is loyal more because of economic fears than from actual reverence. Apparently this figure will also serve the antichrist as his secretary of finance and economics, possibly representing the most powerful position in the future world.

The image of the antichrist is a mysterious figure (Rev. 13:11-18). Somehow a replica of the antichrist is made which comes to life (presumably through demonic powers). The scope of his influence, like that of Satan, the antichrist, and the false prophet, will be largely confined to the Middle East, portions of Europe and northern Africa. The specific duties of this "image" are to assist the false prophet and the antichrist. He also appears to be the Chief Executioner of the antichrist's kingdom.

2. *The Length of the Holocaust:* The duration of this final nightmare for Israel will be three and a half years. Major portions of the biblical books of Daniel and the Revelation are devoted to this period (see Dan. 7; 11:36-45; Rev. 6-19). While the length of this episode seems relatively short, it must be weighed against the fact that 2/3 of Israel's occupants will be mercilessly slaughtered in this period of horror (Zech. 13:8-9).

3. *The Temple Will Be Rebuilt:* Another temple will be constructed for Jewish worship, but the antichrist will seat himself in this shrine and demand the people's worship (2 Thess. 2:4; Rev. 13:1-10).

The destruction of Israel and the scattering of the Jews in A.D. 70 seemed to be a certain sign of the extinction of their national identity. The history of

Israel

this people would be confined to only ancient records. But the amazing saga of the Jewish people has become a contemporary story set against a backdrop of incredible odds. The recent rebirth of the state of Israel is a modern miracle. For the Jew there can only be one place called home, and that is a tiny tract of land in the Middle East given to them by their Lord God nearly 4,000 years ago.

When Israel became an official nation under the leadership of Moses, God instructed them to build a tabernacle to serve as a center for their worship. This was a huge, movable, tent-like structure. In the days of King Solomon the tabernacle was superseded by a more permanent dwelling place, the Temple. But in 586 B.C. this religious house was destroyed by the conquering Babylonians. When the Jews returned from their deportation in 536 B.C., their first ambition was the reconstruction of the Temple. Later, this site was richly embellished, but in A.D. 70 the entire structure was utterly crushed, leaving the Jews with neither a temple nor a homeland.

Today this has all changed. The Jews have returned, and their desire for a temple is a dream that may soon become a reality.

Building a temple is no easy matter, especially if you feel strongly that it must rest on the actual site of the former temple. The chief problem is this. The land is presently occupied by a major Moslem shrine, the Dome of the Rock, which has been there since A.D. 691. The Arabs are no less convinced that this spot is rightfully theirs.

The present solution to this dilemma has been the construction of the Jerusalem Great Synagogue. This structure, acclaimed as the most beautiful in the

ARMAGEDDON 198?

world, is designed to be the central shrine for Jews all over the world. Its location in the Holy Land, its unsurpassed magnificence in design, and its promotion as the central meeting place of worship for all Jews makes this edifice a special structure indeed.

Whether or not this is the Temple predicted by the prophets is uncertain. If it is, then we may be on the literal edge of Jesus' return in the sky; if it is not, then we have the groundwork laid for the construction of Jerusalem's ultimate temple. Regardless of the outcome, we are living in exciting days, when Bible prophecy for the Promised Land is coming to pass before our eyes!

The Bright Side of Israel's Future

The future of the nation of Israel is as bright as the promises of God—and the promises are wonderful indeed. See the details below.

1. *The Two Special Witnesses:* The Christian witness to the Jews will escalate greatly during this three-and-a-half-year period. Throughout the whole episode God will empower two men to preach and to display His mighty power. Unfortunately, their efforts will be met with little positive response (Rev. 11:3-13). These men are apparently sent to offset the perverted ministry of the false prophet, though few seem to care.

The identity of these men is not revealed, but the opinion of most scholars is quite uniform. The team of Elijah and Moses, or the pair of Enoch and Elijah are the most frequent suggestions. The former two are offered because of the similarity between their own earthly ministries and that of the two witnesses; plus, they were seen together with Jesus in His Transfiguration. The latter twosome is selected because neither have tasted death, and therefore, have not

Israel

fulfilled the promise that "it is appointed unto man once to die" (Heb. 9:27). There is little room for dogmatism in either case.

2. *The 144,000 Servants of God:* Another 144,000 men (Christian Jews) will serve God and witness to the Jews during this period before Christ's Second Coming (Rev. 7:1-8; 14:1-5).

This group is mentioned but twice in the Bible. Within these verses lie three items which deserve individual attention.

First, the 144,000 are to receive the seal of the living God. This marking is a symbol of their salvation. Repeatedly, Paul taught that God seals all believers (Rom. 4:11; 1 Cor. 9:2; 2 Cor. 1:22; Eph. 1:13; 4:30; 2 Tim. 2:19). Jesus also pictured the saints as receiving God's special invisible mark (John 3:33; 6:27; Rev. 3:12; 22:4).

There is also another function for the use of this seal. John envisions a period when a host of demons will be released from the abyss. These demons will go forth to bitterly torment men with a sting like that from a scorpion. The recipients of this agony are specifically designated as those "who have not the seal of God" (9:4). Therefore, those who possess God's seal will escape His judgments (cf. 1 Thess. 5:9).

A good illustration of God's sealing, or protecting in the midst of judgment, is seen in Israel's captivity in Egypt. While the Egyptians were afflicted by an innumerable host of frogs, lice, locusts and flies, and while a grievous plague struck the cattle, and the water was turned to blood, and boils covered men's flesh, and great hail fell from heaven, and darkness covered the land, God put a division between His people and Pharaoh's people! Israel was surrounded by God's judgments, and yet, were untouched by all of

ARMAGEDDON 198?

them (Exod. 8-10)! This same effect will occur again.

Second, John is deliberate in identifying this group as 144,000 "servants of God" (7:4). There is no reason for not accepting them as a literal 144,000 (12,000 from each of the twelve tribes of Israel) Christian Jews who serve God (as evangelists?) in the period of the great tribulation.

Third, this group is seen with the Lamb on Mount Zion (that is, heavenly Mount Zion—Heb. 12:22) as "redeemed" from the earth and from among men (Rev. 14:1, 3-4). For this reason they are also called the "first fruits" unto God and the Lamb.[1]

It appears that this company is the first group of Jewish Christian martyrs. After the "woman" (that is, a company of Christian Jews) flees into the wilderness, Satan will make war with "the rest of her offspring, who keep the commandments of God and hold to the testimony of Jesus" (Rev. 12:17). "The rest" may refer to the 144,000 "special servants of God."

3. *Mass Conversions:* Many Jews will become followers of Jesus Christ, especially at the time of Jesus' Second Coming (Zech. 12:10-13:1; Rom. 11:25-29). The greatest Jewish revival of all time is soon to occur. God has not abandoned the Jew forever. Today the Jews stand separated from His gift of salvation (Rom. 10:1-3), but in the near future the Jewish race will see Him whom they pierced and believe in Him as their Messiah!

4. *Mass Evangelism:* After Jesus' return to the

---

[1] Commentators are divided between the martyrdom of the 144,000 (which would cause Mount Zion to be interpreted as referring to heaven) and their preservation (which would refer to Jesus' Second Coming to the earthly Mount Zion). Humility here is most wise.

Israel

earth, and the subsequent conversion of many Jews, these new disciples will eagerly begin to testify to the rest of the world about the salvation that comes through Jesus Christ (Isa. 2:2-4; 66:18-21; Zech. 3:8-10). The Jews will not only be saved in mass, but they will witness in mass as well. It will be a great day of evangelism for the people who are left after the horrible period of the tribulation.

11

The Middle East

The Rise of the Middle East

The term "Middle East" arose around the period of World War II, and it refers to these countries: Morocco, Turkey, Greece, Cyprus, Syria, Lebanon, Iraq, Israel, Jordan, Egypt, Sudan, Libya, Saudi Arabia, Kuwait, Yemen, Oman, Bahrain, Qatar, Tunisia, Algeria, Afghanistan and Pakistan (see map on the following page). Originally the words "Near East" and "Far East" were used for sections of Asia, but today the two words, "Middle East," encompass the area of southwestern Asia between the Mediterranean Sea and India.

Until the twentieth century most of these national entities were non-existent. But this soon changed. Through World War I and the collapse of the Ottoman Empire, these lands began to take on distinct borders. Ten years after World War II these national lines had become fairly well fixed. So, in a valid sense, we can say that the Middle East is a new world, resurrected in just the past few decades. In fact, it was not until the 1960s and the 1970s that this world bloc began to approach any degree of modernization or recognition. But today, in the 1980s, these countries are suddenly among the most important to be found anywhere on the globe.

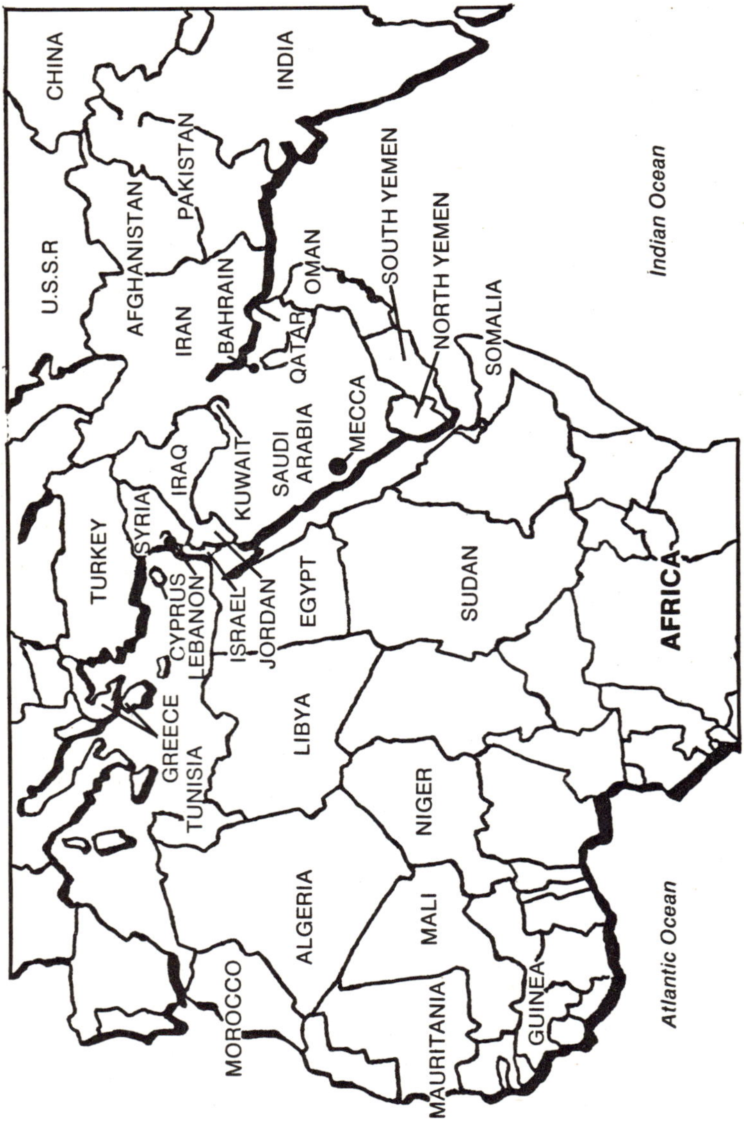
CHINA
INDIA
U.S.S.R
AFGHANISTAN
PAKISTAN
IRAN
BAHRAIN
QATAR
OMAN
SOUTH YEMEN
NORTH YEMEN
Indian Ocean
SOMALIA
MECCA
SAUDI ARABIA
IRAQ
KUWAIT
TURKEY
SYRIA
CYPRUS
LEBANON
ISRAEL
JORDAN
EGYPT
SUDAN
AFRICA
GREECE
TUNISIA
LIBYA
NIGER
ALGERIA
MALI
MOROCCO
MAURITANIA
GUINEA
Atlantic Ocean

The Middle East

A Major Unification of the Middle East

When the Arabs were released from the Ottoman Empire, they sought to unite their interests as an organized body. In order to achieve this goal a conference was held in Alexandria, Egypt (between September 25 and October 8, 1945). Those attending the conference included representatives from Egypt, Iraq, Syria, Lebanon, Trans-Jordan, Saudi Arabia, Yemen, and the Arabs living in Palestine which at this time was under the control of the British.

The result of this conference was the development of a document known as the "Alexandria Protocol." This writing foresaw the formation of a league of independent Arab nations. The aim of this league would be to strengthen the efforts of individual Arab nations by establishing a united bond with other nations of like interests. On March 22, 1945, the league came into formal existence.

The explicit aims of the Arab League are threefold:

1. The advancement of unity and cooperation between the Arab nations.

2. The presentation of a single voice in the affairs of the world.

3. The support of all Arabs in Palestine.

The original membership in the league was small, but today it includes the following countries: Algeria, Bahrain, Djibouti, Iraq, Jordan, Kuwait, Lebanon, Libya, Mauritania, Morocco, Oman, Qatar, Saudi Arabia, Somalia, Sudan, Syria, Tunisia, United Arab Emirates, Yemen, Southern Yemen, and the Palestinian Liberation Organization. At the June 27, 1979, session, the nation of Egypt was absent. Further, all

ARMAGEDDON 198?

the member nations have severed economic and political ties with Egypt because of her treaty with Israel.

The Chief Religion of the Middle East

The chief religion of the Middle East is Islam (a term which means "surrender to the will of Allah/God"). The origins of this religion can be traced to an Arabian prophet named Ubu'l Kassim (or Mohammed, as he came to be addressed). Mohammed lived more than five and a half centuries after the death and resurrection of Jesus Christ (A.D. 570-632), and his influence today affects over 538,000,000 followers! It is one of the largest religions in the world.

Mohammed was a camel driver by trade. This assuredly gave him a broad exposure to the faiths of different people. But by the time he reached the age of twenty-five, he was able to retire—because of a marriage to a wealthy widow. The result of this bond meant that Mohammed could devote himself to multiplied hours of meditation in a secluded cave near the city of Mecca.

Mecca was completely submerged in polytheism, housing over 350 shrines. Still, these idols yielded no satisfaction to Mohammed's quest for meaning. At the age of forty, however, something happened that would alter the rest of his life, and the lives of multitudes as well. While meditating in his cave, Mohammed began receiving frightening revelations and wild convulsions. For the next twenty-two years this experience was to be repeated again and again. Mohammed was uncertain if these experiences were from Allah or demons. But in the end he considered them to be messages from the angel Gabriel.

The essence of the revelations was a combination of

The Middle East

Jewish and Christian beliefs, with a new twist from Mohammed himself. He regarded himself as the final and the greatest of all the prophets.

Winning converts at first was difficult and dangerous. On July 16, 622 (the date from which Muslims start their calendar, and claim the official origins of their religion), Mohammed fled Mecca before a scheme involving his execution could be accomplished.

In the city of Yathrib, Mohammed found success, becoming its governor, general and judge. Soon the name of the city was changed to Medina, which means "City of the Prophet." Naturally, the majority of the people were responsive to his new beliefs.

It was from Medina that Mohammed launched an aggressive military campaign to establish his rule in Arabia. After subduing Mecca, he made it the holy city of the faith. By the time of his death he was ruler of all Arabia. Mohammed's successors were even more ambitious and successful. Through the use of the sword, their conquests brought Mesopotamia, Persia, Egypt, Jerusalem, Syria and portions of Europe and India under their belt. The preaching of "repent or perish," at the mouth of the Muslims (the name for the followers of Mohammed), was to be taken literally. In fact, in the Koran (their holy book) the use of force in spreading their religion is actually encouraged. Those who die as literal soldiers of the faith are guaranteed a place in heaven.

The doctrines of the Islamic faith are found in its 114-chapter book, the Koran (a book slightly smaller than the New Testament). There are five major teachings in this religion:

1. There is only one God—Allah.
2. There are many prophets—Mohammed is the last

and the most important one.

3. There are four inspired books—the Torah (the writings of Moses), the Psalms of David, the Gospels of Jesus, and the Koran. Naturally, this final book is held to be superior to those preceding it.

4. There are many good and bad angels at work in the world.

5. There will be a judgment day, when a pair of scales will weigh our righteous and unrighteous works to determine if we will be admitted to heaven or to hell.

Today there are many sects within the Islamic religion. The major body is called the Sunnites; the next most popular group is called the Shiites (pronounced She-ites). In neither sect is there any priesthood or clergy. The religion is held together by a weekly service, usually in a mosque, and by its four chief duties for all Muslims: prayer five times per day, fasting during the daylight hours one month per year, giving 1/40 of your income to the needy, and visiting Mecca (if at all possible).

The leadership in the Islamic sects is confusing. Generally speaking, the role of leadership is administered by a successor of Mohammed. (Just who is considered to be a legal successor, and what is to be the extent of his authority is debated by Muslims.) Nevertheless, there are successors, and they are called *ayatollahs*.

The trouble now begins. First, there are a number of ayatollahs. Second, any word from an ayatollah is considered final—as though it were directly from God. Third, an ayatollah takes counsel from no one; rather, everyone is to listen to him. Fourth, each ayatollah has his own group of followers. The recent crisis in Iran is a clear example of the muddled, yet powerful, position

The Middle East

such a person holds over the people. It makes one wonder whether or not an ayatollah will be the future antichrist. Such a possibility is entirely possible, especially since his rise to power is from an Arab nation (possibly Iraq).

The Significance of the Middle East

There is a new power in the world that no nation can afford to overlook. The source of this power is not a traditional strength, but no one denies its awesome grip. The new power is the Middle East. And the strength is energy, namely oil. Today this sector of the world represents both the most strategic and the most troubled spot on the earth.

By the end of the 1970s the biggest businesses in the world were oil companies. The profits made by these corporations clearly reflect this statement. Their present multi-billion-dollar profits, say the experts, are but a small percentage of the profits they will soon make. Figures on anticipated profits for oil companies, by the end of the eighties, is estimated at $300 billion!

But what happens if for some reason the Middle East pipeline is plugged up? What would be the effects of a total oil strike?

Presently the United States produces just under 50 percent of all the oil it consumes. That means, should a total oil embargo be put into effect, that one half of our consumption must be eliminated. But the situation for other countries would be far more critical. Japan, for instance, relies upon the Middle East for over 90 percent of her oil energy needs. Within two months the entire country of Japan could be strangled nearly to the point of death. And this is the case in a number of other countries as well.

ARMAGEDDON 198?

Without a doubt the decisions of the Middle East affect everyone in the modern world. Our eyes are firmly fixed on this land because the destiny of our financial and economic future may rest with her stability.

The Future of the Middle East

The hottest spot on earth today is the Middle East. It is the center of the world (Ezek. 38:12) and the center of world politics. Practically every nation on the earth has a keen interest in the decisions that are made by these few countries. But if the attention that is shown today is considered significant, then the attention it will be given in the future must be called absolutely critical.

The prophecies of the Bible envision a period when the Middle East will actually control the economic destiny of numerous countries (Rev. 13:11-18). The precise period for this immense display of power will occur during the years just immediately prior to Jesus' return to this earth. Stated differently, the Middle East will reach its peak economic authority (and disarray) under the leadership of a man whom the Bible calls the antichrist.

Precise and prolonged discussions regarding this figure are provided in a separate chapter (Chapter 15). The highlights from those discussions may be summarized as follows:

1. The antichrist will begin his career as a powerful ruler of a Middle Eastern country, possibly Iraq (Dan. 8:9; Rev. 13:2-3).

2. Some time after coming to power, the antichrist will engage in war with three of his neighbor countries and defeat them. At this point other countries will

The Middle East

align themselves under his powerful influence. In further campaigns the countries of Israel, Egypt, Libya and Ethiopia will become his prey (Dan. 7:8, 20, 24; 11:43).

3. He will be a ruler who is driven with a madness for power. In order to advance his militaristic ambitions he will exercise extremely strict economic regulations. Natural resources from his controlled territories will only be sold to allies (which seems to rule out Russia, China and Trans-Jordan; see Dan. 11:36-45; Rev. 13:1-18).

4. His schemes and successes lead him to believe he is invincible. But numerous countries, including Russia, Iran and China, will boldly challenge his power (Ezek. 38-39; Dan. 11:44). In a devastating conflict (possibly World War III/Armageddon) no one will be left the winner, except Jesus Christ. The Lord will put an end to the ungodly rule of every nation on the earth in his own campaigns at His Second Coming (Rev. 19:11-21).

Conclusion

A short generation ago no one really talked very much about the Middle East. The subject was as dry as its desert sands. Now all of this has dramatically changed. There is scarcely a day when the three major television networks do not report some event coming from this important section of the world.

The world is rapidly changing. The scene is being set. Soon, possibly very soon, we will enter the moments that have been reserved for the end of time as we presently know it. These are certainly great days to hear and heed God's call for a personal salvation in Jesus Christ!

12

Russia

Communism

The term "communism" refers to that theoretical system of government where all property is owned equally by everyone, so that each person might share equally in all the goods of a society. This social ideal is a rather recent political innovation, and the Russians are optimistic that they can reach this unrealistic utopia.[1]

Karl Marx—The Father of Communism

Born on May 5, 1818, to Jewish parents who later became Christians, Karl Marx was to bring to the world the formal groundwork for modern Communism.

Marx studied history, law and philosophy at the

---

[1] Some Christians have attempted to create this form of life, supposing it to be the New Testament standard for a perfectly submitted life (Acts 2:42-46; 4:32-37). For the most part, these efforts have been met with less than ideal results. In a nutshell, here are the fallacies of such a system: (1) It fails to distinguish the unique individuality of each person; (2) It fails to recognize the different calls of God upon people; (3) It fails to understand the carnal nature of people; (4) It fails to integrate others into the system—hence, the result is an exclusive society rather than an inclusive one, which is the opposite of the original goal; and (5) It fails to possess scriptural support (see Prov. 22:2; Matt. 5:39-48; Rom. 13:1-7; 1 Cor. 12).

ARMAGEDDON 198?

Universities of Bonn, Berlin and Jena (where he earned his doctorate). His liberal views, however, soon came to the fore and he was compelled to live in exile. Spending most of his time in Paris and London, Marx worked tirelessly (and usually with poor financial rewards) as a writer. Considered to be extremely arrogant and conceited, he continually researched material to provide even more support for his communistic ambitions.

Marx believed history shows a long and repeated record of struggle between the upper and lower classes. The solution, he said, was to abolish all forms of capitalism and to create an across-the-board equality. He felt that the existence of private property was the source of all social problems. Presumably only a community ownership of property would serve as a remedy for society's many ills. Presently the rich exploit the poor; but in a communistic system (or so the theory goes) there would be no rich-poor distinctions, and therefore, there would be no problems.

Here is a slightly different angle of Marx's views: (1) Create civil revolution in capitalist countries; (2) Elevate the working class to the place of power; (3) Make society classless.

The problems with this distorted brand of reasoning are numerous. For instance, (1) It is overly simplistic; (2) It resorts to revolution to achieve its goals; (3) In countries attempting to produce the communistic ideal, the results have never come close to arriving at the predetermined goals; and (4) The creation of a classless society is as impossible as it is impractical. (Naturally this godless system rules out divine assistance, which is clearly their greatest need in endeavoring to accomplish such a lofty feat.)

Russia

The Formation of the USSR

The Union of Soviet Socialist Republics (USSR or Russia) is a rather modern state in the Eurasian sector of the world. Composed of the largest land mass under one government, modern Russia dates its formal origins to March 12, 1917. On this date rule by the Czars came to an end, and a provisional government was set up in its place.

In a short while another body arose to challenge the new government. Under the leadership of Vladimir Ilyich Lenin, head of the Bolshevik Party (or the Communist Party), the country was destined to submit to the communistic philosophy of society. By January of 1918 the Bolsheviks were the sole power in the nation.

Vladimir Ilyich Lenin

Lenin was born at a troubled time in Russian history—on April 22, 1870, in the small town of Simbrisk. On his seventeenth birthday he graduated from high school as the best student in his class. In that same year, on May 20, 1887, his oldest brother, Aleksandr, whom he deeply loved, was put to death by hanging for attempting to assassinate Czar Alexander III. It was then that Vladimir gave up religion.

The same revolutionary ambition that possessed Aleksandr also consumed each of the four remaining brothers and sisters. They pledged themselves to overthrowing the reign of the Czars.

After attending the University of Kazan for several months, Lenin was expelled for participating in a student demonstration. It was during these days of expulsion that he read the communistic writings of Karl Marx. Soon he fell in love with this philosophy,

ARMAGEDDON 198?

and he organized a Marxist group. Joining with others of a similar persuasion, Lenin tirelessly pursued labors that were directly designed to overthrow the government of the Czars. By 1895 the authorities decided it was time to halt Lenin's campaign for socialism (the Russians equate socialism with communism). He was arrested, sentenced to live in prison for fifteen months, and then exiled to eastern Siberia for another three years.

It was from a prison cell in Siberia that Lenin wrote his first major work on communism, called *The Development of Capitalism in Russia* (1899). The intent of this writing was to unveil to the common Russian the crucial need for a massive revolution, so that a dictator could establish a Socialist state. Lenin constantly cried out for revolution. According to him, "Revolutions are the locomotives of history. Drive them full speed ahead and keep them on the rails!"

When Lenin escaped from prison in 1900, he left Russia and went to Switzerland to begin publishing a Socialist newspaper called *Spark* and a magazine called *Dawn*. (The magazine failed after just three issues.) These papers were then distributed secretly to the major cities of Russia. The result was a rising interest in reforming and overthrowing the government.

During the years between 1900 and 1917 Lenin's success was often mingled with crucial defeats. Many Marxists/Socialists disagreed with his radical and uncompromising views. For a good while Lenin saw himself representing a minority cause (which itself suffered from divisions because of Lenin's unbending philosophy of communism).

At the peak of political turmoil, Lenin returned to

Russia

Russia and announced the need for a complete socialist civil war. In a heated struggle, he found more and more support, but not without the cost of thousands of lives. On November 7, 1917, the provisional government (which was set up after the fall of the final czarist regime earlier that year) officially established a new government called the Russian Soviet Republic. Lenin was made the president of the new party and government.

In the early days of the Lenin regime it was difficult to control the largely illiterate and rebellious people. For instance, Fanya Kaplan, a revolutionary who opposed Lenin's rule, shot and seriously wounded the new leader. Additionally, an anti-Soviet army was formed which made conquests of much Russian territory. Lenin's response was a massive terrorism tactic. A Red Army was created to find suspects and members of a White Army and to have them killed. More than 500 were immediately killed in Leningrad, for instance, because of a protest they made against Lenin. Before his death, more than 250,000 rebels were to be slaughtered in a horrible civil war.

By 1920 the ugly revolts were ended. Communism had won. But the nation was left in a critical condition. Disease, poverty and general confusion were everywhere.

In March of 1923 Lenin experienced his third stroke, leaving him speechless and paralyzed. On January 21, 1924, he died at the age of fifty-three. His death was presumed by some to be due to a poison ordered to be given to him by his successor, Joseph Stalin.

Interestingly, Lenin included these lines in his will: "I propose to my comrades to find some way of

ARMAGEDDON 198?

removing Stalin from position and appointing somebody else who differs in all respects. Someone more tolerant, more loyal, more polite and considerate of his comrades, less capricious."

Joseph Vissarionovich Stalin

Stalin was born on December 21, 1879, to a father who failed to succeed as a shoemaker and to a mother who labored as a washwoman. His early years were spent in terrible poverty, but his economic position did not seem to affect his academic abilities or radical pursuits.

At the age of fifteen Stalin was granted a scholarship to a seminary in Tiflis, where he began studies for the priesthood. Instead of learning theology, however, he found ample discussion directed at a civil revolution designed to overthrow the rule of the Czars. At the age of nineteen he was expelled from the seminary because of his Marxist views. Stalin later blamed the strict rules of the seminary for his cause in turning to the principles of communism!

Like Lenin, he relentlessly pursued the creation of a civil war in Russia (and throughout the rest of the world as well). He published a Marxist newspaper, and went to prison, and eventually to Siberia for these propaganda tactics. After escaping from prison he followed Lenin and the Bolshevik Party from start to finish (excluding five further arrests, exiles and escapes!).

During the days when the Bolshevik Party was gaining momentum, under the leadership of Lenin, Stalin was appointed to the Central Committee. He then founded and edited a newspaper called *Pravda*. After the Communists took control of Russia, Stalin

Russia

served in various high-ranking positions. By the time of Lenin's death he was at the top of the political ladder. He was a logical (though contested) successor.

The reign of Stalin seems to have been dominated by a ruthless madness to protect himself from political enemies[2] and to advance his communistic goals. During his reign, propaganda became a first-rate priority; prison labor camps were overwhelmingly increased in number and in size; private business was taken over by the state; and a vast majority of former officials were purged from office and either put in prison or executed. It was a horrible day for justice and basic human rights. The supposed ideals of communism seemed to be only achievable at the costly expense of an iron-fist dictatorship and the execution of anyone getting in the way. In Russian politics, the end justifies the means. So, if the end meant a totally communistic state, then any means (including deceit, injustice and murder) was to be considered "legal."

On March 24, 1919, Stalin married his second wife (his first wife died in 1905). It was a nearly secret wedding, though the discord in the marriage left little to silence. Arguments were virtually constant. Outraged with Stalin's orders of mass starvation and

---

[2]Shortly after the Communists took office they developed an intelligence agency (or a spy organization). Under Stalin's reign, this group, known as the NKVD, reached its gory height in power. In almost no time it developed a reputation for terror, killing anyone who appeared to not support Stalin. This spy style or tactic has not been altered a great deal in Russia today. The KGB (the name of Russia's modern intelligence agency) has the largest staff and the best financial support of any spy body in the world. Over two billion dollars is spent annually by this group in order to carry out its duties, which include the suppression and persecution of Christians who seek more religious freedom.

ARMAGEDDON 198?

killings, she packed up and left him. Stalin managed to talk her into coming back, but the home would still not know any peace. Finally, she wrote a note accusing him of serious political misjudgments, and then shot herself to death on November 8, 1932.

On March 5, 1953, Stalin died from a brain hemorrhage. He was succeeded by Georgi Malenkov.

Georgi Malenkov and Nikolai Bulganin

On the day following Stalin's death, Malenkov, a key figure in removing dissidents during Stalin's hour of power, was made the new leader of Russia. His stay in office was both short and uneventful. He only held the position from March 6, 1953, to February 8, 1955. Malenkov resigned suddenly, stating that inexperience and inefficiency were his reasons for departing from the position.

Malenkov's short reign was followed by an equally brief role of leadership by Nikolai Bulganin. His authority also proved to be less than dynamic or effective.

Nikita Sergeyevich Khrushchev

Born on April 17, 1894, as the son of a miner, Nikita soon devoted his life to the various causes of communism. In 1918 he joined the Communist Party, and he fought in the Red Army. By 1934 he had advanced to a position in the Central Committee. In succeeding years he served in a number of other high-ranking positions, until he reached the top of the totem pole. This occurred on March 27, 1958.

Russia's policy with the Western (or capitalist) world was a mixture of "peaceful coexistence" and threats to "bury" it in death. Who can forget the

Russia

episode at the United Nations General Assembly in 1959 when Khrushchev removed his shoe and proceeded to pound his desk with it! Despite such words and actions, however, the United States seemed glad to ship his country thousands of tons of wheat and to assist Russia in developing its technology.

Khrushchev served six years as the supreme ruler in the USSR, when suddenly on October 15, 1964, he was removed from his post. It was clearly a forced resignation. Following his ousting an editorial appeared in the official Communist newspaper that stated he was removed because of his "harebrained scheming, immature conclusions, and hasty decisions and actions."

Leonid I. Brezhnev and Aleksei N. Kosygin

In Khrushchev's era the two highest political offices were occupied by himself; following his rule these positions were divided between two men: Brezhnev, who assumed the duties as first secretary of the Communist Party, and Kosygin, who became the premier of the nation. Eventually (by 1970) Brezhnev emerged as the real leader of Russia.

The social, political and economic status inside Russia has changed little since these men assumed office. If it were not for the generosity of Western countries like America, Russia would suffer miserably from hunger and technological backwardness. Freedom of expression is still carefully checked. Many prominent Russians have suffered the agony of exile or arrest for their outspoken views.

Analyzing the Communistic State

There is very little good that can be spoken about the reality of communistic rule in the Soviet Union. Since

ARMAGEDDON 198?

the final civil war that established the Bolshevik Party in politics (1918), there has been a ceaseless parade of atrocities—including an estimated 60,000,000 murders in the so-called interest of the state.

If the communistic system is all it claims to be, then why doesn't it work, especially in the arena of economics and technology, where it is supposed to excel? Here is a partial listing of what the United States would have to do in order to achieve economic and technological equality with Russia:

> Abandon three-fifths of our steel industry.
> Dispense with over 90 percent of our natural gas.
> Destroy fourteen of every fifteen miles of our highways.
> Shut down two-thirds of our hydroelectric plants.
> Eliminate 95 percent of our electric output.
> Scrap two out of three miles of our railroads.
> Junk nineteen of every twenty of our cars and trucks.
> Tear out nine of every ten telephones.
> Transfer sixty million Americans back to the farm.
> Slash all paychecks by three-fourths, and cut our standard of living accordingly.

The Russian governmental system is point-blank totalitarianism. Stated simply, that means there is only one party or only one point of view tolerated in the system. If someone in the state believes or acts in a manner that does not conform to the government's standards, then that party is easily, and often swiftly, exiled or imprisoned or just conveniently lost. A

Russia

massive secret police force is constantly engaged in finding and uprooting such persons. Naturally, this means that much of Russian life is spent in a state of suppressed fear, being aware that they might be spied upon and accused at any time of a non-Communist act.

In matters of religion, the policy is strictly atheistic (except in a few churches that are open to tourists and foreign diplomats). The state condemns all religious training of children, restricts the number of students enrolling in seminary to a minimal level, and prevents the more intelligent boys from entering these schools altogether (most priests come from farms and rural areas). Additionally, the few churches that do exist in Russia are subject to the State Council on Religious Affairs (a body of declared atheists), which has a complete authority over all decisions on the local church level. The communistic state also charges these churches huge sums in order to stay open. Presumably some 80,000 Bibles were printed in Russia during the past twenty years. (That amounts to 4,000 per year for a population of thirty to fifty million supposed believers—a ratio of one Bible for every 10,000 people!)

The facts are clear and repulsive.[3] Perhaps even more discouraging is the seemingly American naiveté toward the USSR, especially in the highest governmental levels. Politicians and presidents have displayed passive, casual and even sympathetic interest in the affairs of this nation. Our negotiations with Russia have often involved a trustworthiness on our part for their integrity. But how can such a horrendous wave

---

[3]Recommended reading: *Russia, The People and the Power*, by Robert G. Kaiser (Pocket Books: New York, N.Y.) 1976.

ARMAGEDDON 198?

of evil, sweeping over all of Russia's communistic history, be overlooked, as though only the present moment amounted to anything? God repeatedly and soundly warned Israel to shield herself from godless alliances (Exod. 23:32; Deut. 7:2; Isa. 30:2-5; Hos. 12:1). A nation professing to be light can no more walk hand-in-hand with a nation proving to be darkness than can a devout Christian spouse follow in the steps of an atheistic mate (2 Cor. 6:14-7:1). The way is different—emphatically and irreconcilably different.

Russia's Future War With Israel
It is the prophet Ezekiel who records the details of a future conflict between what appears to be Russia and the nation of Israel. The writing of this prophecy occurred 2500 years ago, yet it awaits a present-day fulfillment.[4] Below is a four-part analysis of this incredible battle that leaves the invading army utterly crushed.

1. *The Timing of the Battle:*
According to Ezekiel's chronology this battle is to

---

[4]There certainly has been no absolute agreement in the understanding of this passage. Some commentators envision a fulfillment after Israel's return from her Babylonian captivity in 537 B.C. Others see a fulfillment in a yet future time, either just prior to the Great Tribulation or at the close of the Tribulation, namely at the Battle of Armageddon. Still others contend that this prophecy will be realized only at the close of the Millennium, since a reference to "Gog and Magog" is found after Christ's 1,000-year reign (Rev. 20:7-10). A few see a double fulfillment—one at the close of the Great Tribulation, the other at the end of the Millennium. Such a divergence of scholarship should humble the most keen mind. The views of this author are shown above, and they are offered as a careful analysis, not as a dogmatic creed.

Russia

take place "in the latter years" (38:8) and "in the last days" (38:16). This language, unfortunately, provides little assistance in determining the precise time of the confrontation.

There are other considerations offered in our text, however, which help us to pinpoint the probable time of this battle.

First, it will occur only once Israel is restored to her land, after having been scattered among all the nations (39:25-27). Although Israel returned from Babylon in 537 B.C., the context here (chapters 33-39) refers to a fuller and more climactic restoration to the land by all Jews, everywhere. This did not officially occur, in my opinion, until May 14, 1948 (and even this is far from complete). Therefore, the fulfillment of this passage is yet to happen.

Second, the battle will be climaxed with God pouring out the Holy Spirit on the house of Israel (39:29). This will culminate in numerous Jews becoming Christians (39:6-7, 22, 28-29). Elsewhere in the Scriptures we are informed of the precise time of this outpouring and mass conversion—at the Second Coming of Jesus Christ (Zech. 12:10-13:1; Matt. 24:29-31; Rom. 11:25-27; Rev. 1:7).

Third, the details of this battle actually parallel the details found elsewhere for the Battle of Armageddon. For instance, the divine intervention in the battle (38:18-23; 39:2, 6-7, 11-13 with Rev. 19:11-21), the invitation to the fowls of the air to consume the carcasses (39:17-20 with Matt. 24:28; Rev. 19:17-19), and the appearance of hailstones, fire and an earthquake (38:19-22 with 2 Thess. 1:8; Rev. 16:17-21).

Fourth, it is in this battle that God makes himself known, in a special manner, to the nations of the world

ARMAGEDDON 198?

(38:16, 23; 39:6, 21). The revelation of God and Jesus Christ in this battle seem to make them known in two ways—as Judge and as Savior. It is most reasonable to believe, based on Scripture, that a great harvest of people will be won to Christ both *at* and *after* His glorious return (Isa. 66:19-24)!

Fifth, the language used for this battle is climactic. The prophet was clearly told that following this battle God's name would not be profaned any longer (39:7). Therefore, making the time of this conflict any sooner than the Second Coming of Christ seems most improbable. Further, the Lord promises the Israelis that after this military campaign they will now be able to "live securely . . . with no one to make them afraid" (39:26). Neither will God ever abandon them again (39:28-29).

2. *The Place of the Battle:*

The site of the conflict is expressly stated as being "against the mountains of Israel" (38:8; 39:2), "on the open field" (39:5), and "east of the [Mediterranean] sea" (39:11). This rather concise and precise setting fits well with the other description of the Battle of Armageddon. (See Chapter 16 for details.)

3. *The Purpose of the Battle:*

Ezekiel states the cause for this battle will be "to capture spoil" (38:12). In other terms, Israel is holding wealth which a number of nations, including Russia, will seek to possess.

It was not until the fall of 1973 and the winter of 1974 that America, and the rest of the world, became shockingly aware of their survival-dependence upon the natural resources of the Middle East. Since those days the subject of "energy" has become the top

Russia

priority of every modern nation on the earth. Without a doubt, the number one political issue of the eighties will be focused upon energy. With each passing year this subject will become a greater and greater sore, until some nations will be willing to go to war for this substance.

4. *The People Engaged in the Battle:*
Six different countries are itemized as cooperating in this conflict (38:2-3, 5-6; 39:1-2). Here is the biblical citation, along with their current national identities:

Gog [the prince of Rosh, Meshech and Tubal] refers to a king who dwells in the land of Magog, or modern Russia. This is made clear by stating that he dwells in "the remotest parts of the north" (38:6, 15; 39:2). Any map will show that Russia, and only Russia, lies in the distant north above Israel. The reference to Rosh, Meshech and Tubal are believed to be nomadic tribes that lived around the Black and Caspian Seas (Russian territory) and served Gog as their prince (or king). Some lexicographers are confident that behind the ancient spelling of "Rosh" is modern "Russia," behind "Meshech" is "Moscow," and behind "Tubal" is the Russian province of "Tobolsk."

Persia is largely modern Iran. Though she is not very friendly with Russia today, she will someday unite with her in attacking Israel.

Ethiopia (Cush—KJV and NIV) is found in northern Africa, south of Israel.

Put is somewhat obscure. Some see it as a reference to Libya in northeast Africa.

Gomer is in the vicinity of modern Germany.

Beth-togarmah encompasses much of modern Syria and Turkey.

ARMAGEDDON 198?

From an American perspective it appears that the Russians are preparing to achieve the most unprecedented and strategic advantage they have ever held. Their military advancements and negotiations in Europe, the Middle East, and Africa spell out a certain desire to be in a position of global supremacy. Experts predict that in the eighties Russia will be more aggressive, especially in the oil-rich Middle East, than ever before. Recent military campaigns in Afghanistan seem to verify these projections. It is suggested by some that Yugoslavia, Iran and Saudi Arabia will be next on Russia's hit list.

Without the slightest doubt, our present days are serving as a prelude to the hour when Jesus Christ will return to this earth in all of His glory!

13

China

More people live in China than anywhere else in the world (population: one billion people!). About one out of every four births in the world takes place in China. Further, it is the third largest country in area (nearly 4,000,000 square miles), succeeded only by Canada and Russia.

Formation of Modern China
On October 1, 1949, the world saw the end of a twenty-eight-year civil war in China, and the start of the Chinese People's Republic, with Mao Tse-tung serving as president.[1] The next thirty years were to be radical, to say the least.

---

[1]This chapter concerns mainland China, but Nationalist China (or as it is sometimes called, "Free China") should be given some recognition. The Communists defeated the Nationalists in 1949, under Mao. Those who escaped this rule fled to Taiwan, ninety miles from their former territory. Under the leadership of Chiang Kai-shek, these people claimed (and still claim) that mainland China is their land, their home. Initially, the United Nations only recognized Nationalist China, but in 1971 (with support from the United States) these people were expelled from the United Nations, being replaced by the Chinese People's Republic. In 1978 the United States terminated all formal diplomatic relations with "Free China," and we opened the doors to full diplomatic relations with mainland China!

ARMAGEDDON 198?

First, there was economic revolution. When the Communist government assumed control of China, its economic condition was barely alive. Almost immediately the majority of the private businesses were converted to state property. In 1949 the state owned only 15 percent of the agricultural and industrial operations; within three years she managed to gain control over 90 percent of it (today that figure is around 97 percent). Under a relentless and noncompassionate hand, the state drove its citizens into rigid economic programs. As might be expected, due to such massive attention given to this matter, China's economic situation today shows signs of stability.

Second, there was social revolution. The Communists launched the most thorough and intensive propaganda campaign ever conceived by mankind. Their aim was to brainwash the citizens with such heavy doses of Marxism, Leninism and Maoism that all independent thinking would completely cease. All dissidents were considered enemies of the state, for which they could be arrested and/or executed. Some estimates of this sort of killing go as high as 100,000,000 since 1949! In the *Guinness Book of World Records* Mao Tse-tung is stated to have been responsible for more deaths than any other person who ever lived!

Third, there was a foreign revolution. At the start of her ambitious history, China found much mutual favor with Russia. In repeated agreements the two nations vowed to support each other and to defend one another in case of any attack (especially from despised America).[2]

---

[2]Between 1960 and 1964 China-Russia relations grew progressively weak. In 1969 there was a brief exchange of shooting along their adjoining borders. Presently there are no formal ties between these two awesome powers.

China

The Chinese, for example, were quite straightforward in sending troops and supplies into North Korea, North Vietnam and Cambodia. China's desire to be the dominant force in Asia has been no secret. Even so, the United States has signed agreements (between 1972 and 1979), giving China our most advanced scientific and technological expertise (not to mention billions of dollars in commercial and military agreements)! With these new pathways, China anticipates she will achieve a comprehensive modernization on an equal par with the United States by the year 2000.

Fourth, there was religious revolution. The Communists make no pretense about their feelings toward religion. Although they give lip service to religious freedom, the buildings which originally served as meeting places for Confucianists, Buddhists, Taoists and Christians were confiscated and used by the state. Literally hundreds of thousands of Christians (both Catholics and Protestants) were either arrested, imprisoned or killed. The institutional church, representing local assemblies and some 150 denominations from the West, was completely removed.

Despite this truth, W. Stanley Mooneyham states, in his insightful book, *China: A New Day* (Logos, 1979), that God never left China. "Christ stayed with His Church," he writes. Believers may have it rough, but many are meeting in homes for worship. In some places the meetings are even public and well attended today. Jesus said He would build His Church and the gates of hell would not prevail against it (Matt. 16:18). This certainly is the case in China.

A highly inspirational and informative book that gives some of the details of life in Communist China is

ARMAGEDDON 198?

the biography of Watchman Nee by Angus I. Kinnear. It is called *Against the Tide* (Christian Literature Crusade, 1973).

China Joins in Battle at Armageddon
There are only three probable references to China in the Bible.[3] Each of them focuses upon the period immediately preceding the Second Coming of Jesus Christ. Put more specifically, each deals essentially with China's aggression against the new and powerful alliances established by the antichrist.

The first prophecy is taken from the Old Testament: *"Rumors from the East . . . will disturb him [the antichrist], and he will go forth with great wrath to destroy and annihilate many"* (Dan. 11:44).

The nature of these rumors is not stated, but based upon the context (in which we find the antichrist sweeping his armies through Egypt, Libya and Ethiopia), it seems reasonable to assume the reports he receives are severely derogatory of him due to his recent ambitious exploits in Northern Africa. In a fit of rage he will retaliate against those who slander his accomplishments. Whether or not he is successful is not stated in the text. It is entirely probable, however, that this vengeful battle is his final one—the Battle of Armageddon.

The second and third prophecies regarding China are taken from the book of Revelation (9:13-21; 16:12). These references respectively describe the judgments

---
[3] The language of the Bible does not require or restrict these references to nations "from the East" as being China. This is a logical and contemporary interpretation, not a clear-cut linguistic proof. Caution is advised in arriving at premature conclusions, including the ones discussed above.

China

that come from the blowing of the sixth trumpet and the pouring out of the sixth bowl from heaven. These judgments are prophetic pictures of the Battle of Armageddon. In other words, these references to China (as seems to be the case in the previous text from Daniel) involve the final great war on the earth prior to Christ setting up His own Kingdom here.

Now let us consider several of the details regarding this devastating and final battle:

1. The army from the East is said to be staffed with 200,000,000 soldiers (9:16). This is a staggering figure, but as early as 1965 the nation of China boasted of having a two-million-member army. At no other period in history could the literal size of this prophesied army be fulfilled than in our own time.

2. This army will kill one-third of mankind (probably including its own rank and file). The reality of nuclear war is not to be dismissed from this tragic scene. The world has yet to see a major nuclear holocaust, but apparently it is coming.

3. There will be other kings in the East, besides China, to join in this battle (16:12-16). This may include any nation East of Israel.

4. This army, says the Bible, has been prepared specifically for this battle (9:15). God, according to His own sovereign purpose, has ordained this final world war. How thankful we can be that it will be the last war before Jesus Christ returns to establish a rule in which peace will be the order of the day, every day!

14

America

America—"the land of the free and the home of the brave." Is this picture of the United States accurate today? Will this description be true in five years? Fifteen years? Twenty-five years? What does the Bible say about America?

Is America Mentioned in the Bible?

Three approaches have been taken by prophecy scholars regarding the role of America in the last days:

1. The United States *is* to be found *directly* in the scope of Bible prophecy. Those holding to this position contend that the "isles" of Psalm 72:10, the "young lions" of Tarshish in Ezekiel 38:13, and the "eagle's wings" of Revelation 12:14 all refer to America in the last days. An examination of these references, however, requires a pretty extreme imagination to find any allusion to America.

2. The United States *is* to be found *indirectly* in the scope of Bible prophecy. Those holding to this position assert that because America cannot be found in any prophetic passage for the last days, it must not exist at that time as a significant power. Some teachers have gone so far as to suggest that the United States will be

ARMAGEDDON 198?

destroyed by atomic or supernatural power and therefore have no voice in international affairs in the final days. But again, this approach requires a good imagination. Each argument offered in support of this view is based upon the silence of Scripture. Such reasoning seems to be weak and presumptuous.

3. The United States *is not* to be found (directly nor indirectly) in the scope of Bible prophecy. Those who take this view simply declare that for reasons known only to God, He chose to omit any discussion regarding America. This position should not surprise anyone. The Scriptures make no reference to Australia, the Arctic, Canada, Central America, South America, or Antarctica either. (Of the three views, this one has, in my opinion, the proper assessment of the case.)

When you read the Scriptures, you are made constantly aware that only one nation receives the spotlight: Israel. No other nation occupies such a prominent position as this one. In fact, for the most part, any discussion of another nation is done so only in the light of how its influence will affect the nation of Israel. The Bible is Israel-centered.

Some Scriptural Principles for America

Although America is not mentioned by the Prophets, there still remain some scriptural principles that apply to all nations, including the United States. There is no way of accurately predicting the condition of America in the final days, but there are some rules which can be used in order to predict inevitable national consequences:

1. If America will continue to be Israel's friend, then God will bless us; but should the United States ever become Israel's foe, then God will curse us. No stronger

America

or more clear words could be spoken than those found in Genesis 12:3: "I [the Lord] will bless those who bless you [Abraham and his seed], and the one who curses you I will curse."

Thus far America has stood by the side of the Israelis. Based upon current trends, there is reason to believe this interest will continue. The largest population of Jews in the world is to be found in the United States. About 3 percent of our population is Jewish. American policy has been very fair to this minority group. May it always continue to do so.

2. If America will endeavor to be a holy people, then God will bless us; but if we become a nation that does not fear and reverence God, then He must judge us. There is no nation on earth with more Christians than America. Neither is there a country with such a zealous interest in the task of global evangelization as the United States. It might be added that no other nation enjoys greater divine blessings. Still, statistics also indicate a rapid spiritual and moral decline in recent decades. The face of America in the eighties is not the same as it was, say in the fifties.

The Scriptures teach that "righteousness exalts a nation, but sin is a disgrace to any people" (Prov. 14:34). No nation on this earth can resist God's guidelines for life and then expect to prosper in the fullest degree of that term. There are very, very few citizens in America, for instance, who would readily trade their citizenship with someone living in a Communist or Muslim nation. We are the most democratic, the most secure and the most fulfilled people in the world. But these qualities are beginning to dim. And unless America repents of her enormous attitude of self-righteousness and godless living, she will taste the

ARMAGEDDON 198?

bitterness of divine correction!

3. If Christians will pray for America, there is a far greater chance that we will continue to know prosperity and peace. Here is some sound counsel from the Bible:

> First of all, then, I urge that entreaties and prayers, petitions and thanksgivings, be made on behalf of all men, for kings and all who are in authority, in order that we may lead a tranquil and quiet life in all godliness and dignity. This is good and acceptable in the sight of God our Savior, who desires all men to be saved and to come to the knowledge of the truth. (1 Tim. 2:1-4)

Additionally, it should be stated that in the United States, where the freedom of choice still exists, evangelical Christians ought to collectively organize their interests in order to protect both the local community and the nation as a whole from succumbing to anti-Christian legislation. Let us raise a mighty voice for moral and ethical standards that are acceptable to God. There are no less than forty million born-again Protestants and thirty million born-again Roman Catholics in America. It is time to speak; it is time to be heard.

PART IV

BEYOND THE NEWS MEDIA

15

The Antichrist

The worst holocaust of all time—a three-and-one-half-year period prior to the return of Jesus Christ—will be characterized by wars, famines, earthquakes, deceit, economic chaos and so forth. But the greatest cancer will reside in its key personage—the antichrist.[1] Like spokes on a wheel, every event of this cataclysmic epoch will be attached to this single figure.

Four Views on the Antichrist
Concerning the identity of the antichrist, four basic positions have emerged. The first view contends that the antichrist is not an eschatological person but a personification of evil—a mere principle of wickedness. The second position holds that the antichrist is an institution of evil.

Thirdly, it is asserted that the antichrist is an evil person. And fourthly it may be argued that the antichrist encompasses and combines each of the above views into one intensified period of evil, in which an ungodly institution reigns preeminent, with an

---

[1] The most popular title for this figure is the "antichrist," but other significant titles include the "little horn" (Dan. 7-8), the "willful king" (Dan. 11:36-45), the "man of lawlessness" (2 Thess. 2), the "son of destruction" (2 Thess. 2), and the "beast" (Rev. 6-19).

ARMAGEDDON 198?

equally contentious figure as its head. It is this latter view which finds the most abundant support from the Scriptures.

Identifying the Antichrist

Virtually every generation since Christ has determined and pronounced "the identity of the antichrist." Walter K. Price, in his excellent book, *The Coming Antichrist*, has traced the historical attempts to discern this personage. Below is a survey of Price's noteworthy compilation.[2]

1. *The Pre-Nicene Era*

Before the New Testament canon had closed, two Roman emperors had already been "identified" as the antichrist: Caligula (who reigned from A.D. 37-41) was the first nominated when he attempted to place his image in the Jerusalem temple. Nero (who reigned from A.D. 54-68) was the second nominee as the antichrist. He won this title because he severely persecuted the Christians in Rome.

In the second and third centuries the apostolic fathers commonly held that when the Roman Empire fell, it would be followed immediately by the ten-toed kingdom of Daniel's prophecy (see Dan. 2:7). The antichrist was to be in charge of this new kingdom.

Justin Martyr (who lived between A.D. 100-165) viewed the antichrist as "the man of apostasy," as spoken of by Paul in 2 Thessalonians 2. Irenaeus (around the year A.D. 200) surmised that the antichrist would be a Jew from the idolatrous tribe of Dan, and that his appearance would occur three and a half years before

---
[2]Walter K. Price, *The Coming Antichrist* (Chicago: Moody Press, 1974), pp. 18-43.

The Antichrist

the Second Coming. Tertullian (A.D. 150-225) believed in a personal antichrist, though he felt the personage need not be a Jew. Cyprian, having lived through a period of great persecution (around A.D. 200-258) concluded the end was near and the reign of antichrist was upon them. Victorinus, bishop of Pettau, stated that the antichrist would arise from among the Roman Caesars.

2. The Post-Nicene Era

From the time of Constantine (about A.D. 325) attitudes toward prophecy radically shifted. The primary cause for this change was Rome's reversal of policy toward the church. The empire that once persecuted the saints now embraced them and recognized them as the only legalized religion. This favor, however, depended greatly upon the particular emperor who ruled. Emperor Constantius, siding with the Arians, caused Athanasius to believe he was the forerunner of the antichrist. During the same period it was predicted that Constans I, an emperor who had been assassinated, would soon reappear. Hilary (a church leader) taught (along with Athanasius) that the coming of the antichrist was imminent and that his forerunner would be found in the church.

Jerome testified that due to the current breakup of the Roman Empire the antichrist must be near. Adso, the court chaplain to the Queen of France in A.D. 954, assembled all the data on the subject he could find. Adso wrote a pamphlet in which he concluded that the spirit of antichrist had already appeared, though *the* antichrist was yet to appear. He further held that the antichrist must come from the tribe of Dan, and that his birthplace would be Babylon.

ARMAGEDDON 198?

Also during this era, there was a strong conviction that the year A.D. 1000 would mark the end. Even the Muslims were candidates for this satanic title.

3. The Reformation and After

Although the pope had been sporadically branded as the antichrist before the Reformation of the 1500s by such men as Frederick II, Wycliffe and Huss, during the Reformation the papal system and/or the pope himself were consistently identified as such. Men making this accusation included Martin Luther, Philip Malanchthon, John Calvin, Huldreich Zwingli, Nicholas Ridley, Hugh Latimer, William Tyndale, Thomas Cranmer, John Foxe, John Knox and many others.

John Whitgift was awarded his Doctor of Divinity degree from Cambridge. In his dissertation he attempted to prove that the pope was the antichrist. Several confessions, including the Westminister Confession (A.D. 1646), designated the papal system as antichrist.

King James I, who authorized the writing of the "Authorized Version," at the age of twenty, wrote *A Paraphrase Upon the Revelation of the Apostle St. John*, in which he identified the locusts as the different orders of monks, and their king was the pope. Samson Lennard wrote a six-hundred-page volume proving that the pope was the antichrist. John Field (in 1581) wrote, "To prove the pope is antichrist is needless considering how it is a beaten argument in every book." Francis Potter (in 1642) attempted to prove mathematically that the number 666 represented the pope.

Naturally, during this period the popes made their counterattacks by charging that the Reformers and their movement was antichrist. Nevertheless, the Puritans continued the Reformation identification and

The Antichrist

it has largely prevailed until this present day (though such men as Napoleon, Nietzsche, Hitler and Mussolini have been offered as fulfillments).[3]

Scriptural Usages of the Term "Antichrist"
The actual word "antichrist" is used but five times in the Scriptures, and only by John in his first and second letters. Each of these usages is quoted below from the New American Standard Bible.

> Children, it is the last hour; and just as you heard that antichrist is coming, even now many antichrists have arisen; from this we know that it is the last hour. (1 John 2:18)

> Who is the liar but the one who denies that Jesus is the Christ? This is the antichrist, the one who denies the Father and the Son. (1 John 2:22)

> And every spirit that does not confess Jesus is not from God; and this is the spirit of the antichrist, of which you have heard that it is coming, and now it is already in the world. (1 John 4:3)

> For many deceivers have gone out into the world, those who do not acknowledge Jesus Christ as coming in the flesh. This is the deceiver and the antichrist. (2 John 7)

Six explicit conclusions may be drawn from these biblical references:

---

[3] A fine table which summarizes the various identities ascribed to the antichrist and those who hold such positions may be found in Raymond Ludwigson's volume, *A Survey of Bible Prophecy*, pp. 25-26.

ARMAGEDDON 198?

1. There are many antichrists (those within whom abides the spirit of antichrist).
2. The *last hour* (probably a designation for the whole church age) is at hand when antichrists are present.
3. A denial of the Father or the Son or the Messiahship of Jesus constitutes one as being an antichrist.
4. Everyone not acknowledging the full deity and humanity of Jesus Christ is an antichrist.
5. The antichrist is a deceiver.
6. The Christians of John's day anticipated the appearance of one particular antichrist, who apparently had not yet arrived.

According to John, then, the coming antichrist of antichrists will be a man of deception and denial, repudiating and disowning the person and work of Jesus Christ by means of speech and/or personal egotistical ambitions. But let's look still deeper, into the actual word itself.

The term "antichrist" is a clear compound of two parts: "anti" and "Christ." The prefix "anti" generally carries one of two meanings; it denotes either "face to face," in the sense of opposition toward something, or it means "in place of," in the sense of substitution. Hence, the antichrist will either parade about in open hostility toward the Father and Son, or he will attempt to pawn himself off as the fulfillment of the long-awaited Messianic dreams. The former view is by far the more probable for five essential reasons:

1. Nowhere is the antichrist said to be worshiped as the Messiah. The antichrist is always and only worshiped as "God" (Dan. 11:36-37; 2 Thess. 2:4; Rev. 13:1-10).
2. The antichrist, in all likelihood, will be a Gentile.

The Antichrist

This would automatically eliminate his eligibility for such a title.

3. Repeatedly, the antichrist is viewed as blaspheming the God of the Jews (Dan. 7:8, 25; 11:36; Rev. 13:5-6). Such speech will hardly promote Jewish worship.

4. The very title "antichrist" is used by John of those who "deny the Father and the Son." To deny the Father is to reject the sole God of the Jewish faith. Such blasphemy would never be tolerated by even unorthodox Jews.

5. Richard C. Trench, writing on the distinction between "false Christs" (Matt. 24:24; Mark 13:22) and the "antichrist" makes the observation that if the antichrist were intended to duplicate the Messianic role, another word would have been employed. He writes,

> The pseudochristos (false Christ) does not deny the being of a Christ; on the contrary, he builds on the world's expectations of such a person; only he appropriates these to himself, blasphemously affirms that he is the foretold One, in whom God's promises and men's expectations are fulfilled. The distinction, then, is plain. The antichristos (antichrist) denies that there is a Christ; the pseudochristos (false Christ) affirms himself to be the Christ. Both alike make war against the Christ of God, and would set themselves, though under different pretences, on the throne of his glory.[4]

For a detailed contrast between this eschatological figure and Christ note the listing on page 137. This data is quoted from my earlier book entitled,

---

[4]Richard C. Trench, *Synonyms of the New Testament* (Marshallton, Delaware: The Foundation for Christian Education), pp. 101-103.

ARMAGEDDON 198?

The Victor Bible Source Book (Wheaton, Ill.: Victor Books, 1977) pp. 189-190.

Now we will consider the antichrist himself—his character, his rise to power, his rule as a dictator and his ultimate doom.

His Character
1. *He will strongly oppose God and His people (Dan. 7:11, 20, 25; 11:36-39; 2 Thess. 2:4; Rev. 13:5, 7).* Every allusion to the antichrist reveals that central in his character is an absolute hate for God and Christians, especially Jewish Christians.

One of the principal activities of the short-lived reign of the antichrist will be the extermination of the Jews. The prophet Zechariah, in describing the death toll in the tribulation period, declares that two-thirds of the Jewish population in and around Jerusalem will be slaughtered, while one-third will be refined and become strong believers (Zech. 13:8-9).

Persecution is ahead. The Church has known such difficulty since its foundation. And so have the Jewish people. The merciless killings of the present and past are not to cease; rather they will be intensified, especially in the land controlled by the antichrist.

2. *He will be a very proud and arrogant man (Dan. 7:8, 20, 25).* The antichrist will make incredible boasts. His speeches will ring with clever, yet self-centered, diplomacy. He will fear no one, not even God. For some, this line of communication will have a strong appeal. They will quickly rally around such a self-confident political statesman.

3. *He will be a deceiver (2 Thess. 2:9-10; 2 John 7).* No one who ever lived will ever have been filled with more lies, propaganda and craftiness than the antichrist.

Contrasts Between Antichrist and Christ

Antichrist

1. Has ten horns
   Rev. 13:1
2. A king of earth
   Dan. 7:8, 24
3. Claims deity
   Dan. 11:36
4. Proud
   Dan. 7:25
5. Blasphemous speech
   Rev. 13:5
6. Deceiver
   Dan. 8:23
7. Fights saints
   Dan. 7:21
8. Sheds blood
   Rev. 6:2-10
9. Devours earth
   Dan. 7:23
10. Speaks great words
    Dan. 7:25
11. Reign is limited
    Dan. 7:25
12. Rules from Jerusalem
    2 Thess. 2:4
13. His power is not his own
    Dan. 8:24
14. Called a prince
    Dan. 9:26
15. Breaks covenant with Israel—Dan 9:26-27
16. Acts according to his will
    Dan. 11:36

Christ

1. Has seven horns
   Rev. 5:6
2. Ruler of earth's kings
   Rev. 1:5
3. Is deity
   John 20:28
4. Meek
   Matt. 11:29
5. Speech controlled by the Father—John 14:10
6. Guileless
   1 Pet. 2:22
7. Comforts saints
   Rev. 7:7-17
8. Gave His blood
   Rev. 5:9
9. Smites nations
   Rev. 19:15
10. Speaks words of life
    John 6:63
11. Reign is limited
    1 Cor. 15:24-28; Rev. 20:4-6
12. Rules from Jerusalem
    Isa. 2:2-4
13. His power is not His own
    Matt. 28:18
14. Called the Prince of princes—Dan. 8:25
15. Fulfills covenant with Israel—Zech. 12:10-13:1; Rom. 11:25-27
16. Acts according to Father's will—Mark 14:36

	Antichrist		*Christ*
17.	Is worshiped Rev. 13:4	17.	Is worshiped Rev. 5:8-14
18.	Son of perdition 2 Thess. 2:3	18.	Son of God John 1:14
19.	Man of sin 2 Thess. 2:3	19.	Sun of righteousness Mal. 4:2
20.	Called wicked one 2 Thess. 2:8	20.	Called Lord of glory James 2:1
21.	Wears a crown (*stephanos*) Rev. 6:2	21.	Wears crowns (*diadems*) Rev. 19:12
22.	Rides white horse Rev. 6:2	22.	Rides white horse Rev. 19:11
23.	Has bow in his hand Rev. 6:2	23.	Has sword Rev. 19:15
24.	Gathers armies for Armageddon—Rev. 16:13-16	24.	Brings armies to Armageddon—Rev. 19:14
25.	Ascends from the pit Rev. 11:7	25.	Descends from heaven Rev. 19:11
26.	Symbolized as a leopard, bear, lion and beast—Rev. 13:1-2	26.	Symbolized as a lion and lamb—Rev. 5:5-6
27.	Wounded to death Rev. 13:3, 12, 14	27.	Wounded to death Rev. 5:6
28.	Death wound healed Rev. 13:3, 12, 14	28.	Death wound healed Col. 2:12
29.	Hailed as a king Rev. 13:4	29.	Hailed as a king Luke 19:38
30.	Demon-possessed Rev. 16:13-14	30.	Spirit-controlled Luke 4:1
31.	Mark of antichrist Rev. 13:15-18	31.	Mark of Christ Rev. 3:12
32.	Comes in his own name John 5:43	32.	Came in His Father's name—John 5:43.
33.	Comes to destroy Rev. 13:1-10	33.	Came to save Luke 19:10

The Antichrist

His ability to misguide the masses will be performed with a matchless degree of finesse. The most subtle device at this leader's disposal will be his tool of false appearances—that is, he will persuade people that what he tells them is true, when in actual fact it is just a lie made up for the occasion. Unfortunately, powerful leaders have often relied upon this tactic to gain their following. The antichrist will be no exception.

4. *He will not desire women, but war (Dan. 11:37-38).* It is natural for men to have an affection for women, but this will not be the case with the antichrist. Instead, he will be devoted solely to his god of war. There will not be a warm spot in this man's heart for people. Natural affections will not be a part of his personality.

5. *He will be indwelt and controlled by demons (Rev. 17:8).* This should come as no surprise. The antichrist will be Satan's pawn, by his own choosing. Jesus was offered by Satan this same egotistical position of momentary power, but he flatly refused it (Matt. 4:8-10). The antichrist, not being so wise, will not turn down this once-in-a-lifetime offer. Regrettably, it will cost him his soul in eternal hell.

His Rise to Power

1. *The antichrist will rise to power only after a ten-state federated body is organized in the region of the old Roman Empire (Dan. 7:8, 20, 24).* In other words, before you can expect to see the kingdom of the antichrist, you will first see the formation of some political alliance between ten countries. The fulfillment of this prophecy has been seen by some as coming in the ten-nation-body known as the European Common Market. Whether or not this is the intended fulfillment is uncertain at this time. It is possible that another union,

composed of ten nations, will yet be established (possibly between some of the Middle East nations). At any rate, proof of the modern realization of this prediction may or may not be among us (though no one denies its potential for a soon appearance, if it is not yet here). Once this ten-member-body is established, it will submit (at some point in time) to the leadership of a terrible harlot, called "Mystery Babylon" (Rev. 17). The identity of this latter body is debated by biblical interpreters. The major views are these: (a) it is papal Rome; (b) it is an apostate world church with its headquarters in Rome; (c) it is the reconstructed city of Babylon on the Euphrates River in modern Iraq; (d) it is a symbolization of secular godlessness; and (e) it is the city of Jerusalem. Each view has its claims. Perhaps the best solution is to wait and see. Our arguments may sound convincing today, but only time will prove our views to be correct or in error.

2. *The antichrist will come to power in a country represented by one of the four divisions in the old Greek Empire, namely the Syrian (or Seleucid) section (Dan. 8:9; Rev. 13:2-3).* When Alexander the Great died, his kingdom was subsequently divided into four sections by his four leading men. According to Daniel's prophecy the prototype of the antichrist was to arise from the Syrian segment of the former Greek nation. This happened in the years 175-164 B.C. during the reign of a Syrian king called Antiochus IV.

This ruler's activities perfectly correspond to the yet future antics of the antichrist. This kind of prophecy which foretells future events through current happenings is called "typology." In the mind of Daniel, the occurrences under the rule of Antiochus IV would be repeated under the reign of the antichrist. This con-

The Antichrist

clusion is confirmed by the writing of John, in about A.D. 100. Each of these men saw the antichrist coming from old Greece (or more specifically, the Syrian element of this former empire). The original Syrian section was considerably larger than modern Syria. Today it includes portions of Turkey, Syria, Lebanon and Iraq. Based upon this evidence, it seems reasonable to conclude that both the antichrist and his kingdom will arise somewhere within this original territorial boundary. It is conceivable that he will be a future ruler of one of these modern nations. Since the Scriptures also state that this nation's size will be rather large (in contrast to its neighbors—Dan. 7:20), the possibility of Lebanon and Syria seem unlikely.

My personal opinion is that Babylon, in Iraq, will be reconstructed and serve as the original headquarters of the antichrist.

While it may be difficult to imagine rebuilt Babylon as playing any significant role in world affairs, it must be remembered that her rise to recognition comes only after the ten kings yield their power to the antichrist. This change in loyalty from Rome to Babylon will make it automatically the new economic capital of the world. Such an awesome overnight shift in power will be of no small import.

There has been little interest in the Middle East until recent years. Now it is practically the center of world attention. Why? Because oil is the world's chief source of energy, and over one-half of the earth's supply is located here. In 1938 Iraq was virtually unknown. Today she is, along with her neighbors, the fastest changing land on our planet.

The nations of the Middle East are rapidly becoming

ARMAGEDDON 198?

excessively wealthy. In fact, some economists are calling this area the money center of the world.

So much money has been poured into these countries that a whole new life style is being created—a new society is being established. The most ambitious construction projects ever undertaken are now in progress. On the outskirts of Saudi Arabia's capital, Riyadh, for example, a new university is being erected with more than ten million square feet of teaching space—that's larger than Harvard. Additionally, a city is being built to accommodate 200,000 people. An airport is being constructed that is larger than London's airport. And on it goes.

There is little surprise then that on March 29, 1971, a news release from Beirut, Lebanon, ran an article announcing the reconstruction of ancient Babylon. It reads as follows:

> Iraq plans to "resurrect" the ancient city of Babylon, whose great walls and hanging gardens were among the seven wonders of the world, according to the Iraq news agency.
>
> The government has approved a $30,000,000 fund-raising campaign to meet the costs of the "resurrection plan," the agency reported. UNESCO and the Gulbenkian Foundation will be invited to share in the costs.
>
> The ruins of the 4,000-year-old city, once the capital of the Babylonian Empire, are still a main tourist attraction in Iraq.
>
> They will be rebuilt in their original architectural designs under the new plan, the agency reported.

The Antichrist

To date, less than 10 percent of the actual building process is completed. It has been estimated that the year 1982 will see its completion, but political unrest may keep this from becoming a reality.

Some commentators do not envision Babylon ever being rebuilt. But here are eight reasons that support the idea of its reconstruction:

a. *The Day of the Lord:* Babylon is said to be destroyed during "the day of the Lord" (Isa. 13:1-13). This unique eschatological terminology has particular reference to the Great Tribulation and the Second Coming of Christ. Therefore, it must be rebuilt before this prophecy can be fulfilled.

b. *Heavenly Signs:* Babylon's destruction will come with the accompanying signs of stars from heaven not shining, the sun becoming black and the moon not giving its light (Isa. 13:1-10). These identical signs will precede the Second Coming (Matt. 24:29-31; Rev. 6:12-17; 16:17-21).

c. *Sinners Removed:* All sinners will be removed from Babylon at its doom (Isa. 13:1-10). When Babylon fell to Medo-Persia (538 B.C.), this certainly never occurred. It has yet to happen as prophesied.

d. *Like Sodom and Gomorrah:* God's judgment of Babylon will be so severe that it is compared to His judgments of Sodom and Gomorrah (Isa. 13:19; Jer. 50:39-40; cf. 51:26). This was not the case with historical Babylon (Dan. 5:25-11:35). In fact, in the conquering of Babylon, the city was never destroyed at all!

e. *Habitation:* No one will ever inhabit Babylon once it is destroyed (Isa. 13:20). Again, this has no historical fulfillment.

f. *Flee:* The Jews were admonished to "flee from the midst of Babylon" in order to escape her divine punish-

ment (Jer. 51:6, 45). This never occurred in Babylon of old, but it will happen in rebuilt Babylon (Rev. 18:4).
    g. *Commercial Center:* Zechariah prophesied the future building of a commercial center in Shinar, Babylonia (Zech. 5:5-11). We should be looking for this new site in the very near future.
    h. *Literal City:* The prophecies of John speak of a literal city with the name of Babylon. This city is to be destroyed by God at the Second Coming (Rev. 18). It would be exceedingly difficult to pass over all these predictions by calling them symbolic. A literal fulfillment is most possible.
    3. *The antichrist will gain significant power after fighting and conquering three nations (Dan. 7:8, 20, 24).* Some time after the (previously discussed) ten-nation alliance is established, he will go up to fight with three of these members. Apparently his militaristic and diplomatic skills are so impressive and persuasive that the remaining seven nations will also forsake their loyalty to the "harlot" of Mystery Babylon and yield their faithfulness to the antichrist. Once this happens, the little-known leader will become an overnight superpower. Anyone controlling significant segments of the Middle East, as will the antichrist, cannot be called anything less than a major world power—possibly greater than the current Big Three (the United States, Russia and China).

His Rule as a Dictator
    1. *He will desire to be absolutely sovereign (Dan. 7:25).* With an ambitious arrogance the antichrist will attempt to have everything run his own way. There will be no room for democracy in his administration. According to the prophet Daniel, he will even attempt

The Antichrist

to change traditionally significant calendar dates. This may mean he will desire to make a new calendar that honors his own birth and notable events in his life.
2. *He will subdue Jerusalem, making it his personal headquarters (Dan. 11:41, 45).* The Bible calls Israel the center of the world (Ezek. 38:12). Doubtless this tyrant will seek to be exalted in the most prominent place available to him. There is even clear prophetic evidence stating that the antichrist will demand his subjects to bow their knees and worship him, as though he were God (2 Thess. 2:4). The response will be obedience to such commands, but this will be probably due more to fear than to reverence.
3. *He will exercise a tight-fist economic policy (Rev. 13:17).* The politics of the latter days will be dominated by crucial economic interests. And right now economic interests mean oil—Middle East oil. Whoever controls the oil fields of the Middle East will also control the destiny of many modern nations. Few countries today can bring themselves to the place of even imagining what life would be like without the oil that is supplied to them from outside their borders.

There is an extremely significant prophecy from Daniel's writing that states the antichrist will sell strips of land—oil-rich land—for the kind of resources that will beef up his aggressive army (Dan. 11:39). And if you cannot supply him the type of goods and allegiance he requires, you will be eliminated from the marketplace—both on the international and local levels.[5]

---

[5]Everyone within the antichrist's domain wishing to live will be required to receive an imprint on either his forehead or right hand. Whether this mark applies to the beast's name, number or something other than these is not certain (see Rev. 14:9; 15:2-4; 20:4). Interestingly, there is now a process whereby a number can be imprinted invisibly and irremovably on the hand or forehead by an electronic device. This number can be read by another instrument at a glance.

ARMAGEDDON 198?

4. *He will generate a worldwide influence, but his kingdom will never closely resemble a one-world government.* The scope of the antichrist's domain is said to be "over every tribe and people and tongue and nation . . . and *all* who dwell on the earth will worship him" (Rev. 13:7-8). If this is to be taken literally, then no one at all will be outside the antichrist's immediate grasp. But this is not the case, as we shall see.

What does the Bible mean when it uses such expressions as "every" and "all"?

Of Nebuchadnezzar it is written that God made him ruler over "all" men (Dan. 2:37-38; 4:1, 11-12). Yet history testifies that Babylon only ruled a very small portion of the then-known world.

Greece is prophesied to "rule over all the earth" (Dan. 2:39), but there are many lands Greece never conquered.

Rome, too, is described as devouring the "whole earth," but again this is not the actual case.

The exaggerated use of "all," "whole," and "every" could go on and on (see Josh. 6:21-25; 2 Sam. 6:5, 15; 1 Kings 11:16-17; Matt. 3:5-6; Luke 2:1-3; etc.). These words are clearly used as a common figure of speech. The same practice occurs today. For example, when we go to the state fair, it is easy to say that it was so crowded that *everyone* must have been there. This is a normal and clearly understood exaggeration.

A more accurate understanding of the terms "all" and "every" would be to consider them as expressing "a large portion" or a "sizable quantity." These words do not need to be understood in the absolutely literal sense. The word "many" is the more proper intention.

The book of Revelation never suggests that antichrist's territorial boundaries will ever exceed those

The Antichrist

of the ten kingdoms (the Revised Roman Empire). The antichrist is pictured as a man mighty in war, but not a single account is recorded in the book of Revelation of his annexing more kingdoms under his banner than the ten previously discussed.

Daniel 11:40-43 specifically states that Israel, Egypt, Libya and Ethiopia will fall under his control. But in the same account, Moab, Edom and Ammon are said to be "rescued out of his hand" (v. 41). Daniel's last remarks on the battles of the antichrist reveal that a nation from the North (Russia) and a nation from the East (China) will greatly disturb him (11:44). This is hardly the language of a completely sovereign political dictator.

A final proof that the antichrist's kingdom is unquestionably restricted can be found in Isaiah and Zechariah. These prophets teach that there will be multitudes in the world *after* the Second Coming of Christ who have not even so much as heard of Jesus Christ (Isa. 66:19; Zech. 8:23). Certainly the kingdom of the antichrist will not spread farther in three and a half years than the Kingdom of Christ, which has been operative for nearly 2,000 years!

The final line is this: The scope of antichrist's boundaries can probably be fixed to only segments within Europe, western Asia and northern Africa. He will control the ten nations who yield to him their power, and a few additional nations which he conquers. Beyond this, Scripture is silent. This does not mean that America will remain unaffected by the antichrist's power, however. For whoever controls this much territory will hold an awesome economic grip on the destiny of many countries.

ARMAGEDDON 198?

His Ultimate Doom

The duration of the antichrist's reign is repeatedly stated as lasting only 1,260 days or forty-two months (Dan. 7:25; Rev. 11:2; 12:6, 14; 13:5). At the close of this short rule he will be utterly crushed by invading nations at the Battle of Armageddon, and by the heavenly armies accompanying Jesus Christ at His return (Rev. 16:13-16; 19:11-21). He will end up where every misguided and rebellious person goes—to death and to hell, forever (Rev. 19:20).

Conclusion

Forty years ago only a few persons were taking Bible prophecy seriously. For most, the predictions of Scripture were as insignificant as the desert regions of the Middle East. But today every nation has its eyes on the newly formed nation of Israel, and her oil-producing neighbors.

Could it be that your eyes are being opened too? Is it possible that this generation could be the one to see Christ's return to earth? I believe so!

16

The Second Coming of Jesus Christ

Christ's return to earth will be *personal* (John 14:3; Acts 3:19-21; 1 Thess. 4:16-17; Phil. 3:20-21; Heb. 9:28; 2 Pet. 3:3-4; James 5:7-8; 1 John 2:28), *sudden* (Matt. 24:25-28; 1 Cor. 15:51-52; Heb. 10:37; Rev. 22:12), *unexpected* (Matt. 24:32-51; 2 Pet. 3:8-10), *with angels* (Matt. 16:27; 25:31-46), *with saints* (1 Thess. 3:13; 4:14), *triumphant* (Luke 19:11-27), *visible* (Rev. 1:7), *in fire* (Isa. 66:15-16), *in chariots* (Isa. 66:15), and on *dark clouds* (Joel 2:1-18).

There is no more dramatic event recorded in the Scriptures than the Second Coming of Jesus Christ. His descent is not only the basis for the "blessed hope" of all who believe (Titus 2:13), it is also the subject of rejoicing for all creation (Ps. 96:12-13; 98:7-9; Isa. 11:6-9; 35:1-7; 55:10-13; 65:25; Hos. 2:18; Rom. 8:20-21).

There are more than 1,400 passages devoted to the single theme of Christ's return and rule on this earth. In the New Testament there are more than 300 direct references to His Second Coming alone. And when you consider the fact that there are only 216 chapters in the New Testament, you are suddenly made aware that this event occupies a paramount position.

For the Christian this data is abundantly exciting because if Christ can fulfill to the letter the numerous

ARMAGEDDON 198?

prophecies of His first coming (and He did!), then He will equally fulfill the many faceted prophecies regarding His Second Coming, too!

The Marriage of the Lamb
Often the Scriptures describe the relationship between God and His redeemed in the terms of a marital union. The use of the figures of the bridegroom (referring to Christ) and the bride (referring to all the saints)[1] are common (Matt. 9:15; John 3:29; Rom. 7:4; 2 Cor. 11:2; Eph. 5:25-33; Rev. 19:7-8; 21:2, 9). The purpose for this identification is simple, yet it is by far the most profound and exhilarating hope of the saint—Jesus Chist will marry His bride and love her for the duration of eternity!

The time and place of this marriage, in all likelihood, will be in heaven and after the Rapture (or the first resurrection) (Rev. 19:7). This service will then be followed by the saints' descent to earth (Rev. 21). Once the various battles of the Second Coming are fought, guests from all over the world will be invited to the marriage supper (Rev. 19:9).

This chronology of events is in perfect accord with the oriental pattern of marriages. First, there was the betrothal—which speaks of the saints' acceptance of

---

[1] Who the Lamb marries has been a subject of much debate. Dispensationalists hold that only the Church—those saved between Pentecost and the pretribulational rapture—will be the bride. They view the Old Testament saints as only being guests at this service.

Non-dispensationalists would more commonly accept the bride as referring to the saints of *all* ages. This view seems to be the more probable, since both Israel and the Church are called the Lord's wife (Isa. 54:1-10; Jer. 3:1-19; Ezek. 16:1-63; Hos. 2:1-3:5; and so forth).

The Second Coming of Jesus Christ

Jesus Christ as their personal Savior (2 Cor. 11:2). Secondly, the bridegroom came for his bride—this is pictured in the Rapture (1 Thess. 4:13-18). And thirdly, guests were invited to the marriage feast—this refers to the plea which goes out after the Battle of Armageddon to all those left on the earth (Matt. 22:1-14; Luke 14:15-24).

The marriage of Christ to the saints will constitute the most unique and wonderful event the universe has ever known! Is it not possible that the thirty minutes of silence, occurring in heaven at the seventh seal, refers to this unspeakable service (Rev. 8:1)?

The Day of the Lord

Of the seventy-two designations referring to the events of the Second Coming of Jesus Christ, this one, "the day of the Lord," is probably the most descriptive. And the reference which best clarifies the issues involved in this period is 2 Peter 3:10-13. This passage contains six main thoughts:

1. *Notice whose day it is.* This is "the day of the Lord." It is the Lord's day. It belongs to Him alone. No one else can claim that day. The Lord—Father, Son and Spirit—will occupy the spotlight by himself. This day is reserved for the members of the Trinity, for their activities. The only thing that will matter on that day is what is done by the Lord. It is His glorious moment to move dramatically into the affairs of the nations of the earth. This will be the most profound day in history (next, of course, to the day Jesus paid for each person's sins by hanging on the cross).

2. *Notice how unprepared the people will be at the coming of this day.* Prophecy means very little to most of the earth's occupants. They either ignore or scoff at

ARMAGEDDON 198?

such predictions as this one. But disbelief will not halt its perfect fulfillment. And when all this happens, many people will be shocked and totally unprepared. Jesus will have come and found them as unexpecting of His glorious arrival as the appearance of thieves to their homes. How unfortunate that most of the earth's people will not be ready to meet Jesus when He returns! But this need not happen. We can be ready (see 1 Thess. 5:1-8; Rev. 16:15).

3. *Notice what will happen in this day.* Here is the most climactic and devastating language found anywhere in the Bible—"The elements shall melt with fervent heat; the earth also, and the works that are therein shall be burned up" (KJV). This could well refer to nuclear warfare.

The word for "elements" refers to the single component of which all matter is composed—the atom. The term translated "melt" literally means to separate, to take apart, to destroy. The image is clear to the late-twentieth-century reader—atomic/nuclear explosions that burn the earth with its dreadful effects. Doubtlessly earth's final war (World War III?) will involve the use of earth's most powerful and dreaded weapons.

4. *Notice the call to holiness.* Since these events are inevitable, we are exhorted to join the winning side—the Lord's. And the way this is done is by allowing the Lord to change our life style to one patterned after holiness and godliness. Honestly, this is the best life possible—both now and forever more!

5. *Notice the effects of holy living.* In some mysterious manner the way we live actually affects the time when the Lord's day will occur. Through holy, peaceable and spotless conduct the time of Christ's return can be "hastened." Therefore, if we truly want Jesus to return

The Second Coming of Jesus Christ

in our generation, then we ought to live as though we want this occurrence in our lifetime.

6. *Notice the ultimate end of the Lord's day.* The final result of the Lord's day is a new heaven and earth, in which only the righteous will be found. Sin will not reign forever. It will end. And all that is right will take the throne and rule forever. This is our dream, and when Jesus comes the second time, it will become a great and wonderful reality.

Second Coming Judgments

There are seven judgments that will occur at the time of Christ's Second Coming.

The First Divine Judgment: Against Edom

The land of Edom received its name from Esau and his descendants who inhabited the area. It is located just south of the Dead Sea.

For many years the Edomites and Israel were archenemies. Fighting between the two countries was vicious and costly. But in a yet future battle the Lord himself will engage in conflict with the people of this tiny land. Alone, He will vent His wrath and rescue those who have hidden themselves there from the slaughtering arm of Satan and the antichrist (see Isa. 34:1-15; 63:1-6; Matt. 24:16-20; Rev. 12:6, 14).

It is difficult, if not impossible, to locate with precision the site of this divine judgment. It is just as hard to determine whether this event is associated or not with the second judgment below.

The Second Divine Judgment: Against the Jews

When Christ returns to this earth, His primary intent will be to set up His own kingdom of universal

ARMAGEDDON 198?

righteousness and peace. Since the very beginning God has desired that men should live together harmoniously and in a garden of perfect bliss. This is still God's plan. And it will be fulfilled. But in order to create this new kingdom, there must first be some judging of earth's people and powers.

The second judgment will be executed against the Jews. You can read the details in Ezekiel 20:34-38 and in Malachi 3:1-5. The essence of the judgment is this. All living Jews will be examined by God's spiritual eye to determine if their hearts are still hard toward Christ, or if they have yielded their hearts to Christ's lordship. Those who have not become Christians will be cast into outer darkness. And those who have become Christians will be privileged to enter the kingdom age (or the Millennium).

The exact place of this Jewish judgment is not indicated, but from the text in Ezekiel it appears it will transpire just outside of Jerusalem. It also appears to be entirely feasible that the saved Jews will then follow their Lord, Jesus Christ, to the city of Jerusalem for a third Divine Judgment.

Paradox always plays a significant role in Scripture. Here we find the judgment of unbelieving Jews. But we also know from other Scriptures that this time will mark the greatest period of Jewish salvation (Rom. 11:1-36). Many will be saved, and many will be lost.

There are many Scriptures which teach that the Jews will be restored to their land (Isa. 11:11-12; 35:8-10; 49:18-22; 51:11; 55:12; 60; 62:10; 66:20; Jer. 3:18-19; 23:3; 24:6-7; Ezek. 36-37; Hos. 1:10-11; 2:23; Amos 9:13-15; Mic. 4:6-7; Zeph. 3:9-13, 18-20; and so forth). This regathering process will take place *prior* to the Second Coming and have its climax with Israel's

The Second Coming of Jesus Christ

judgment *after* Christ returns (Ezek. 20:33-38; Zeph. 3:11; Zech. 13:8-9; Matt. 25:1-30). This judgment on Israel will purge all unbelievers from among them so that only the saved will enter the promised land and the millennial period.

Zechariah writes of a day when God will pour out the Spirit of supplication and prayer upon all the house of David and the inhabitants of Jerusalem (12:10-14). It is in that day when the Lord will open a fountain to them for the removal of sin and uncleanness (13:1). All Jerusalem will be saved.

When will this happen? The explicit evidence of Scripture declares it will occur immediately after the Second Coming (compare Zech. 12:10 with Matt. 24:29-31 and Rev. 1:7). The broader testimony of Scripture is plain in its statement that there will be numerous conversions of Jews after the Lord returns (Isa. 11:1-12). It is at this time that they will have their partial blindness removed and they will be converted (Rom. 11:25-29; cf. Isa 4:3-4; 27:9; 60:21; 62:11-12; Jer. 50:20; Ezek. 11:17-21; 36:24-33; 37:11-14; Joel 2:28-32; Mic. 7:8-20; Zech. 3:8-10).

These converted Jews are then sent into all the world to declare His glory among the nations and invite them to the marriage supper (Isa. 2:2-4; 66:18-21; Zech. 3:8-10; Rev. 19:9). Apparently, there will be people on the earth, even after Armageddon, who have not so much as heard of the Lord's fame nor seen His glory (Is. 66:19). The result of this witnessing will be numerous conversions. In fact, it will be one of the most successful evangelistic campaigns ever conducted (Isa. 66:18-21; Zech. 2:11; Rom. 11:12). Nevertheless, some will come to the supper not being converted, while others will refuse to come (Matt. 22:1-14; Luke 14:15-19).

ARMAGEDDON 198?

The Third Divine Judgment: Against the Armies Holding Jerusalem

When Jesus leads His army to Jerusalem, He will stand on the Mount of Olives. The Bible says a new valley will be created by a devastating earthquake. And then Christ will bring safety to Jerusalem by utterly crushing her enemies. You can read of this specific battle in the following references: Joel 3:13-17; Zech. 8; 12; 14.

The Fourth Divine Judgment: Against the Armies Gathered at Armageddon

The most discussed divine judgment of the Second Coming centers on the Battle of Armageddon. The word "Armageddon" itself only appears once in the entire Bible—Rev. 16:16. But its site is alluded to in many other references, such as: Dan. 2:44-45; Zech. 12:3-11; 14:1-3; Rev. 6:12-17; 11:15-19; 14:17-20; 16:17-21; 19:11-21. All of these references discuss the great Battle of Armageddon.

The designation "Armageddon" is the Greek form of the Hebrew word *har Megiddo*. The word *har* means "mountain," and *Megiddo* means "a place appointed for meeting, an appointed meeting." Hence, Armageddon is God's predetermined location for the final battle.

Armageddon is located in north central Palestine. It is approximately ten miles southwest of Nazareth, fifteen miles east of the Mediterranean coast, and fifty-five miles north of Jerusalem. If you were to look for it on a modern map, it would be called Megiddo. It is a fourteen-by-twenty-mile tract of land which Napoleon appraised as the most ideal place on earth for a military battle.

The Second Coming of Jesus Christ

Megiddo has long been the great battlefield of Israel. It was here that Gideon defeated the Midianites (Judges 7), that Saul met his death (1 Sam. 31:8) and Josiah was killed in battle (2 Kings 23:29-30; 2 Chron. 35:22).

Lehman Strauss, quoting Fredrich L. Brooks, writes,

> Here (at Armageddon) many of the most noted military generals have fought. Thothmes fought here, 1500 B.C.; Rameses, 1250 B.C.; Sargon, 722 B.C.; Sennacherib, 710 B.C.; Nebuchadnezzar, 606 B.C.; Antiochus Epiphanes, 168 B.C.; Pompey, 63 B.C.; Titus, 70 A.D.; Khosru, the Persian king, 614 A.D.; Omar, 637 A.D.; the Crusaders under St. Louis of France, 909 A.D.; Saladin, who conquered Richard the Lionhearted in 1187 A.D.; the Ottoman Forces, 1516 A.D. And here, possibly at the climax of World War III, Christ will return in His own judgment.[2]

Now let me point out to you four interesting matters about this terrible battle:

First, the battle will be demonically inspired. In Revelation 16:13-14 we read that "demons . . . [will] go out to the kings of the whole world, to gather them together for the war of the great day of God, the Almighty."

A careful examination of Scripture will reveal that all wars have a demonic base. Behind every nation are angels and demons. It can be scripturally proven that at the heart of every military campaign is an invisible

---
[2]Lehman Strauss, *The End of this Present World*, p. 90.

ARMAGEDDON 198?

conflict among the angels and demons. Whoever wins the invisible battle will also win the visible battle between the nations. Everything depends upon the righteousness and prayers of the people engaged in the conflict. God will defend a holy nation, but judge the guilty. Read Daniel 10 and 11 for a clear confirmation of these statements.

Second, the Battle of Armageddon will principally involve three figures (or nations):
1. The kingdom of the antichrist (a territory encompassing much of Europe and the Middle East).
2. A northern kingdom (always identified by commentators as Russia).
3. An Eastern kingdom (always identified by commentators as China).

Here are several principal references:

Daniel 11:44. "Rumors from the East [China] and from the North [Russia] will disturb him [the antichrist], and he will go forth with great wrath to destroy and annihilate many." This is a picture of the fleeting moments before the Battle of Armageddon.

Revelation 16:12. "The sixth angel poured out his bowl upon. . . the Euphrates; and its water was dried up, that the way might be prepared for the kings from the east." This is just another picture of how the events before the Battle of Armageddon will synchronize and result in earth's worst battle. Revelation 9:16 describes this eastern army as being 200 million strong.

Today there can be no debate that two of the world's most lethal powers lie directly north and east of Israel. Someday—possibly very soon—these powers will engage in the bloodiest atomic battle ever known in the history of mankind.

The third interesting fact about the Battle of

The Second Coming of Jesus Christ

Armageddon is that while to the human eye there will be three major parties engaged in this conflict, a fourth, and unsuspected kingdom, will enter the battle. This will be the kingdom of God, led by its King—Jesus Christ, and accompanied by His army of glorified saints.

There are eight ways in wich the antichrist and the earth's armies will meet their doom at Megiddo.

1. By the sword that goes out of Christ's mouth—2 Thess. 2:8; Rev. 19:15.
2. By the stone which is cut out without hands—Dan. 2:34-35, 44-45.
3. By the brightness of His coming—2 Thess. 2:8.
4. By great hailstones—Rev. 16:21.
5. By a flaming fire—2 Thess. 1:7.
6. By the angels—2 Thess. 1:7.
7. By the breath of His mouth—Isa. 11:4; 2 Thess. 2:8.
8. By glorified saints—Ps. 149:5-9; Zech. 14:5; 1 Thess. 3:13; Jude 14; Rev. 19:14.

When Jesus Christ enters the Battle of Armageddon, all of earth's armies will fall helplessly to the ground beneath His feet. No human army will be a match for this heavenly host.

What a personal joy it will be, as a glorified saint in the army of Christ, to fight at Armageddon under the command of Jesus Christ!

One final interesting note should be made regarding this battle. Certain Scriptures tend very seriously to support the notion that *earthly saints* will join with the *heavenly saints* in this final battle:

> The Lord says to my Lord: "Sit at My right hand, Until I make Thine enemies a footstool

for Thy feet." The Lord will stretch forth Thy strong scepter from Zion, saying, "Rule in the midst of Thine enemies." Thy people will volunteer freely in the day of Thy power; In holy array, from the womb of the dawn, Thy youth are to Thee as the dew. (Ps. 110:1-3)

Could it be that teen-agers—Christian teen-agers—will assist Christ at the Battle of Armageddon? It's entirely possible!

The Fifth Divine Judgment: Against Satan and the Demonic Host
Once the dust is settling from the Battle of Armageddon, Satan, the fallen angels, and all the demons will be cast into the abyss. There they will be confined for a period of 1,000 years—allowing the earth to be free of their diabolic schemes. For details read Rev. 20:1-3, 7-10.

The Sixth Divine Judgment: Against All Gentiles
All the "nations" will be gathered for judgment too. The time of this judgment is probably just before the marriage supper (Isa. 2:2-4; 34:1-3; Jer. 46:28; Mal. 3:1-6; Matt. 12:18-20).

The word translated "nation" in Matthew 25:32 is the source of undue confusion. The word literally means "the heathen" or "Gentiles." It is simply used to distinguish Israel from all other nations or peoples. In other words, all non-Jewish people who are living on the earth will be gathered and judged. This is proven sufficiently by the context of the judgment itself (Matt. 25:31-46).

Another area of confusion in this regard is the basis

of this judgment. How will God determine the righteousness or unrighteousness of those under trial? A quick reading of Matthew 25 gives the impression that *works* are the sole criteria. A closer examination, however, reveals that the righteous ones are those who supported Israel in her times of distress (Matt. 25:35-40; cf. Zech. 14:16; Gen. 12:1-3). The sheep of this judgment probably become such through the witness of the Jews who are converted at the Lord's return. (One must remember that if the post-tribulational view of the Rapture be correct, then there will be no saved person on the earth when Jesus returns. Therefore, the sheep at the time of the Rapture, only days earlier.)

The Seventh Judgment: Against the Believer's Works
The time of rewarding the glorified saints is known as "the judgment seat of Christ" (1 Cor. 3:10-15; 2 Cor. 5:10). No one will be lost or become lost in this judgment. The judgment is solely designed to determine each individual's eternal rewards and his or her position in the kingdom (Job 19:25, 27; Dan. 12:2a, 3; Mal. 3:1-3, 16-17; Matt. 25:20-23; Luke 14:13-14; 19:11-26; Rom. 2:7, 10; 1 Cor. 4:5; 9:25-27; 2 Cor. 5:10; 1 Thess. 2:19-20; 2 Tim. 1:12, 18; 4:8; James 1:12; 2:23; 1 Pet. 5:2-4; 1 John 4:17; 2 John 8; Rev. 2:20, 17, 26-27; 3:11; 11:18b).

It is the believer's *works* that are judged, not the believer (1 Cor. 3:13). These works of the saints are classified as either "gold, silver and precious stones" or as "wood, hay and stubble." Fire will be used to test every man's work. All the works of the flesh (wood, hay and stubble) will be burned to ashes. All the works of the Spirit (gold, silver and precious stones) will

ARMAGEDDON 198?

remain forever in the personal glory of the saint's new body (Dan. 12:2-3; 1 Cor. 3:11-15; 15:41-42).

There are also five crowns which will be given to the worthy bearers:

1. *Crown of Life:* This crown is awarded to those who, under great tribulation or temptation, remain faithful unto the very end (James 1:12; Rev. 2:10).

2. *Crown of Glory:* This is given to the pastors who have been faithful in feeding their sheep God's Word (1 Pet. 5:2-4).

3. *Crown of Rejoicing:* This crown will be presented to soul winners (1 Thess. 2:19-20; Phil. 4:1; cf. Dan. 12:3).

4. *Incorruptible Crown:* Those who do not yield to Satan, self, or the world, but strive to be holy in all manner of life, will be awarded this crown (1 Cor. 9:25-27).

5. *Crown of Righteousness:* Every saint who longs for the return of Jesus Christ shall wear this crown (2 Tim. 4:8).

It is during this time that the twelve apostles will be seated on their thrones (Luke 22:28-30; Rev. 20:4a). Their task will be to judge (or rule) Israel during the Millennium. The other saints will rule over the nations (1 Cor. 6:2; 2 Tim. 2:12; Rev. 2:26-27; 3:21; 20:5-6).

The Marriage Supper

It is not difficult to believe the whole earth will be gathered for the wonderful celebration of the marriage supper of Christ to all the believers (Rev. 19:9). The number of guests could be relatively small, considering the vast number who will be killed during the Great Tribulation, plus those who are removed at the various judgments after the Second Coming. In any case, the

The Second Coming of Jesus Christ

number will not catch God unprepared to accommodate those who are present.

The Lord will at this time inform all the nonglorified saints of the earth's new political structure and the bliss that shall be theirs (Zech. 14:16-21). It is also at this point that the earth will be released from its curse. It seems likely that the earth will now become the "new earth" of Rev. 21:1.

Faithfully Watching and Waiting!

Shep, a Shepherd pup owned by Francis McMahon, of Erie, Illinois, during the early 1920s learned his lessons well.

McMahon suffered a fractured skull in a fall. As he was taken into St. Anthony's Hospital, he reached out, patted Shep, and told the dog, "Wait here, I'll be back for you."

It wasn't to be. McMahon took a turn for the worse in the hospital and died of his injury early the next morning. An undertaker removed his body by a rear door; so Shep, waiting patiently by the front door, never saw his master again.

That didn't deter Shep, who kept up his vigil. Hospital officials tried to chase him away, but he always returned. The nurses soon began to take pity on Shep, virtually adopting him. They began feeding and caring for him. He normally would lie by the door, watching and waiting. Every time it opened, he would jump up, expecting his master to emerge.

Occasionally, Shep would take a short walk for exercise, but he would always return. It was on one of his walks, however, that he was hit by a car. His spine was shattered. That didn't stop the dog from returning to his post. He dragged himself back to the front door

ARMAGEDDON 198?

of the hospital, despite his pain. By the time the nurses discovered his injuries, Shep couldn't be helped.

The dog died. Shep had waited for McMahon, his only master, for twelve years!

Regarding His Second Advent, the Lord Jesus had admonished His followers to "watch" (Matt. 24:42; 25:13) and "be ye also ready, for in such an hour as ye think not the Son of man cometh" (Matt. 24:44 KJV). For those who are faithful in watching and in occupying till He comes, the Lord has a special reward (2 Tim. 4:8)!

Let us be found ready and waiting!

17

Hell

The Duke of Wellington and Napoleon Bonaparte were both born in the same year, 1769. Each was born on an island; each became fatherless in early boyhood; each had four brothers and three sisters; each attended military school in France at the same time; both became lieutenant colonels within a day of each other; both excelled in mathematics; both were great soldiers; both commanded great armies. And finally, both are remembered for what happened at Waterloo, where one became the victor in war and the other was defeated!

The lives of these two men were almost identical—until the defeat of Napoleon. In this final hour one man won, while the other lost.

How much our lives are like this. We are similar to each other in many respects. But some day, when our appointed hour for death arrives, there will be a very vast difference. Some will enter into the presence of God and Jesus Christ, but others will make their journey into regions of torment and hell!

The most serious subject in all of the Bible is the judgment of God. It is real—as real as life itself. Condemnation is as much a part of God's overall plan for the human race as is justification. We cannot have one

ARMAGEDDON 198?

and reject the other. They are not given to us as optional doctrines. Rather, both destinies have been firmly established by God. If we believe in Him, then we must also believe in a personal heaven and hell! There is nothing more marvelous than to know for sure that God has forgiven and accepted you. Nothing! But conversely, there is nothing more terrifying at that final hour, than to be without God's forgiveness and acceptance. Nothing!

The Liberal's Position About Hell

The most subtle danger this world has ever known is to be found in liberal "Christianity." No other enemy has so cleverly divested the genuine Church of the truth. In many circles the so-called "Christian church" is but a shell—an exterior with the appearance of Christ, and an interior with the deceptions of the spirit of antichrist (see 1 John 2:18, 22-23; 4:3; 2 John 7).

It is both interesting and significant that the first sign Jesus gives concerning His Second Coming is religious deception. You can be wrong about tomorrow's weather, the current price of beef, the winner of last year's World Series, or a thousand and one other matters of minor significance. But if you should be wrong in religious matters, the consequences could be quite permanent, even fatal! There are some things you just cannot afford to be wrong about. Christianity is one of them!

No one is immune to spiritual deception and religious lies—including Christians. If genuine Christians were exempt from false beliefs there would be no warning to "see to it that no one misleads you" (Matt. 24:4). Neither would Jesus have said, "Do not fear those who kill the body, but are unable to kill the soul;

Hell

but rather fear Him who is able to destroy both soul and body in hell" (Matt. 10:28). But these warnings do exist. And the reason for them is clear—since believers, you and I, can be led away from the truth by religious men.

Religious deception comes in seven major canisters: (1) liberalism; (2) cultism; (3) agnosticism; (4) occultism; (5) world religions; (6) atheism; and (7) Satanism. The worst of these is liberalism, because of its subtle attacks. It parades about, in the words of the apostle Paul, as "deceitful workers, transforming themselves into the apostles of Christ . . . [as] an angel of light. . . . as the ministers of righteousness" (2 Cor. 11:13-15 KJV).

What is liberalism? John Henry Newman defines liberalism as "the doctrine that there is no positive truth in religion but that one creed is as good as another." Harry Emerson Fosdick wrote, "At the very center of liberalism is the conviction that nothing fundamentally matters in religion except those things which create private and public goodness."

Let me attempt to crystalize these definitions and focus our thoughts for a moment. Liberalism is a "religious" interpretation of the words "God," "Christ," "Spirit," "Man," "Sin," "Salvation," "Heaven" and "Hell." And it interprets (or defines) these words with the dictionary of human experience and knowledge. According to liberalism there is no single person or book that can be considered absolutely reliable. That means the Bible, while useful, is not without errors. For the liberal then, truth is relative, conditional, subject to change, and for a large part, yet to be found.

The guiding light of liberalism is the logic of computerized scientific proofs. If something cannot be demonstrated scientifically, then it is to be rejected. The human brain, coupled with our latest scientific discoveries, becomes the liberal's god, or at least the instrument by which God (if indeed one or many exist) can be proven and understood.

Why is liberalism so treacherous? The chief cancer in liberalism resides in how it handles the Bible. It is one matter to claim the Bible is *the sole source* for establishing Christian doctrines. It is a totally different matter to state that the Bible is *one source* for establishing Christian doctrines.

Liberals (in part or in whole) do not accept the authority of the Bible. They contend that the Bible contains truth, but it is not the only source or the only measuring stick for all truth. In other words, the message of the Bible, according to the liberal, must be weighed against the "proofs" of the various sciences before it can ever be accepted. Should the Bible "fail" the tests, then its statements must be considered false.

Here is an example of one test the liberals use to show the Bible has failed. The accounts of Jesus' Resurrection from the dead and His subsequent Ascension into heaven cannot be accepted as true. The reasoning is simple. Dead men don't rise. Science proves this; therefore, Christ did not rise. In the Thomas Jefferson version of the Bible this point is made most emphatic by concluding each of the Gospel stories with Christ still in the tomb!

Such a fundamental departure from the biblical text must be considered a serious mistake. J. Gresham Machen went so far as to state, "Despite the liberal use of traditional phraseology, modern liberalism not only is a different religion from Christianity, but belongs in a totally different class of religions. It is not the Chris-

Hell

tianity of the New Testament."

In other words, liberal "Christians" are not Christians at all. They are pseudo-Christians—false Christians. Not everyone bearing the name Christian actually possesses what he professes.

Who is a liberal? Without the slightest hesitation, liberals consider themselves to be fine Christians. Recently I assisted a prominent local pastor at a funeral. I spoke first and then sat to listen to his fifteen-minute discourse on nature. I was shocked. This man talked about the beauty of the world and of life. He never once mentioned the words "God," "Jesus" or "death." In his closing prayer he addressed "the spirit of life and love," not God. There was not a speck of hope in his message—none!

After the service I confronted him and asked how he could, with a sincere attitude, present such a hopeless talk. His response was straightforward: "We don't know what happens at or after death. Why should we speculate?" He felt that the Bible could not be trusted in these unproven areas. Still, he thought of himself as being a faithful Christian.

Perhaps the words of Jesus fit this situation most appropriately. "Not every one who says to Me, 'Lord, Lord,' will enter the kingdom of heaven; but he who does the will of My Father who is in heaven. Many will say to Me on that day, 'Lord, Lord, did we not prophesy in Your name. . . .' And then I will declare to them 'I never knew you; depart from Me, you who practice lawlessness'" (Matt. 7:21-22).

What do liberals believe about hell? Nothing, or practically nothing. You see, once the authority of the Bible is challenged, then you can believe whatever you

ARMAGEDDON 198?

want to believe. This, in a nutshell, is the liberal position.

The Biblical Position About Hell

Jesus called hell a place of "everlasting punishment" (Matt. 25:46 KJV), and "outer darkness" (Matt. 8:12). He also called it "a furnace of fire" (Matt. 13:42), where there would be "weeping, and gnashing of teeth" (Matt. 13:42). Elsewhere Jesus called it an "everlasting fire, prepared for the devil and his angels" (Matt. 25:41; also see Matt. 5:22, 29-30; 8:12; 10:28; 11:22-24; 12:31-32; 13:40-42; 18:6-9; 22:13; 23:13, 33; 25:30, 41; 26:24; Mark 12:40; 16:16; Luke 12:47-48; 16:19-31; John 3:16-17; 5:28-29; 8:21, 24; 15:6; 17:12). In brief, Jesus not only believed in the doctrine of hell, He actually taught on the subject more than anyone else. He discussed it more frequently than the topic of heaven.

The following is a short discussion on the seven major biblical words that must be understood in order to grasp the doctrine of hell:

(1) *Sheol*—occurs sixty-five times and is translated "grave" thirty-one times, "hell" thirty-one times and "pit" three times. The idea suggested by "grave" does not convey the word's actual meaning, and really should not be translated as such. The general meaning is "the place of the dead." It has reference to both the righteous dead (Ps. 16:10; 30:3; Isa. 38:10; etc.) and the wicked dead (Num. 16:33; Job 24:19). It is a place of conscious existence (Deut. 18:11; 1 Sam. 28:11-15; Isa. 14:9). It was regarded as being temporary, a place from which the righteous ones were to be resurrected (Job 14:13-14; 19:25-27; Ps. 16:9-11; 17:15; 49:15; 73:24). *Sheol* is said to be located "beneath the oceans" (Job 26:5), and in the "lower parts of the earth" (Ps. 63:9).

Hell

(2) *Hades*—occurs eleven times and is translated "hell" ten times (Matt. 11:23; 16:18; Luke 10:15; 16:23; Acts 2:27, 31; Rev. 1:18; 6:8; 20:13-14) and "grave" once (1 Cor. 15:55). *Hades* is the temporary or intermediate abode of only the unrighteous dead. It is located in a "down" region (Matt. 11:23; Luke 10:15), "in the heart of the earth" (Matt. 12:40).

(3) *Tartarus*—occurs only once (2 Pet. 2:4) and is translated "hell." It is probably another word for the "bottomless pit" since fallen angels reside there (cf. 1 Pet. 3:19; Jude 6-7).

(4) *Pit*—occurs nine times and is translated "deep" (Luke 8:31; Rom. 10:7) and "bottomless pit" (Rev. 9:1, 2, 11; 11:7; 17:8; 20:1, 3). With the possible exception of Romans 10:7 this is a reference to the abode of imprisoned fallen demons. This pit will be opened during the tribulation period to release a host of these evil spirits. Equivalent expressions for the pit are "the abyss" and "Abaddon."

(5) *Gehenna*—occurs twelve times and is only translated "hell" (Matt. 5:22, 29, 30; 10:28; 18:9; 23:15, 33; Mark 9:43, 45, 47; Luke 12:5; James 3:6). *Gehenna* is the Greek form of the Hebrew *hinnom*, the Valley of Hinnom. This valley encompasses Jerusalem on its western side.

In the southern section of the Hinnom Valley the Jews worshiped Molech (2 Kings 23:10; 2 Chron. 28:3; 33:6; Jer. 7:31; 19:2-6). This god, who was worshiped by the Moabites and Ammonites, was a fire god of the Assyrians and Canaanites. Jewish tradition describes this deity as being hollow and made of brass. Its appearance was like a huge man with the face of a calf, with his hands stretched out. The worship of Molech consisted of casting little children into a fiery furnace.

King Josiah attempted to put an end to this abominable worship by destroying the altars and making it a place where dead bodies were thrown and burned (2 Kings 23:13, 14). Later it became the refuse center for Jerusalem. Its furnace fires were always burning in order to consume what was dumped there.

Gehenna is identical in meaning with the "lake of fire" (Rev. 19:20; 20:10, 14-15) and the "second death" (Rev. 20:14; 21:8).

The distinction between *hades* and *gehenna* is found in their duration. *Hades* is the temporal or intermediate state, while *gehenna* is eternal. All those in *hades* will be resurrected at the close of the Millennium, judged, and cast into their everlasting abode, *gehenna* (Rev. 20:11-15).

Lastly, gehenna "has been prepared for the devil and his angels" (Matt. 25:41). That is, it was originally designed only to house the satanic host but has been enlarged to include those humans who fail to choose the way God has made available to them.

(6) *Abraham's Bosom*—occurs twice (Luke 16:22-23). The righteous dead, *before* Christ's resurrection, went to a separate abode in *sheol* bearing this name. Between the righteous dead and the unrighteous was a "great chasm" which could not be crossed.

(7) *Paradise*—occurs three times (Luke 23:43; 2 Cor. 12:4; Rev. 2:7). Paul was "caught up to the third heaven . . . up into paradise." Paradise is obviously in the immediate presence of God. If Abraham's bosom is to be identified with paradise, then it can be said that at Christ's ascension the location of the righteous dead shifted from within the earth to God's presence (Eph. 4:8-10). All who die "in Christ" today go immediately to be with Christ in heaven or paradise (2 Cor. 5:8; Phil. 1:23).

Hell

Only one additional matter needs attention: the scriptural descriptions of hell. Below, in outline fashion, are the seven basic aspects of this terrible site.

(1) *Vision*—Luke 16:23
(2) *Torments*—Luke 16:23
   a. *levels of hell*—Matt. 23:14; Mark 6:11; Luke 12:47-48; Rom. 2:5-6; 2 Cor. 5:10; 11:15; 2 Tim. 4:14; Rev. 2:23; 20:11-15.
   b. *darkness:*
     1. outer darkness—Matt. 8:12; 22:13; 25:30
     2. chains of darkness—2 Pet. 2:4
     3. mist of darkness—2 Pet. 2:17
     4. under darkness—Jude 6
     5. blackness of darkness—Jude 13
   c. *prison:*
     1. bars—Job 17:16
     2. gates—Isa. 38:10; Matt. 16:18
     3. chains—Jude 6; Rev. 20:1
     4. keys—Rev. 1:18
   d. *smoke:*
     1. ascends forever—Rev. 14:9-11
     2. burning sulfur—Rev. 14:9-11; 19:20
   e. *fire:*
     1. everlasting burning—Isa. 33:14
     2. unquenchable—Isa. 66:24; Matt. 3:12
     3. flames—Luke 16:24
     4. furnace of fire—Matt. 13:42
     5. eternal fire—Matt. 18:8
     6. lake of fire—Rev. 20:14-15
   f. *no rest*—Rev. 14:9-11
   g. *weeping and wailing*—Isa. 38:3, 10, 15; Matt. 22:13

ARMAGEDDON 198?

    h. *grinding of teeth*—Matt. 22:13
    i. *place of wrath*—Deut. 32:22
    j. *naked before God*—Job 26:6; Prov. 15:11; Ps. 139:8
    k. *eternal/unending*—Mark 9:45-48; Dan. 12:2; Rev. 20:10
    l. *worm dies not*—Isa. 66:24; Mark 9:44-48
  (3) *Speech*—cf. Matt. 22:18
  (4) *Remembrance*—cf. Isa. 65:17
  (5) *Great chasm*—Luke 16:26
  (6) *Prayer*—Luke 16:27; cf. Jon. 2
  (7) *Burden for lost souls*—Luke 16:28

If you were to die in five minutes, where would you go—to heaven or to hell? Would you consider your death to be a personal blessing or a personal judgment? What would you want to do over? What would you wish to have erased from your past?

Regrettably, our minds have been so overexposed to sin in our world (through television, newspapers, radio, movies, magazines) that the threat of hell's fires seem unreal to many of us. We must guard ourselves from this threat of casual belief! The reality of eternal judgment must awaken each of us to the seriousness of how we live our daily lives. Jesus put it this way:

> If thy hand offend thee, cut it off: it is better for thee to enter into life maimed, than having two hands to go into hell, into the fire that never shall be quenched: where their worm dieth not. . . .

> If thy foot offend thee, cut it off: it is better for thee to enter halt into life, than having two feet to be cast into hell, into the fire that never shall be quenched: Where their worm dieth not. . . .

Hell

If thine eye offend thee, pluck it out: it is better for thee to enter into the kingdom of God with one eye, than having two eyes to be cast into hell fire: Where their worm dieth not and the fire is not quenched. (Mark 9:43-48 KJV)

THIRD HEAVEN OR PARADISE

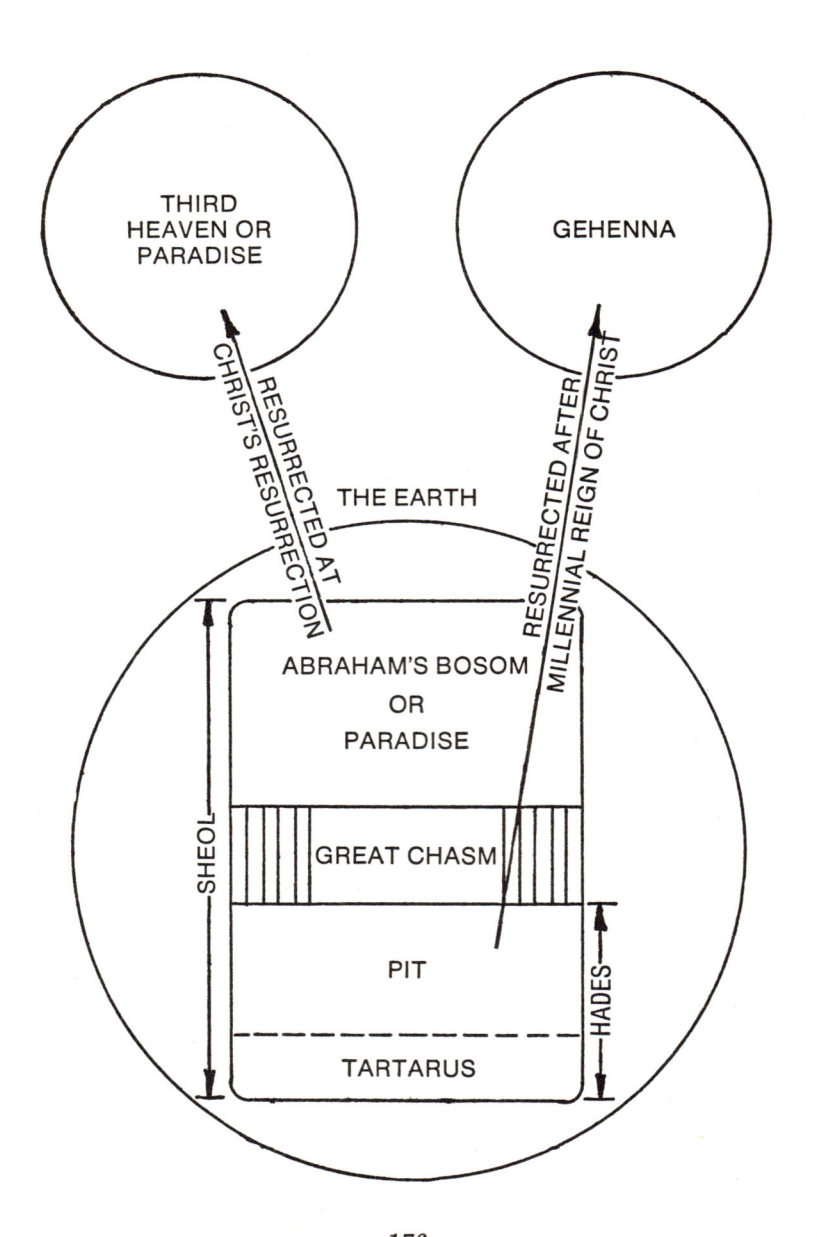

GEHENNA

RESURRECTED AT CHRIST'S RESURRECTION

RESURRECTED AFTER MILLENNIAL REIGN OF CHRIST

THE EARTH

ABRAHAM'S BOSOM OR PARADISE

GREAT CHASM

PIT

TARTARUS

SHEOL

HADES

18

Heaven

The words "heaven" and "heavens" appear over 700 times in the Bible. Jesus said, "Lay up for yourselves treasures in heaven" (Matt. 6:20). Paul said, "our citizenship is in heaven" (Phil. 3:20). John writes of seeing heaven, "I saw a new heaven and a new earth; for the first heaven and the first earth passed away" (Rev. 21:1).

Yes, heaven is a real place. And it has been especially prepared for real people, like you and me. But what do we actually know about this site? We've sung numerous songs about its glory and we've frequently talked about its reality with a strong confidence. But again I ask, what do we honestly know about this place, the most longed after spot in the universe?

The purpose of this chapter is to answer these kinds of questions. We want to explore the sacred Scriptures in search of the nature of heaven. Below, in a question and answer format, are the major gleanings of the teaching of the Bible on this always timely subject.

1. *What does the word "heaven" mean in the original Hebrew and Greek languages?*

There is not any significant difference between the meanings of this word in the Hebrew *(shamayim)* and

ARMAGEDDON 198?

the Greek *(ouranos)*. The essential idea is that which is high, lofty or above the earth and out of man's grasp. The earth is below our feet, while the heavens are above our heads.

2. *What did Paul mean when he said he was caught up to the "third" heaven (2 Cor. 12:2)? How many heavens are there?*

The term "heaven" is used in the Scriptures to describe three distinct realms:

The *first heaven* refers to earth's atmosphere. It is within this heaven that birds fly (Prov. 23:5), rains fall (Deut. 11:11), dew comes (Deut. 33:13), thunder roars (Ps. 18:13), winds blow (Zech. 2:6), clouds abide (Ps. 147:8) and hailstones fall (Josh. 10:11).

The *second heaven* refers to the cosmic universe. Included in this heaven is our solar system and the numerous galaxies beyond our own (Gen. 1:1, 14; 15:5; Heb. 1:10). Statistics regarding the size of this domain are staggering. The only practical unit of measurement is the light-year. (This is the total distance light travels in the time span of one year—5,880,000,000,000 miles!) Our solar system has a diameter of about 660 light-minutes. But our galaxy, of which the solar system is only a small part, has a diameter of 100,000 light-years! The distance across the entire universe (if it should have limits) is considered to be multiplied billions of light-years in diameter! In brief, the second heaven is a very big place.

The *third heaven* refers to the abode of God. It is referred to in the Scriptures as the tabernacle (Rev. 21:3), temple (2 Sam. 22:7), sanctuary (Ps. 102:19), house (John 14:1-3), throne (Ps. 103:19), and city in which God dwells (Heb. 11:10, 16). It is to this heaven

Heaven

that Paul has made reference.

3. *Who and what can be found in heaven today?*

Regarding "who" occupies heaven today, these names may be noted: God (Deut. 26:15), Jesus Christ (John 14:2-3), Holy Spirit (Rev. 4:5), living creatures (Rev. 4:6), archangels (1 Thess. 4:16), seraphim (Isa. 6:2-7), cherubim (Exod. 25:18-22), angels (Acts 18:10), Satan (Rev. 12:10), and the spirits or souls of departed saints (Luke 23:43; 2 Cor. 5:8; Phil. 1:21, 23; Rev. 6:11).

With reference to "what" can be found in heaven, these items may be noted, though they may merely represent symbols rather than actual realities: key and chain (Rev. 9:1; 20:1), harps (Rev. 5:8; 14:2; 15:2), rainbows (Rev. 4:3), chariots (2 Kings 2:11; 6:17), horses (2 Kings 2:11; 6:17), rivers of water (Rev. 22:1), fountains of water (Rev. 7:17), thrones (Dan. 7:9-10; Rev. 3:21; 22:3), four sets of books (Ps. 56:8; Mal. 3:16; Rev. 20:12), swords (1 Chron. 21:16), trumpets (Rev. 8:2), a sickle (Rev. 14:17), seven bowls (Rev. 15:7), golden censers (Rev. 8:5), food (Ps. 78:24-25; Luke 22:30), a tear bottle (Ps. 56:8), trees (Rev. 22:1-3), many rooms (John 14:1-3), altars (Isa. 6:6-11), tongs (Isa. 6:6), fire and coals (Isa. 6:6), stones (Rev. 2:17), crowns (Rev. 4:4), palm leaves (Rev. 7:9), a temple (Rev. 7:15), and the ark of the covenant (Rev. 11:19).

4. *When do Christians go to heaven?*

This one is simple to answer. Christians enter the third heaven immediately upon their natural death. Paul writes, "For to me to live is Christ, and to die is gain" (Phil. 1:21). And what is there to "gain" at the moment of death? We "depart and to be with Christ; which is far better" (Phil 1:23 KJV). When the time comes for us to be "absent from the body" (that is, to leave this body behind us for the ground), then we will be ushered by the angels "to be present with the Lord" (2 Cor. 5:8; Luke 16:22).

5. *Are the spirits or souls of the saints in heaven conscious or unconscious?*

According to some Bible interpreters death is equivalent to going to sleep, except for the fact that you never wake up. They content themselves with the passages that call death a sleep (Matt. 27:52; Acts 7:60; 1 Thess.4:13; etc.), and with other references that state the dead possess no consciousness (Ps. 115:17; Eccles. 9:10; etc.). But these references do not speak of our spirit or soul (see Luke 16:19-31; John 17:24; Heb. 12:23; Rev. 5:9; 6:10; etc.); instead they refer only to the body of the one who has departed. Certainly this portion of our being is asleep and unconscious, but our soul or spirit will never sleep; it cannot.

6. *What are Christians doing in heaven?*

The Scriptures approach this question from both negative and positive angles. They tell us what they are *not* doing, as well as what they *are* doing.

Christians are not being married to one another (Matt. 22:30); they are not hungering or thirsting (Rev. 7:16); neither are they crying nor sweating (Rev. 7:16-17; 14:13; 21:4); and they cannot sin (Rev. 21:24-27), experience pain (Rev. 21:4) or die (1 Cor. 15:53-54; Rev. 21:4).

The saints of heaven are worshiping God, face-to-face (Rev. 19:1-3; 22:4), serving Him in His temple (Rev. 7:15; 22:3) and preparing to reign with Him forever (Rev. 2:26-27; 22:5). Apparently there is a temporary consciousness of the affairs of earth that goes with us into heaven (Rev. 6:9-11), though this will ultimately be erased and replaced with the mind of

Heaven

God (Isa. 65:17; 1 Cor. 13:12).

7. *Do the saints in heaven know what is happening on earth? Are they able to help people still living on the earth?*

No is the answer to both inquiries. While spiritualists contend that contact with a departed person is possible, God strictly forbids such practices, calling them demonic (Deut. 18:9-14; 1 Chron. 10:13). Some suggest that prayer may be profitably offered to certain heavenly saints. Again, the Scriptures denounce this practice by stating that prayer is to be offered to God, and to no other (Matt. 6:9 ff.). There is not a shred of evidence to support the notion that departed spirits or souls have any direct awareness of current events upon the earth (Job 14:21; Eccles. 9:10; Isa. 63:16).

8. *Will we know one another in heaven?*

Yes, we will know one another in heaven, but the source of our knowledge will not stem from our earthly roots. That is, at some point in time in heaven, God will erase our memories of all the events that occupied the first heaven and earth, and then fill it with His very own mind (Isa. 65:17; 1 Cor. 13:12). Such an occurrence will naturally cancel any unique friendships (including marriage—Matt. 22:30) that we have established on earth in this life. Our identities in heaven will not be the same as they were on earth. We will be given new names (Rev. 2:17). Even Jesus will have a new name (Rev. 3:12).

9. *Where do children go when they die?*

Extreme Calvinistic teachers contend that only the children of at least one saved parent will enter heaven. Others, from the same school, suppose that only those

ARMAGEDDON 198?

whom God elected before the foundation of the world will be saved to enjoy heaven. Catholicism endorses the view that only baptized children will see God. What do the Scriptures teach?

The testimony of the Bible indicates that all children who die will be eternally saved. Jesus said, "Suffer little children, and forbid them not to come unto me, for of such is the kingdom of heaven" (Matt. 19:14 KJV). Paul, describing himself as a child, states that at that period in his life he was "alive." It was not until he saw and understood God's laws that he became aware of any need of salvation (Rom. 7:9).

This position does not imply that children are sin free and therefore innocent before God. No. They do sin, and they need God's grace as desperately as anyone else. The difference resides in the fact that children are extended a special grace.

Also read these passages: Acts 17:24-30; Rom. 2:14-16; 5:18; 1 Tim. 4:10; 2 Pet. 2:1; and 1 John 2:1-2.

10. *What does the Bible mean when it says God will create a "new heaven and a new earth"?*

There are four explicit appearances of this prophetic announcement in the Bible: Isaiah 65:17; 66:22; 2 Peter 3:13; and Revelation 21:1.

Isaiah emphasizes the contrasts between the present order and the one that is to come. He sees in the new heavens and earth a whole new life, with the former existence being removed from our memories. It will also be a final or permanent creation. There will be no further need for any renovations.

Peter brings in the idea of righteousness for the new order. There will no longer be any practicing of sinfulness. The former heaven and earth will be

Heaven

cleansed. This will naturally include the removal of Satan and his host from the heavens, and the unrepentant sinners from the earth.

John tells us when all of this will happen—at the Second Coming of Christ. With the descent of Jesus will come a new world government for heaven and earth. He will reign supreme, enforcing righteousness everywhere.

19

Getting Ready for the Last Days

"You yourselves know full well that the day of the Lord will come just like a thief in the night. But you, brethren, are not in darkness, that the day should overtake you like a thief" (1 Thess. 5:2, 4).

A Thief in the Night
   Not one of us sits up night after night waiting for a thief to come. Instead, we sleep. We trust that all will be well, secure and at peace. Unfortunately, however, every single night there were many persons who went to sleep thinking they were safe, only to discover they had been robbed.
   In the last days there will be many persons who think they are spiritually secure. Their position, possessions and generally good character have lulled them into a tightly wrapped security blanket called humanism. Their interests in the things of the world will have taken priority over spiritual matters. The home, the job, the children, hobbies, school, friends, and so forth, will all receive prime attention. And for most persons, these items will have precedent over the matter of being a spiritually prepared person.
   In the last days (as in all periods, for that matter) some people will be ready to face the worst tests, while

ARMAGEDDON 198?

others will have difficulty trying to keep the pieces of life together.

Once when I taught on the subject of the last days I noticed a lady who looked quite disturbed. The longer I talked the more distraught she became. Finally, I approached her. She was literally shaking and unable to stand. She was really terrified. "I could never face the last days," she said. It was all too much for her emotions to receive without going into a near state of panic. (I certainly didn't teach with any sensational aims, but she caught wind of a cold future that she couldn't handle.)

I have seen other persons practically shrug off this message, as though it really won't happen. They listen passively and without much thought that it might actually touch them. In this category I have found both Christians and non-Christians.

This fearful trembling on the one hand, and this carefree attitude on the other, pretty much represent the way many persons react. Both reactions are extreme. Thinking realistically about the prophesied future seems either impossible or unnecessary to too many persons. But this is not the case at all.

Getting Ready Today

If you are going to make a great trip ten or twenty years from now, you probably will not need to prepare for it yet. But if a wonderful trip could be just around the corner for you, then you should start getting ready right now—today.

No one knows the precise hour when the antichrist will appear, or when Jesus Christ will return. These dates have been kept a secret by God. Neither do we know the times of our deaths. These facts are also

Getting Ready for the Last Days

unknown to us. Most of us plan to be around and enjoy many years of retirement, but approximately 100,000 people every year (in America alone) find that their time is up before these years ever arrive. If you are going to be ready for whatever comes, whenever it comes, then you must be prepared today and every day. It may sound difficult to be constantly prepared, but it is not. You can become equipped in a matter of moments. And you can stay prepared with a little effort each day. Here are a few matters you need to take care of:

1. *Genuine Conversion:*
This is where everything begins. You need a *know-so salvation*. That is, you need to be saved from sin, self and Satan. And you need to know this can happen to you personally. In order for this to occur, you must first change your opinion about Jesus and about yourself. You need to turn away from self-management and instead place Jesus in the highest chair of authority in your life. Make Jesus the president of your many-faceted life. If you have yet to do this, then lay down this book and pick up your Bible. Turn to the Gospel according to John (the fourth book of your New Testament) and read chapter three. Then pray to God as though He were in the same room with you—He really is, you know. Ask to be forgiven of your sins. And God will forgive you. He will also make you His very own child.

2. *Church Membership:*
Some people think they can get along without the church, but this is not true. The Bible teaches that regular church attendance is a must (Heb. 10:24-25).

ARMAGEDDON 198?

Look around until you find a good Christian church. Do not take this advice lightly. Not any church will do. Some churches actually fail to teach the Scriptures. Many pastors of "Christian" churches are not Christians themselves. This is a fact! So search until you find a church that teaches the Bible and strengthens its people in spiritual matters.

3. *Baptism in Water:*
Once you find a good church, you need to confess your faith to the people there. With warm hearts they will want to welcome you into the family of God. Your next step should be to request baptism in water. This profound act demonstrates your co-death and co-resurrection with Jesus Christ. It is a wonderful experience. Do not neglect or postpone this step. (Read Romans 6 for a good explanation of this service.)

4. *The Infilling of the Holy Spirit:*
You will soon discover (if you have not yet discovered it) that you will have difficulty living the Christian life if you rely upon your will power to accomplish God's will. This is a most frustrating experience. The harder you try, the worse things sometimes get. God has a cure for this lack of power. It is called the infilling of the Holy Spirit. Here is what happens when you are filled with the Holy Spirit. You are actually tapped into the resources of the throne of God. When you need help, He is there to assist you. By surrendering your whole life to Him (with its many compartments: social, domestic, financial, emotional, physical, intellectual, vocational, etc.). He begins to work in these areas and to help you be successful in them. You will need this help daily. Don't be backward about asking for this power

Getting Ready for the Last Days

from heaven every day! See Acts 2; 8; 19 and Ephesians 5:18-21 in your Bible.

5. *Confession of Sins:*
You may think that with God's power inside, you will now never sin, but this is not the case. Christians—all Christians—sin from time to time. We are not perfect, and we can never claim to be such. So when you sin, admit it immediately to God. And if it is needful, tell others your faults and ask for their forgiveness too. Never permit a single night to pass with unconfessed sin to dwell inside you. Get rid of it as soon as possible. Be sure to memorize 1 John 1:9.

6. *Close Fellowship:*
You will also need (and I do mean *need*) close fellowship with *spiritual* people. Friends are nice, but you will need more than this in order to become the kind of Christian that pleases both God and yourself. Become acquainted with as many tremendous Christians as possible. Listen to Christian radio and view Christian television programs. Attend special meetings where speakers are invited to share. Take advantage of all the services provided by your church. From these contacts you should find some special Christian people who are just right for you. Invite some of these persons over for a snack or a meal. Go to their homes. Share together. Cultivate a meaningful, spiritual fellowship, one where you can tell the whole truth about yourself without feeling like a fool afterwards. Meet often. Share deeply. Remember the words found in Acts 2:42-46.

7. *Devotional Life:*
Regular fellowship is a wonderful thing, but it is not

ARMAGEDDON 198?

a substitute for daily communion with God. Make prayer and Bible reading a meaningful, daily habit. Talk to God and to Jesus about everything. Give them the opportunity to talk with you, through the Holy Spirit and the Holy Bible. Ask God for help for daily needs. Read the Bible slowly, looking for personal statements. God will speak to you. Meditating on Psalm 1 and 23 is a good place to begin.

8. *Meaningful Involvement:*
Do you realize there are people who need *your* fellowship and encouragement? It is true! You may not be as mature as you desire to be, but remember these two matters: First, you will never be as mature as your desire. There will always be room for more growth. Someone will always be ahead of you to challenge you to press on still farther. Second, no matter where you are, you are always a little higher up the ladder of maturity than someone else who can be helped by you. It may be a lost person needing Christ or a Christian needing encouragement, but regardless, there are people in your daily world who need your help. Get involved with people. The promises found in 1 Corinthians 12 are very encouraging.

These simple eight steps will carry you through your entire Christian life. Read them again and again, until they become an unconscious part of your daily life. These ingredients will prepare you for the present days, the last days and eternity itself!

APPENDIXES

Appendix 1
Blueprints for the Last Days

An Elementary Approach to the Last Days
Our understanding of prophecy should begin at a very simple stage. The two major events of the last days are the first and second comings of Jesus Christ. (See the chart below.)

1. *First Coming.* In a study of the first coming of Christ we learn about the Savior's birth, ministry, death and Resurrection. Here we focus intently on how Jesus paid the price at Calvary for our sins—past, present and future (1 John 2:1-2). This is simple enough to excite each of us, and yet it is quite profound.

2. *Second Coming.* In a study of the Second Coming of Christ we learn that at this event Jesus will exercise His kingship to the fullest degree. Sin will be punished, and righteousness will be rewarded. It will be a vastly different world after Jesus comes to earth again (Rev. 19:11-16).

AN ELEMENTARY APPROACH TO THE LAST DAYS

```
                    First Coming      Second Coming
                      of Christ         of Christ
                          |                 |
                          ▼                 ▼
The
Beginning─────────────────────────────────────
```

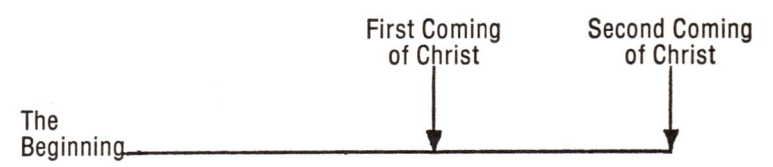

This is an elementary approach to the study of the last days. It is enriching, but it does lack an obvious degree of finesse. There is a great deal more that should be said regarding the end of this world system as we presently know it.

ARMAGEDDON 198?

A Secondary Approach to the Last Days
In the secondary approach to prophecy of the last days we start to pick up a few of the fine points. Here are four additional notes. (Notice the diagram on page 195.)

1. *Great tribulation.* Before Jesus returns to reign on this planet there will be a terrible period of political, economic, demonic and natural unrest, such as has never existed. Paradoxically, it will also be a time of massive evangelization. The duration of this upheaval and revival will be three and a half years. (This dark and light period is explained in detail in Appendix 5.)

2. *The Rapture.* The Rapture is that stupendous time when all true Christians—whether they be dead and in the grave, or alive and on the earth—will be caught up into the sky to meet the Lord Jesus Christ (1 Thess. 4:13-18). The actual sequence will be discussed at length in Appendix 3. You will also be shown the five different views that are held regarding the precise time when it is believed the Rapture will occur. At this present level, however, we only need to recognize that prior to Jesus' return to earth all Christians will be caught up to meet Him in the sky.

3. *Battles.* At the Second Coming of Christ there will be three battles. One battle will involve the rescuing of Jews in the ancient territory of Edom, just south of the Dead Sea (Isa. 34:6-15; 63:1-6). Another battle will deliver Jerusalem from her hostile enemies (Joel 3; Zech. 12:9). And the final battle, at Armageddon, will bring an end to all of earth's wars, at least for a thousand years (Rev. 16:16-21; 19:11-21).

Blueprints for the Last Days

4. *Satan is bound.* Once Jesus returns, there will be no room left on earth for Satan, nor for his fallen companions. This diabolic company will be rounded up and dumped into the abyss (Isa. 24:21-23; Rev. 20:1-3). No longer will we, or the nations of the world, be deceived. No longer will satanic temptations distract us from a pure walk of obedience to earth's greatest King—Jesus Christ.

A SECONDARY APPROACH TO THE LAST DAYS

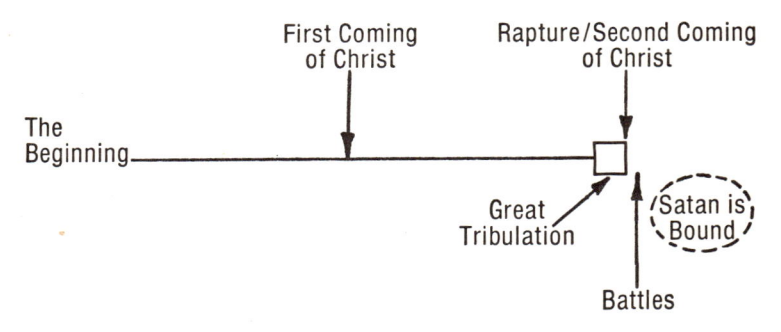

An Advanced Approach to the Last Days

There are other matters to be learned in the advanced study of prophecy. Here are four more items that need to be added to your chart of the last days. (See the following chart.)

1. *Seventy-Five Days.* This busy little period is divided into two sections—a thirty-day section (Dan. 12:11) and a forty-five-day section (Dan. 12:12). It is difficult to determine with any firm degree of dogmatism what occurs during this period. The following events are offered as suggestions of what could possibly fill this time span.

A. The judgment of unbelieving Jews (Ezek.

20:33-38; Zeph. 3:11).
B. The salvation of believing Jews (Zech. 12:10-13:1; Rom. 11:25-29).
C. The witnessing of the converted Jews to Gentiles who have not heard of Christ (Isa. 2:2-4; 66:18-21; Zech. 2:11; 3:8-10; Rom. 11:12).
D. The judgment of unbelieving Gentiles (Matt. 15:31-40).
E. The rewarding of all resurrected believers (Luke 14:14; 2 Cor. 5:10).
F. The marriage supper (Rev. 19:9; Matt. 22:1-14; Luke 14:15-29).
G. The inauguration of the new heavens and new earth (2 Pet. 3:10-14; Rev. 21, 22).

2. *A Thousand Years.* This millennial period refers to that time when Christ will rule the whole earth, allowing for no resistance to His will (Ps. 2; 110:1, 2; Dan. 2:44, 45; Rev. 20:1-6). The specific details of this grand reign of Christ will be catalogued in a separate chapter near the close of this book.[1]

3. *Little Time.* At the close of the thousand-year reign of Christ upon the earth, the abyss will be

---

[1]The position of this book is premillennial (that is, the belief that Jesus will return to the earth and set up a kingdom, over which He will rule for 1,000 years). Some scholars follow an amillennial approach (which holds that Christ will not reign on the earth for a thousand years—instead, the number is symbolic, they say, and refers to His heavenly reign). Others are postmillennial (believing the Church will, in effect, establish the Kingdom on the earth, after which Christ will return in final judgment). For a detailed analysis of these views see *The Meaning of the Millennium*, edited by Robert G. Clouse (InterVarsity Press, 1977).

Blueprints for the Last Days

AN ADVANCED APPROACH TO THE LAST DAYS

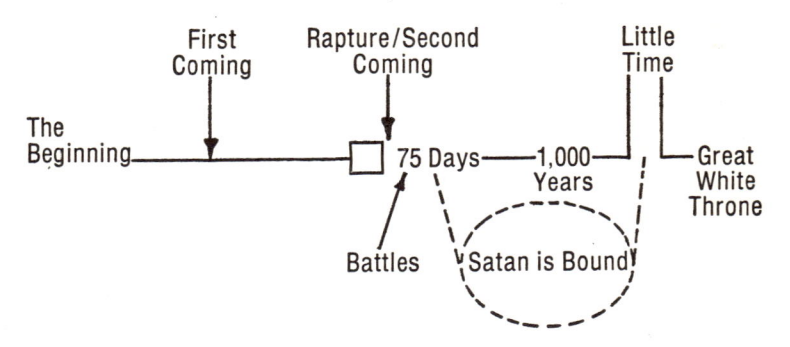

```
         First          Rapture/Second                Little
         Coming         Coming                        Time
The
Beginning ─────────────▼──────□  75 Days ── 1,000 ──┐  ┌─ Great
                              ╱         ╲   Years   │  │  White
                              ╱           ╲---------│  │  Throne
                          Battles    ╲Satan is Bound╱
                                      ╲_____╱
```

opened, releasing Satan and his host to prey one final time upon the inhabitants of this planet. He will go out to deceive the people. In ambitious haste he will gather together a feeble army of supporters. These pathetic soldiers will march to Jerusalem for earth's final war. God will consume them instantly and put an everlasting seal on any further such disturbances on the earth.

4. *Great White Throne Judgment.* The very last act of God against sinners is viewed here at this terrible and awesome judgment seat. All those who have stiff-armed Christ out to the maximum limits of their life—those who have resisted God's offer of salvation through Christ—will be resurrected, sentenced to their appropriate level of punishment, and cast into the lake of unending fire (Rev. 20:11-15). The sad facts of this event will be discussed at length in another chapter.

A Jewish Approach to the Last Days

In 605 B.C. God brought the armies of Babylon to Jerusalem. Within moments Israel was her captive prey. This defeat had often been foretold by the prophets. With solemn repetition they warned Israel of her approaching doom. In fact, the precise time of her dominion by Babylon was even stated to the year—seventy (Jer. 25:11).

When the seventy-year captivity was nearing its completion, God spoke to the prophet Daniel about another period, using the unit of seventy (Dan. 9:24-27). This time the theme was not judgment, but salvation through the long-awaited Messiah.

Starting in either 538 B.C. (if the seventy weeks are to be taken symbolically) or 458 B.C. (if the seventy weeks are to be taken literally), Israel could count her days until God's complete restoration for her would be brought to fulfillment.

There are three interesting aspects to these weeks that you should notice:

First, the seventy weeks are divided into four sections:

    A. Israel's restoration—seven weeks;
    B. Israel's silent rest between this restoration and the baptism of Jesus, the Messiah—sixty-two weeks;
    C. The first half of the seventieth week—the three and a half years of Christ's earthly ministry; and
    D. The remaining three and a half years, which will transpire immediately prior to Christ's Second Coming.

Second, it should be noted that a rather sizable gap exists between the first half and the last half of the seventieth week. Within this gap is the New Testament Church.

Blueprints for the Last Days

Third, it should be observed that this three-and-a-half-year period before the Second Coming of Christ is a time of severe judgment, especially for the land and people of Israel (2 Thess. 2:1-12; Rev. 6-19). See the chart on this page. Also, consult Appendix 3 for a precise analysis of this date.

A JEWISH APPROACH TO THE LAST DAYS

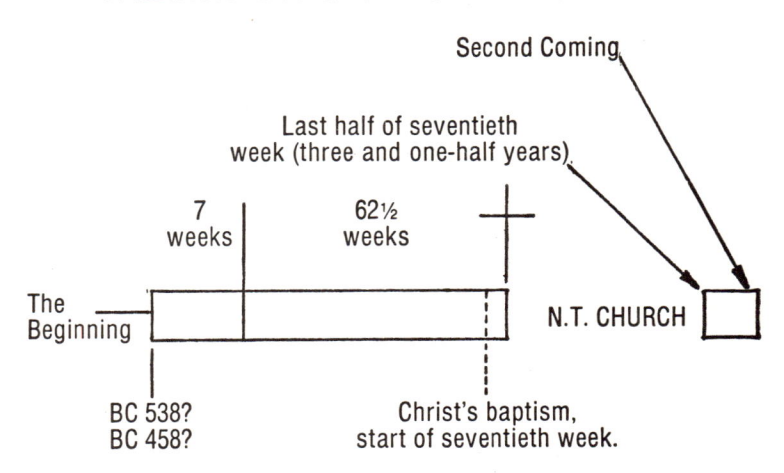

```
                            Second Coming
              Last half of seventieth
              week (three and one-half years)
       7              62½
       weeks          weeks
The
Beginning                              N.T. CHURCH

       BC 538?             Christ's baptism,
       BC 458?             start of seventieth week.
```

A Topical Approach to the Last Days

When we think of the last days, we're inclined to think only of the major events that headline this study—such as the Second Coming of Christ and the Battle of Armageddon. But actually every doctrine of the Bible is dealt with in this momentous study. Just as Genesis opens the doorway to all the teachings of the Bible, so a study of the last days brings each of these topics to the end of their journey.

Let me illustrate my point. There are only nine major facets of biblical knowledge:

ARMAGEDDON 198?

1. Theology: The study of God
2. Christology: The study of Christ
3. Pneumatology: The study of Holy Spirit
4. Anthropology: The study of Man
5. Hamartiology: The study of Sin
6. Soteriology: The study of Salvation
7. Ecclesiology: The study of Church
8. Angelology The study of Angels
9. Eschatology: The study of Last Day Prophecy

Each of these doctrinal seeds finds its birth in the record of Genesis. Throughout the entire Old Testament these seeds of truth are seen growing and developing, until they reach their peak of maturity in the cross of Christ. But from here they must travel to their ultimate destinies.

1. Knowledge of God will be made complete (1 Cor. 13:12);
2. All things will be made subject to Christ (1 Cor. 15:24-27);
3. The Spirit will finish His work of conviction and witness (John 16:8-15);
4. Man will be resurrected and judged or rewarded (John 5:28-29);
5. Sin will be forever ended (Dan. 9:24; Rev. 21-22);
6. Salvation will be capped off with glorification (Rom. 8:29-30);
7. The church will be translated into the new heaven, the holy city (Rev. 21:9-27);
8. And finally, the angels will be judged (1 Cor. 6:3).

All of this is the message, the rather complex message, of the last days. (Please notice the diagram on the next page.)

A TOPICAL APPROACH TO THE LAST DAYS

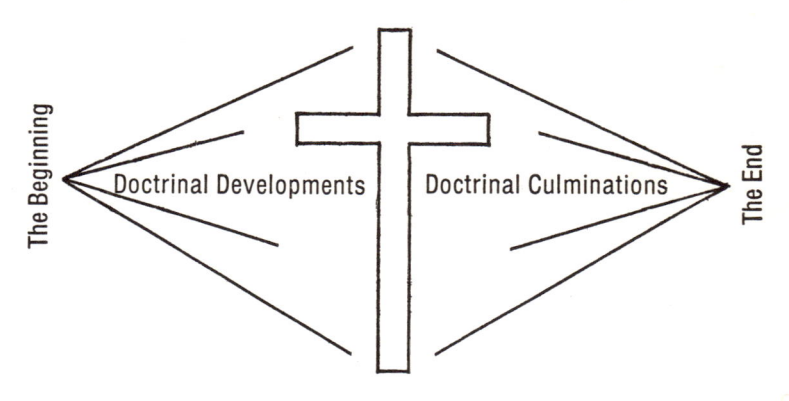

The Beginning ◁ Doctrinal Developments │ Doctrinal Culminations ▷ The End

The Last Days—A Multi-faceted Structure

Often when we think of "the last days,"[2] we are naturally inclined to perceive the matter in climactic terms. We don't normally envision the final stages of anything as being a series of prolonged periods. But this type of thinking will not fit into the multi-faceted structure of the Bible's last-day teaching. This field actually covers a lengthy period of time—a span of no less than 3,000 years.

With so many years in view when you talk about the last days, it is essential to recognize that not all of it is referring to the same event. The Bible uses either similar or identical terminology to describe totally different events. For instance, the New Testament uses the phrase "last days" to describe at least three distinct periods. In all, there are nine logical units (or events) in the last days—some distinct from others, and some overlapping with others. Below is this

---

[2]See Appendix 2 for a thorough listing of "last day" terminology.

ARMAGEDDON 198?

listing in its chronological sequence, along with a few leading Bible passages. On the following page is a chart to help you visualize this data.
    1. The time of the Gentiles, which spans a period from 605 B.C. to the Second Coming of Christ (Luke 21:24; Dan. 2; 7).
    2. The first coming of Christ (Gal. 4:4; Heb. 9:26).
    3. The church age (Acts 2:17; 1 Cor. 10:11; James 5:3; 1 John 2:18).
    4. The last phase of the Church age (1 Tim. 4:1; 2 Tim. 3:1; 2 Pet. 3:3; Jude 18).
    5. The Day of Resurrection (John 6:39-40, 44, 54; 11:24; 1 Thess. 4:13-18).
    6. The Second Advent of Christ (Jer. 23:20; 30:24; 1 Cor. 1:8).
    7. The earthly phase of God's Kingdom (Isa. 2:2; Ezek. 38:8, 16; Hos. 3:5; Mic. 4:1; Rev. 20:1-3).
    8. The day of final judgment (Rev. 20:11-15).
    9. The eternal state (Rev. 21:1ff.).

The hope of the last days is never presented climactically, in the sense of an absolute cessation of one order and the initiation of some new existence. To the contrary, the last days are always pictured as transpiring in phases, with each phase bringing one closer to a new, but non-detailed, culmination. Carefully examine the following chart.

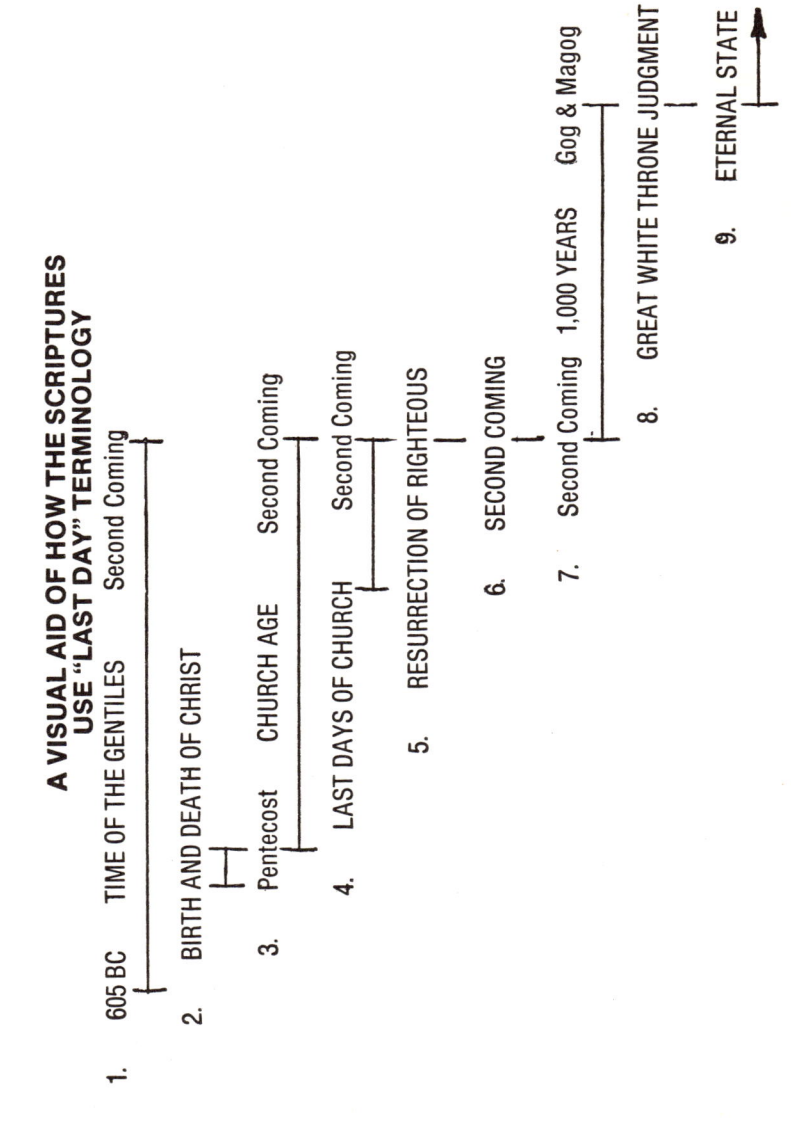

A VISUAL AID OF HOW THE SCRIPTURES USE "LAST DAY" TERMINOLOGY

1. 605 BC — TIME OF THE GENTILES — Second Coming
2. BIRTH AND DEATH OF CHRIST
3. Pentecost — CHURCH AGE — Second Coming
4. LAST DAYS OF CHURCH — Second Coming
5. RESURRECTION OF RIGHTEOUS
6. SECOND COMING
7. Second Coming — 1,000 YEARS — Gog & Magog
8. GREAT WHITE THRONE JUDGMENT
9. ETERNAL STATE

203

Appendix 2
"Last Day" Terminology in the Bible

There are numerous words and expressions used throughout the Scriptures to refer to the period generally known as the "last days." The following is a fairly exhaustive listing of the biblical terminology used for the close of our present world system.

A. *Old Testament Terminology*
  1. That day—1 Sam. 3:12; 8:18; 2 Chron. 18:24; Isa. 2:11, 17, 20; 3:7, 18; 4:1, 2; 5:30; 7:18, 20, 21, 23; 10:20, 27; 11:10, 11; 12:1, 4; 17:4, 7, 9; 19:16, 18, 19, 21, 23, 24; 20:6; 22:8, 12, 20, 25; 23:15; 24:21; 25:9; 26:1; 27:1, 2, 12, 13; 28:5; 29:18; 30:23; 31:7; 52:6; Jer. 4:9; 25:33; 30:7, 8; 39:17; 46:10; 48:41; 49:22, 26; 50:30; Ezek. 29:21; 30:9; 38:14, 19; 39:11, 22; Hos. 1:5; 2:16, 18, 21; Joel 3:18; Amos 2:16; 8:3, 9, 13; 9:11; Obad. 8; Mic. 2:4; 4:6; 5:10; Zeph. 1:10; 3:11, 16; Hag. 2:23; Zech. 2:11; 3:10; 9:16; 12:3, 4, 6, 8, 9, 11; 13:1, 2, 4; 14:4, 6, 8, 9, 13, 20, 21.
  2. The day of His anger—Job 20:28.
  3. The last day—Job 19:25.
  4. The day of calamity—Job 21:30; Jer. 18:17; 46:21; 51:2; Amos 6:3.
  5. Time of distress . . . day of war and battle—Job 38:23.
  6. Today—Ps. 2:7; cf. Acts 13:33.
  7. Day of wrath—Prov. 11:4; Zeph. 1:15.
  8. The day of evil—Prov. 16:4.
  9. The day of the Lord—Isa. 13:6, 9; Ezek.

205

ARMAGEDDON 198?

13:5; 30:3; Joel 1:15; 2:1, 11, 31; 3:14; Amos 5:18, 20; Obad. 15; Zeph. 1:7, 14; Mal. 4:5.
10. Day of reckoning—Isa. 2:12.
11. Day of punishment—Isa. 10:3.
12. The day of His burning anger—Isa. 13:13.
13. The day—Isa. 14:3; Ezek. 34:12; 36:33.
14. Day of panic, subjugation and confusion—Isa. 22:5.
15. The day of the great slaughter—Isa. 30:25.
16. Day of vengeance—Isa. 34:8; 61:2; 63:4; Jer. 46:10.
17. The day of distress—Jer. 16:19; Hab. 3:16.
18. The woeful day—Jer. 17:16.
19. The day of disaster—Jer. 17:17, 18.
20. Time of Jacob's distress—Jer. 30:7.
21. The day of the wrath of the Lord—Ezek. 7:19; Zeph. 1:18.
22. Day of Jezreel—Hos. 1:11.
23. Day of rebuke—Hos. 5:9.
24. The day of battle—Hos. 10:14; Amos 1:14; Zech. 14:3.
25. Day of darkness and gloom . . . clouds—Joel 2:2; Zeph. 1:15, 16.
26. Day of tempest—Amos 1:14.
27. Great day of the Lord—Zeph. 1:14.
28. The day of the Lord's anger—Zeph. 2:2, 3.
29. The day of His coming—Mal. 3:2.
30. Days of punishment . . . retribution—Hos. 9:7.
31. Last days—Isa. 2:2; Mic. 4:1.
32. Latter days—Deut. 4:30; 31:29; Jer. 30:24; 48:47; Dan. 2:28; 10:14.
33. Latter years—Ezek. 38:8.
34. Seventy weeks—Dan. 9:24.

"Last Day" Terminology in the Bible

35. Latter period—Dan. 8:23.
36. After many days—Ezek. 38:8.
37. End—Dan. 8:17, 19; 9:26; 11:27, 35, 40; 12:4, 6, 9, 13.
38. End of that period—Dan. 4:34.
39. Time of the end—Dan. 8:19.
40. Many days—Dan. 8:26.

B. *New Testament Terminology*
1. Day of redemption—Eph. 4:30.
2. Day of God—2 Pet. 3:12.
3. Day of our Lord Jesus Christ—1 Cor. 1:8.
4. Day of the Lord Jesus—1 Cor. 5:5; 2 Cor. 1:14.
5. Day of Christ Jesus—Phil. 1:6.
6. Day of Christ—Phil. 1:10; 2:16.
7. Day of the Lord—1 Thess. 5:2; 2 Thess. 2:2; 2 Pet. 3:10.
8. The day—Luke 17:30; Rom. 2:16; 13:12; 1 Cor. 3:13.
9. That day—Matt. 24:36; 26:29; Mark 13:32; 14:25; Luke 10:12; 17:31; 21:34; 1 Thess. 5:4; 2 Thess. 1:10; 2 Tim. 1:12, 18; 4:8.
10. A day in which He will judge the world—Acts 17:31.
11. Last day—John 6:39, 40, 44, 54; 11:24; 12:48.
12. Last days—Acts 2:17; 2 Tim. 3:1; Heb. 1:2; James 5:3; 2 Pet. 3:3.
13. The great day—Jude 6.
14. The day of judgment—Matt. 11:22, 24; 12:36; 2 Pet. 2:9; 3:7; 1 John 4:17.
15. His [Christ's] day—Luke 17:24.
16. Great and glorious day of the Lord—

ARMAGEDDON 198?

Acts 2:20.
17. Great day of their wrath—Rev. 6:17.
18. Later times—1 Tim. 4:1.
19. Last time—1 Pet. 1:5; Jude 18; 1 Pet. 1:20.
20. Later rains—James 5:7.
21. Last trumpet—1 Cor. 15:52.
22. The time—1 Cor. 4:5.
23. Fulness of the times—Eph. 1:10; cf. Gal. 4:4.
24. Difficult times—2 Tim. 3:1.
25. Proper time—Titus 1:3.
26. Fulness of the Gentiles—Rom. 11:25.
27. Times of the Gentiles—Luke 21:24.
28. End of the age—Matt. 13:39, 40, 49; 24:3; 28:20.
29. Time of refreshing—Acts 3:19.
30. Restoration of all things—Acts 3:21.

Appendix 3
ISRAEL'S SEVENTY WEEKS

Few books of the Bible reveal the intimate activity of our Lord in the affairs of the earth in such a variety of ways as the writings of Daniel. First, He is introduced as the One who raised up King Nebuchadnezzar in order to humble the sinful inhabitants of Judah by deporting certain members of the royal family and nobles to Babylon. Next, He is seen honoring the piety of four young captives by granting them profound wisdom and favor. Following this, the Lord gives Nebuchadnezzar a prophetic dream which only Daniel, after fervent prayer, can explain.

Then there are the episodes of God's protection of Shadrach, Meshach and Abed-nego in the fiery furnace; Nebuchadnezzar's abasement at God's powerful hand; the mysterious handwriting on the wall which only Daniel could interpret; the conspiracy to kill Daniel, and his miraculous preservation in the lion's den; and the visitations of the angels to speak with Daniel. The height, depth, width and breadth of these dramas provide a maximum of superb devotional information.

In addition to these inspirational adventures, the Lord reveals to Daniel some of the most detailed prophecies found anywhere in the Scriptures. This book is a gold mine for the child and the scholar alike. It is filled with precious nuggets—many which lie on the surface for easy removal, and many more which require most exacting care. A good example of the latter is the prophetic account of Israel's seventy weeks, which we will now put under the microscope for a penetrating observation.

ARMAGEDDON 198?

Seventy Weeks Are Decreed

Within one chapter, Daniel 9, are two references to a prophetic period which involves the number seventy. The former citation (9:2) refers to a time span of seventy years, while the latter reference (9:24-27) speaks of a seventy-week period of time. The relationship between these two units of seventy is quite striking.

Israel, at the time of Daniel's writing, was culminating her exile in captivity to Babylon—a deportation that had been predicted to last seventy years (Isa. 23:15-17; Jer. 25:11-12; 29:10). in the sixty-seventh year of this exile Daniel is given a prophecy which again involves the measurement of seventy. The correspondence between these identical numbers is clear—*for each year of dispersion in Babylon, Daniel is given a corresponding prophetic week toward Israel's ultimate restoration* (cf. Num. 14:32-34; Ezek. 4:5-6). For seventy years Israel had been afflicted under God's rod; now for seventy weeks she could joyfully anticipate God's blessing for a final and complete redemption. Note the simple chart below.

THE TWO SETS OF SEVENTY

JUDGMENT |—— 70 YEARS DISPERSION ——▶ RETURN TO ISRAEL |—— 70 WEEKS ANTICIPATION ——▶ MESSIAH

By far the most difficult and crucial segment of Daniel's prophecy is located in the four closing verses of chapter 9. Within this passage we see Israel's history from 538 B.C. to the Second Coming of the Messiah. Between these points prediction is made of

Israel's Seventy Weeks

Jerusalem's restoration in troublesome times, the advent and death of the Messiah, the appearance of a cruel desolator and the destruction of Jerusalem. The prophecy of Daniel 9:24-27 is obviously compact. Its details are exacting, but also sweeping and panoramic. The language is explicit, yet its syntax is shrouded with ambiguity. The intent is plain, but its fulfillment occupies reams of debate. In brief, these magnificent predictions of hope are tightly wrapped in the garments of scholarly disagreement, thus requiring no small portion of meekness in our search for their complicated fulfillments.

Explaining the Designation of "Seventy Weeks"

The expression "seventy weeks" is a bit misleading. The immediate impression we receive is that seventy weeks, of seven days each, are in view. This would represent 490 (70 x 7 = 490) days. The word translated "weeks" however, only means "sevens." It would be more accurate, and less confusing, to translate the first part of verse 24 in this manner: "Seventy sevens (or units of seven) are determined upon thy people and upon thy city." This is the approach that is used in the New International Version of the Bible.

The "sevens" then must either refer to literal days or years. The most common and satisfactory explanation is to take the sevens as units of years. This would indicate a measurement of 490 years. Each day would stand for a year.

It was not uncommon for the Jew to think in the terms of a day representing a year. Take for example the "sabbatical year" (Lev. 25:1-7). For six years the Jew was to sow, prune and gather his crop, but on the seventh year the land was to have a "sabbath rest."

ARMAGEDDON 198?

It is readily apparent that this "sabbatical year" for the land coincides with God's sabbath for man. For six days man is to work; on the seventh he is to rest. For six years the land was to be worked; on the seventh it, too, was to rest. Man's sabbath was one day out of seven days. The land's sabbath was one year out of seven years. The analogy is obvious.

In the same chapter there is a further progression of this theme of sevens. The Lord told Moses "to count off seven sabbaths of years . . . seven times seven years, so that you have the time of the seven sabbaths of years, namely, forty-nine years" (Lev. 25:8).

The year following the forty-ninth was to be a year of "jubilee" (Lev. 25:8-17). It was a year of rejoicing and liberty. Two things occurred during this year:
1. The land was to rest. There was no sowing or reaping.
2. Those who had become poor and were forced to sell their property, and even themselves, were now released from all their debts. Their former possessions and freedom were restored to them without charge.

THE DAY-YEAR PARALLEL FOR THE SABBATH

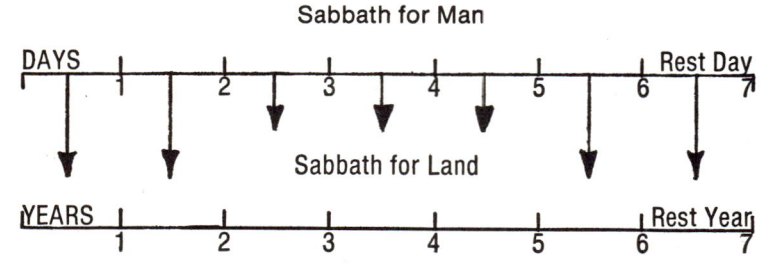

Sabbath for Man

DAYS | 1 | 2 | 3 | 4 | 5 | 6 | Rest Day 7

Sabbath for Land

YEARS | 1 | 2 | 3 | 4 | 5 | 6 | Rest Year 7

Again, the comparison is clear. While the weekly sabbath served as the pattern for the sabbatical year, this latter sabbath served as the pattern for the year of jubilee. These two events—the sabbatical year (which occurred every seventh year) and the year of jubilee (which occurred at the end of seven sabbatical years, or forty-nine years)—amply illustrate that "seventy sevens" could easily refer to seventy sevens of years, or 490 years. (See chart on page 212.)

The Six Main Prophecies in the Seventy Weeks
The prophecy of the seventy weeks (or 490 years) is an oracle of the greatest imaginable hope. At the climax of these years is to be a time of absolutely perfect bliss. With the coming of the Messiah, six specific matters are to be forever resolved:

1. *Finish the transgression.* The verb "to finish" carries the idea of bringing to a complete end, to finish, accomplish, cease and vanish. "Transgression" signifies a revolt or an insubordination to authority. Quite clearly the Messiah, Jesus, the Christ, came to offer Israel and the world a salvation that would result in obedience to God (Matt. 1:21; 2:11; 9:13; Luke 3:6; John 1:29; 3:16-17; 5:35).

2. *Make an end of sins.* "Make" is the Hebrew term for sealing something up which had been left open, so as to remove it from one's sight (cf. Job. 14:16-17; Dan. 12:4). The word for "sin" simply denotes falling short of the acceptable mark. Therefore, the seventy weeks were to usher in a period where one's spiritual shortcomings could be sealed up and removed from God's vision (Col. 2:14; Heb. 9:27; 10:14).

3. *Make atonement for iniquity.* The word "atonement" conveys the idea of covering, hiding, washing away, rubbing off and obliterating. "Iniquity" has

ARMAGEDDON 198?

reference to the resultant nature in man that is caused by practicing evil (cf. 1 Sam. 20:30; 2 Sam. 7:14; 19:19; 1 Kings 8:47). In other words, the Messiah came to offer a covering or washing away of iniquity, and to provide a freeing from sin (Jer. 18:23; Rom. 5:10; 2 Cor. 5:18-21; Col. 1:20; Heb. 2:17).

4. *Bring in everlasting righteousness.* While the first three items of God's redemptive dealings speak essentially of the negative aspects of sin and its removal, this point emphasizes the positive result of sin's covering. The "righteousness" referred to here is that judicial state (Isa. 53:11; Rom. 3:21-22; 1 Cor. 1:30; 2 Cor. 5:21; Phil. 3:9; Heb. 9:12-14) and ethical standing (Job 35:2; Prov. 1:3; 2:9; Jer. 22:13; Hos. 10:12) that attaches itself to God's forgiveness and pardon.

5. *Seal up vision and prophecy.* The sealing of vision and prophecy (literally the prophet) has to do with the consummation of the Old Testament covenantal hope that reached its vertex in the coming of the Messiah. In Him is the fulfillment of the Law and the prophets (Matt. 5:17; 11:13). The end of all redemptive prophecy came with the advent of Jesus Christ.

6. *Anoint the most Holy.* The translation of the Hebrew into "holy place" (as suggested by some authors) is not easily justified. The preferred translation is "Most Holy One." Proof that this rendering has precedence is fourfold.

a. In 1 Chronicles 23:13 the same word is used of Aaron—"to sanctify him as most holy."

b. The title "Messiah" means "anointed one." Since the Messiah is the theme of this unit of Scripture, it is probable that the association between Him and the anointing is deliberate.

c. Jesus Christ is frequently referred to as receiving

Israel's Seventy Weeks

God's anointing (Ps. 2:6; 45:6-7; Isa. 61:1; Luke 4:18-21; John 1:41; Acts 4:27; 10:38; Heb. 1:8-9).

d. Jesus Christ is also often called the Holy One (Mark 1:24; Luke 1:35; Acts 3:14; Heb. 7:26; Rev. 3:7). Hence, the Messiah, God's holy one, is the recipient of this anointing (probably at the time of Jesus' baptism—cf. Luke 3:21-22; John 1:32-33; Acts 10:38). (See chart on following page.)

The Four Divisions of the Seventy Weeks

The seventy weeks are not an unbroken chain with only one destination. That is, they do not stretch from week number one to week number seventy without any intervening predictions. Instead, four divisions (or units of time) are located within these seventy weeks:

1. *Seven weeks.* "From the going forth of the commandment to restore and to build Jerusalem... shall be seven weeks: the street shall be built again, and the wall, even in troublous times" (Dan. 9:25 KJV).[1]

It took seven weeks (literally, seven sevens, or seven x seven, which equals forty-nine years) to accomplish the task of restoring and rebuilding Jerusalem. The reference to "the wall" (actually, the plaza and moat)

---

[1] More than twelve dates have been offered for the time when this commandment was issued, though only three times have received much attention—538, 458, and 445 B.C. Any thorough commentary on Daniel will supply you with ample discussion on this point. Pinpointing this date is not critical since it does not affect the interpretation of the prophecy itself. Personally, I doubt that the popular date—445 B.C.—is correct since the decrees suggested for this date do not adequately fit the prophetic requirements; neither does this date culminate in Jesus' appearance (as the prophecy seems to indicate) but, instead, in His death.

ARMAGEDDON 198?

THE HOPE OF THE JEWS

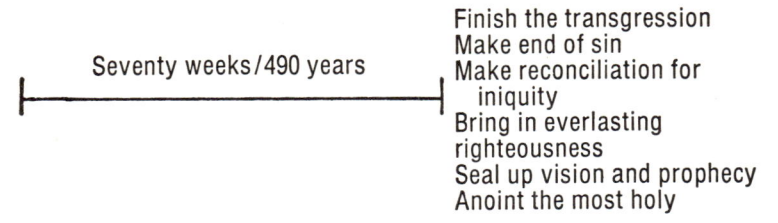

Seventy weeks / 490 years
|——————————————|

Finish the transgression
Make end of sin
Make reconciliation for iniquity
Bring in everlasting righteousness
Seal up vision and prophecy
Anoint the most holy

seems to depict a wide street, the main street, or the public square in Jerusalem, and a ditch to assist in her fortification. The mentioning of "troublous times" indicates the turmoil that would accompany this restoration work (cf. Ezra 9-10; Neh. 4; 6; 9:36-37; 13:1 ff.).

2. *Sixty-nine weeks.* "After threescore and two weeks [plus the former seven weeks, totaling sixty-nine weeks, or 483 years] shall the Messiah be cut off" (v. 26 KJV).

Carefully observe that the Messiah was to be "cut off" (or crucified) some time after the close of the sixty-ninth week. Therefore, some notable event must appear to separate the sixty-ninth week from the seventieth week. Daniel makes it clear just what event is in view by stating, "from the going forth of the commandment. . . unto the Messiah, the Prince, shall be seven weeks and threescore and two weeks" (v. 25 KJV).

In other words, the manifestation of the Messiah was to take place at the climax of the sixty-ninth week. In the vertex between the termination of the sixty-ninth week and the initiation of the seventieth week, Jesus—"Messiah, the Prince"—was to appear. The precise event that separates these weeks is, in all

Israel's Seventy Weeks

likelihood, the baptism of Jesus, which is the focal point for the start of His glorious ministry (Luke 3:21-22).

THE WEEKS BEFORE THE MESSIAH APPEARS

```
7 weeks   +   62 weeks    =   69 weeks
49 years  +   434 years   =   483 years
```
|—————————|————————————————————| MESSIAH
                                     THE PRINCE

3. *Middle of the seventieth week.* In the middle of Israel's seventieth week the Messiah was "cut off" (v. 26). The term used here comes from a common Hebrew word that was used of the death penalty (Lev. 7:20; Ps. 37:9). It is an unmistakable reference to the Crucifixion of Christ.

4. *Last half of the seventieth week.* Thus far the succession of time in Israel's seventy weeks has been consecutive, without any breaks in the time flow. There were the seven weeks (forty-nine years) for restoring Jerusalem; the sixty-two weeks (plus the former seven weeks, totaling 483 years) for the introduction of the Messiah; and the first half of the seventieth week (three and a half years) for confirming the covenant. There remains but the last half of the seventieth week (also three and a half years).

There are two possible approaches to this final period: it either continued naturally, as the first sixty-nine and a half had so done, or God's clock for the final half of the seventieth week stopped and will not resume until some indefinite time in the future. It is this latter alternative which seems the more probable. Below are four simple points in support of this conclusion:

a. Repeatedly, in the two books of Daniel and

ARMAGEDDON 198?

Revelation, there is mention of a yet future three-and-a-half-year period that centers its attention on Israel (forty-two months—Rev. 11:2; 13:5; 1,260 days—Rev. 11:3; 12:6; time, times and half a time—Dan. 7:25; 12:7; Rev. 12:14). It is highly probable that these three-and-a-half-year references should be identified with the latter half of Israel's seventieth week.

    b. Paul makes it clear that "God has not rejected His people," though for the present dispensation "a partial hardening has happened to Israel." According to the apostle's chronology, at some future period this hardening will be removed and all Israel will be saved. These future dealings are doubtless just prior to and during Christ's Second Coming campaigns (Rom. 11:1-32; Isa. 11:1-16; 66:15-19; Zech. 12:9-13:1, 8-9; Matt. 24:29-31; Rev. 1:7; 7:3-8). Again, God's dramatic, future dealings with Israel could readily fit within the last phase of her seventy-week history.

    c. The number "seventy" is often associated with God's work in the world. After the flood, the world was repopulated through the seventy descendants of Noah (Gen. 10); seventy persons went to Egypt in the days of Joseph (Gen. 47:27); seventy elders helped Moses administer the affairs of Israel (Num. 11:16); Judah spent seventy years in exile at Babylon (Jer. 25:11); and Jesus commissioned seventy disciples to be His witnesses (Matt. 18:22). Therefore, it would not be unnatural to consider the seventy weeks of Israel's history as the full period of God's redemptive dealings with this nation. And since her major redemptive experience is yet future, as noted above, the culmination of the seventieth week has yet to transpire.

    d. Perhaps the strongest argument to be presented is in observing the unique manner in which God

Israel's Seventy Weeks

reckons Jewish time. Sir Robert Anderson, in his provocative book, *The Coming Prince* (Kregel Publications), has noted that God's Jewish calendar only runs while the Jews are not in a state of being "cast off" by God, due to their sins. Let me illustrate my point.

In 1 Kings 6:1 it states that in the fourth year of Solomon's reign he began to build the magnificent temple for God. This took place in the 480th year after the children of Israel had come out of the land of Egypt.

The apostle Paul, giving dates for the same period in Acts 13:18-21, declares that Israel spent forty years in the wilderness, 450 years under judges, and forty years under King Saul. This totals 530 years. To this must be added the forty years of David's reign (2 Sam. 5:4), along with the three completed years of Solomon's reign (1 Kings 6:1), in order to calculate the same time period recorded by the writer of 1 Kings 6.

Stated precisely, Paul saw the period of time from Israel's deliverance in Egypt until the building of the temple under Solomon as encompassing a span of 573 years. The writer of 1 Kings 6:1 describes the same period as being 480 years. This is a difference of ninety-three years! How can these figures be reconciled?

The answer to this dilemma is located in the book of Judges. On five different occasions God is said to have given Israel up and sold them into the hands of their enemies. They were slaves to the king of Mesopotamia for eight years (3:8), to Moab for eighteen years (3:14), to Canaan for twenty years (4:2-3), to the Midianites for seven years (6:1) and to the Philistines for forty years (13:1). The sum of eight plus eighteen plus twenty plus seven plus forty is exactly ninety-three years.

ARMAGEDDON 198?

The writers of Kings and Acts are in perfect harmony. While Paul's figures are based on the regular, progressive calculation of time, the writer of Kings does his reckoning on God's basis of measuring time (which is obviously different from Paul's and ours). Sin stopped God's clock in the period of the Judges. In all likelihood it stopped it again at the rejection of Christ in His Crucifixion. The Jews still have three and a half years of time on God's redemptive calendar.

The next chart will assist you in grasping the details of the above discussion.

THE FINAL WEEK OF THE COVENANT

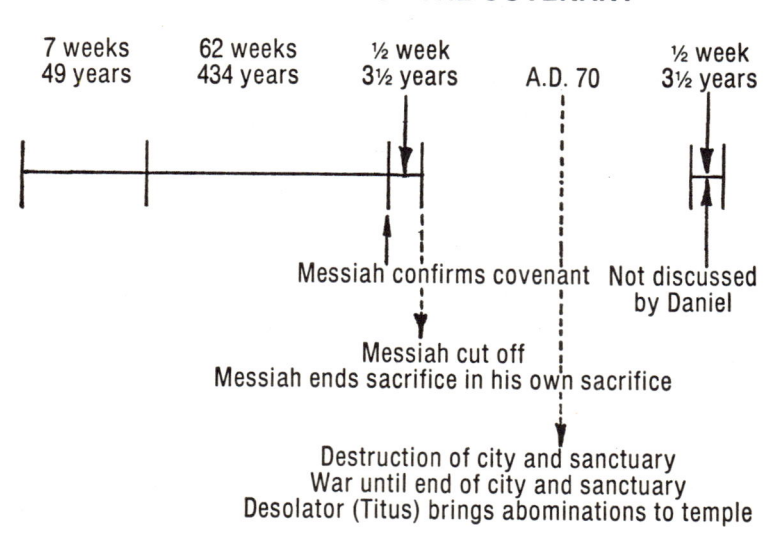

```
7 weeks      62 weeks       ½ week                    ½ week
49 years     434 years      3½ years      A.D. 70     3½ years
```

Messiah confirms covenant   Not discussed by Daniel

Messiah cut off
Messiah ends sacrifice in his own sacrifice

Destruction of city and sanctuary
War until end of city and sanctuary
Desolator (Titus) brings abominations to temple

Identifying the Two Princes

In the discourse of the seventy weeks, two references are made to a prince: "Messiah the Prince" (v. 25), and "the prince who is to come" (v. 26; cf. 11:22). The former reference is quite obviously a prediction of the Lord Jesus Christ. The identity of the latter prince, however, is not so easily determined. The major consensus sees this prince as referring either to the Roman general, Titus Vespasianus, or to the antichrist. It is crucial at this juncture to accurately dissect verses 26 and 27. In the two preceding verses the narrative has continued in a progressive and sequential manner. In the final two verses, however, there is an obvious shift in the flow.

In verse 26a the theme is the advent and death of the Messiah, as portrayed from a human point of view. This section should be identified with verse 27a, which speaks of the same identical events, except that it is now seen from a divine perspective. In the former verse the Messiah is displayed as God's eternal Sacrifice, while in the latter He is viewed as the consummator of all sacrifices.

Verse 26b and 27b are also corollary units and speak of corresponding events in the reign of General Titus (and not the antichrist, as we shall see later) over Jerusalem. The following diagram gives a clear picture of these facts.

CONTRASTING THE MESSIAH AND TITUS IN DANIEL 9:26-27

Human Perspective	Divine Perspective
v. 26a Messiah Passive Consumed as Sacrifice	v. 27a Messiah Active Sacrifices Consummated
v. 26b Titus Destroying Jerusalem	v. 27b Titus Desolating Temple

While the above data, at first glance, may appear inconclusive, a closer examination of the whole matter

ARMAGEDDON 198?

will greatly enhance one's understanding and appreciation for the complexities involved. Verse 27a reads, "And *he* will make a firm covenant with the many for one week." Question: Who is this "he" referring to? Is it the Messiah, Titus or the antichrist? Let's make two observations.

First, regardless of which of the positions one takes, the "he" clause of verse 27a must be viewed as a recapitulation statement because verse 26 runs from the time of the Messiah to "the end." Verse 27 does not pick up the flow of the preceding verse; rather, it starts again at the beginning of the seventieth week. Seeing this is indispensable. Hence, if the "he" refers to the antichrist, then the Messiah must have been "cut off" after the sixty-ninth week but before the seventieth week ever began. However, as has already been stated, it is more probable to envision the manifestation of the Messiah as occurring immediately after the close of the sixty-ninth week. This, therefore, would easily make the "he" of 27a refer back to the Messiah of the preceding verse, since the theme of the whole passage is the Messiah. This is the most grammatically acceptable interpretation.

Second, there is a translation dispute in verse 27a. The phrase, "And he shall confirm the covenant," (Authorized Version) is accurate. Or, "he will cause the covenant to prevail," is another acceptable translation. But some (many!) want to translate this phrase as follows: "he will make a firm covenant." This translation is highly questionable.

The notion that some new covenant is being made between the "he" of this verse and the "many" (Israel) is a very weak argument, especially if we believe the "he" refers to the antichrist. The normal Hebrew words

Israel's Seventy Weeks

for making a new covenant are strictly standardized, and they do not appear here in this passage. If the author had in mind a future covenant between Israel and the antichrist, he chose the least likely terms in the Hebrew language to convey this event. Instead, the words that are used clearly depict the confirmation of an already understood covenant.

If the "he" referred to the antichrist, then the seventieth week of Israel's history would begin with a covenant between himself and them, but there is not another hint in the Scriptures which speaks of such a treaty. There is a basic rule of interpretation involved here. Any teaching of Scripture must be confirmed by the testimony of two or more witnesses (cf. Deut. 19:15; Isa. 28:9-10; 1 Cor. 2:13). Since this is the only evidence for a supposed treaty between the antichrist and Israel, it should be seriously questioned as being a proper interpretation of the text.

If the "he" refers to the Messiah (this is my contention), then what covenant did He confirm? The answer to this inquiry is not a difficult one. Repeatedly, the prophets spoke of an everlasting covenant that God would give to Israel (Isa. 55:3; Jer. 32:40; cf. Heb. 8:6-13; 9:15-28; 10:4-18; 12:22-24; 13:20-21). Perhaps the most significant of the Old Testament passages is found in two verses from Isaiah's prophecy: 42:6 and 49:8. After reading these references it becomes explicitly plain that these citations are unquestionable references to the person of Jesus Christ, God's servant. In Jesus resides all the promises for Israel (2 Cor. 1:20). God's great redemptive covenant (already discussed in verse 24 of Daniel 9) came in the person of the Messiah, who confirmed the testimony of the prophets. But in the midst of His work he was "cut off" or crucified.

ARMAGEDDON 198?

In concluding this point, let me make several points to further establish the fact that Titus is the second "prince" in Daniel's prophecy, and not the antichrist.

1. Some interpreters state that the "people" of the prince and the "prince" himself, while associated in nationality, are disassociated in time. Hence, the "people" are the Roman soldiers of Titus, but the "prince" is the antichrist. Such a slicing of the puzzle pieces just so they will fit a particular eschatological framework is an obviously poor approach to interpretation. Grammatically, there is no justification for separating the "people" from the "prince" who is to come. It is more natural, from the perspective of the Hebrew language, to see them united into one single event—the destruction of Jerusalem in A.D. 70.

2. Because it is most likely that the "he" of verse 27a refers to the Messiah, it is not necessary for Titus or the antichrist to make any covenant with Israel.

3. Jesus used this passage of Jerusalem's desolation as a prediction of A.D. 70 (Matt. 24:15 with Luke 21:20-24).

Note the following chart.

ISRAEL'S SEVENTY WEEKS
Daniel 9:24-27

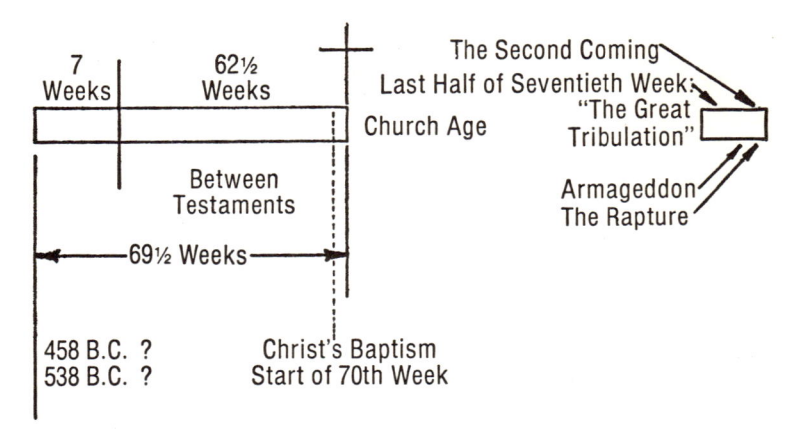

7 Weeks	62½ Weeks		The Second Coming

Last Half of Seventieth Week:
"The Great Tribulation"

Church Age

Between Testaments

◄—— 69½ Weeks ——►

Armageddon
The Rapture

458 B.C. ?
538 B.C. ?

Christ's Baptism
Start of 70th Week

Appendix 4
The Great Holocaust

"Tribulation"—A Definition
1. *Latin:* The English term "tribulation" is derived from the Latin *tribulum*, "an agricultural implement employed for separating the husks from the corn by a rigorous process."[1] The imagery of roughness and intensity is important.
2. *Greek:* In the New Testament there is but a single word with this translation—*thlipsis*. Used literally the term means "to press," "squash," "rub" and "hem in." Figuratively, it denotes the idea of "to afflict," "oppress" and "harass."[2] It is used both of distress that is brought about by outward circumstances (Acts 11:9, Rom. 5:3b; 12:12; 2 Cor. 1:8; 6:4; 8:2; Rev. 1:9; 2:9, 22) and of distress that is mental and spiritual in nature (2 Cor. 2:4; Phil. 1:16).[3] Raymond Ludwigson notes that this word is applied six ways. It describes the state of:
   1. Those hard pressed by siege and calamities of war (Matt. 24:21, 29; Mark 13:19, 24).
   2. Those pressed by want and poverty (2 Cor. 8:13; Phil. 4:14).
   3. A woman in childbirth (John 16:21).
   4. Afflictions Christ had to undergo (and from

---

[1] Lawrence Duff-Forbes, "Tribulation" in *Baker's Dictionary of Theology*, ed. Everett F. Harrison (Grand Rapids: Baker Book House, 1973), p. 530.

[2] Heinrich Schlier in *Theological Dictionary of the New Testament*, Gerhard Kittel ed., Volume III (Grand Rapids: William B. Eerdmans Publishing Company, 1965), p. 139.

[3] William F. Arndt and F. Wilbur Gingrich, ed., *A Greek-English Lexicon of the New Testament and other Early Christian Literature* (Chicago: The University of Chicago Press, 1957), pp. 362-363.

ARMAGEDDON 198?

which His followers must not shrink—Col. 1:24).
5. Anxiety, burden of heart (2 Cor. 2:4).
6. A period of tribulation out of which a great multitude will be saved (Rev. 7:14).[4]

Of the fifty-four occurrences of this word (including both verb and noun forms) it is variously translated in the King James Version: *narrow* (Matt. 7:14); *throng* (Mark 3:9); *afflicted/affliction(s)* (Matt. 24:9; Mark 4:17; 13:19; Acts 7:10, 11; 20:23; 2 Cor. 1:6; 2:4; 4:17; 6:4; 8:2; Phil. 1:16; 4:14; Col. 1:24; 1 Thess. 1:6; 3:3, 7; 1 Tim. 5:10; Heb. 10:33; 11:37; James 1:27); *trouble/troubled* (1 Cor. 7:28; 2 Cor. 4:8; 7:5; 2 Thess. 1:6, 7); *tribulation(s)* (Matt. 13:21; 24:21, 29; Mark 13:24; John 16:33; Acts 14:22; Rom. 2:9; 5:3; 8:35; 12:12; 2 Cor. 1:4; 7:4; Eph. 3:13; 1 Thess. 3:4; 2 Thess. 1:4, 6; Rev. 1:9; 2:9, 10, 22; 7:14); *anguish* (John 16:21); *persecution* (Acts 11:19); and *burden* (2 Cor. 8:13).

3. *Hebrew:* The Hebrew equivalents for *thlipsis* are "words derived from the related roots *suq*, which ... means 'to straiten,' 'to distress' (Deut. 28:53, 55, 57); *sur*, 'to bind up,' 'to press upon,' 'to beset'; and *sarar*, 'to oppress,' 'to persecute' (Num. 10:9)."[5] Derivatives from this last root are found in Deuteronomy 4:30, a passage keenly associated with Jewish eschatology. Hence, the Messianic Age was to be brought in by tribulation (see Dan. 12:1ff.).

"Tribulation"—Applying the Word
1. *Non-Prophetic Tribulation:* The multiple usages of the term "tribulation" are quite uniform. They

---

[4]Raymond Ludwigson, *A Survey of Bible Prophecy* (Grand Rapids: Zondervan Book House, 1973), p. 184.

[5]Lawrence Duff-Forbes in *Baker's Dictionary of Theology*, ed. Everett F. Harrison, p. 530.

The Great Holocaust

inevitably describe a period of pain, pressure or persecution. In the general sense, therefore, *tribulation* depicts the distress and trials of all Christians in every period of history (Matt. 7:14; John 16:33).

2. *Prophetic Tribulation:* More specifically, however, it is clear that the word *tribulation* possesses a distinctly eschatological aspect. In the book of Revelation, John records seeing a great multitude from every nation who were standing before the throne of God and before the Lamb (7:9ff.). Then John is given the identity of this heavenly host. "These are the ones who come out of the great tribulation" (7:14). The context makes it plain that these saints are the converts of a three-and-a-half-year span which immediately precedes the Second Coming of Christ (see Rev. 6:9; 13:1-7; 20:4).

The chronology is, therefore, very plain:

First: general tribulation for all saints in all periods of church history;

Second: specific tribulation immediately before the Second Coming; and

Third: the Lord's return to earth.

Descriptions of Prophetic Tribulation

The Scriptures describe this future period as a time of "punishment" (Isa. 24:20-21), "wrath" (1 Thess. 1:10; 5:9; Rev. 6:16-17), "judgment" (Rev. 14:7; 15:4), "darkness" (Joel 2:2; Amos 5:18; Zeph. 1:14-18), "destruction" (Joel 1:15), "indignation" (Isa. 26:20-21), "trouble" (Jer. 30:7), and "desolation" (Dan. 12:11-12). Without doubt, it will be the bleakest period in the earth's history.

But there is a bright side too. There is much more than political and economic chaos and Christian martyrdom during the reign of the antichrist. It is also the most productive period of soul-winning ever to exist

ARMAGEDDON 198?

on this earth! The number who will meet Christ and make Him their personal Lord is virtually numberless. John describes the situation in this manner:

> After this I beheld, and, lo, a great multitude, which no man could number, of all nations, and kindreds, and people, and tongues, stood before the throne and before The Lamb, clothed with white robes. . . . These are they which came out of the great tribulation, and have washed their robes, and made them white in the blood of the Lamb. (Rev. 7:9, 14 KJV)

Before Jesus returns there will be two phenomena—unprecedented evil, on the one hand, and glorious evangelism on the other. Both will walk together through the moments that immediately precede Christ's reign over the nations of this globe.

Purpose of the Prophetic Tribulation
The tribulation is essentially Jewish in its center of activity (Rev. 12:1ff.). The focus on Israel is for one paramount purpose—to prepare her for the Messiah. Once the tribulation is past and Christ returns, then "all Israel will be saved" (Rom. 11:26; cf. Isa. 11:1-2; Zech. 12:10-14; 13:1; Matt. 24:29-31).

God has not finished His work with the Jews—national Israel. His covenant with them is still incomplete. So, during this period God will again deal with this nation in order that they might receive Jesus as their long-promised Messiah.

The Dark Events of the Great Tribulation
It is during this period that Satan, the antichrist, the

The Great Holocaust

false prophet and the image of the beast will have unhindered liberty to blaspheme God, kill His saints, wage war, and attempt converting the neighboring world to their ways of worship. It is also during this time that God will pour out His wrath with unparalleled fury. The events of these brief forty-two months are staggering in both individual horror and quantity.

The Chronological Architecture of Revelation 6-19

Most of the details concerning the Great Tribulation are located in the book of Revelation. Unfortunately, this book has been subjected to a rather broad variety of interpretations, making its meaning a subject of debate. Well, here is another presentation on this vitally important book.

I. The Fifty-Two Visions of Chapters 6-19

On the Lord's day (c. A.D. 68-95),[6] John was in the Spirit when he received instructions from Jesus Christ to write in a book what he *saw* (1:11). Consequently, John *saw* and recorded numerous, detailed visions. Fifty-two of these visions appear in chapters six through nineteen (the section containing the seals, trumpets and bowls).

Verbs of "seeing" appear 140 times in this quickly paced twenty-two-chapter letter. With the brevity of about twenty-second movie clips, John's fifty-two visions quickly flash before the reader. When the astonishing presentation is finished, one's response is mixed. Initially he is both aghast at the magnitude of

---

[6]Whether John wrote before or after the fall of Jerusalem in A.D. 70 has no consequences upon the literary structure of his book. Interpretative conclusions always follow an analysis of the book's compositional nature.

ARMAGEDDON 198?

the catastrophies and ecstatic over Christ's triumph. His emotions are stretched to their limits, but once he descends from this stage and begins to assimilate the data he has seen, he is perplexed that the presentation did not follow a more thematic or sequential route. While some of the visions possessed an apparent chronological continuity, the majority frequently seemed to be independent from what preceded or followed them. But even this is not wholly true, because the contents of these detached visions would often reappear later, only in a somewhat modified style.

With these overwhelming initial impressions, let us consider the fifty-two scenes again. This time we will look for some unifying principles and chronological architecture. Below are three observations which almost immediately become apparent.

A. *Three Series*

Out of these fifty-two visions, twenty-one are arranged into three sets of seven. These three groupings of seven consecutive scenes constitute the seal, trumpet and bowl judgments. The remaining visions surround these three episodes in a parenthetical or nonsequential manner. In other words, the seal, trumpet and bowl series explicitly suggests some order, at least within their own individual sets, while the remaining thirty-one visions are without any explicit unifying principle; they are interludes in the sequence.

B. *Within Each Series Is an Interlude*

In the seal, trumpet and bowl series there is a division in each chain between the sixth and seventh judgments. Some parenthetical vision is invariably interjected before this final member is presented.

The Great Holocaust

C. *Each Series Is Independent*
Following each of these three series are more non-sequential visions. See the diagram on the following page.

II. *Similarity in the Seals, Trumpets and Bowls*
   A. *Their Nature*
   The most common trait within these three series is their devastating characteristic. Each set focuses upon judgment, calamity and death. (See 6:1-17; 8:1 for seals; 8:2, 7-9:21; 11:15-19 for trumpets; and 16:1-12, 17-21 for bowls.)
   B. *Their Number*
   Each chain in these series is comprised of seven members. The number seven is not uncommon to the Bible and particularly to the writing of Revelation, where it appears forty-five times. It is universally acknowledged that this number is frequently used to depict completeness or finality. The case in point is no exception. There is both a wholeness and a natural culmination at the close of each seventh member. This completeness within each series strongly suggests their autonomous and nonsequential nature.

   The popular notion that the trumpet series emerges from the seventh seal, thus "proving" a successive nature to the three series, is far from conclusive. First, the text does not say the trumpets are the product of the seventh seal. This is explicitly clear. Only "silence"—nothing more, nothing less, nothing else—is said to accompany this seal (8:1). While the trumpet series follows in the text, along with an interluding vision, this does not, by any means, necessitate succession—especially in Revelation, where the multiple visions so rapidly appear and disappear. Secondly, such an

233

AN OUTLINE OF THE LAST HALF OF ISRAEL'S SEVENTIETH WEEK ACCORDING TO THE BOOK OF REVELATION

1a. Six Seals—6:1-17
(Three parenthetical
visions—7:1-17)

1b. Seventh Seal—8:1
(Two parenthetical
visions—8:2-6)

2a. Six Trumpets—8:7-9:21
(Four parenthetical
visions—10:1-11:14)

2b. Seventh Trumpet—11:15-19
(Nine parenthetical
visions—12:1-15:8)

3a. Six Bowls—16:1-12
(One parenthetical
vision—16:13-16)

3b. Seventh bowl—16:17-21
(Twelve parenthetical
visions—17:1-22:21)

A. Each section begins with the start of Israel's last three and one-half years of prophetic history, and each will run for the entire period.

B. In each section satanic forces are seen at odds with the saints, sinners and God.

C. In each section God is seen as being victorious over Satan and in the presence of His saints. As such, there are earthly judgments and heavenly victories in each section.

D. The seals, trumpets, and bowls give a complete account of the last half of Israel's seventieth week *without the parenthetical visions.* While the seals, trumpets, and bowls run chronologically, the related visions are not chronological, but rather, serve to review and add the finer details within this period, enriching our understanding as to *how* and *when* all these matters will fit together.

The Great Holocaust

arrangement breaks the natural flow which the first six seals have created. With the sixth seal culminating in the Battle of Armageddon, it would be illogical, and, in fact, impossible, to start a new chronological series which antedates this event, as the trumpets would do, if viewed sequentially. Thirdly, it disrupts the clear parallel and concurrent nature of the three sets. It is much more natural to view each of the three series of sevens as self-sustaining entities which compose the whole period under consideration.

C. *Their Correspondence*

If the three sets are arranged in a triple-decker fashion, so that the successive numbers of each series are parallel to each other, an unmistakable relationship is observed. First, the initial five judgments in each set involve the domain of the beast (6:8; 8:7-8, 10; 9:4, 15; 16:10). Secondly, the sixth judgment in all three cases focuses its attention on the events immediately surrounding Armageddon. Thirdly, the seventh seal, trumpet and bowl concern themselves with the Second Coming of Jesus Christ. There is little debate over these simple observations.

There is ample evidence (from a futurist's interpretation of Revelation) to support the conviction that the antichrist will *not* control the whole inhabited earth—which would necessarily make these judgments non-universal. Consider the data: 1. Daniel prophesied the fall of Israel, Egypt, Libya and Ethiopia to the antichrist, but he also announces that Moab, Edom and Ammon will be "rescued out of his hand" (11:40-43). 2. Daniel's final remarks on the struggles of the antichrist reveal that a nation from the North (Russia?) and a nation from the East (China?) will "greatly disturb" him (11:44). These two prophecies from the

ARMAGEDDON 198?

pen of Daniel hardly suggest a universally sovereign situation. 3. The prophecies of Isaiah and Zechariah make it plain that there will be multitudes in the world *after* the Second Coming of Christ who have not even so much as heard of Him (Isa. 66:19; Zech. 8:23)! Certainly the kingdom of the antichrist will not spread farther in three and a half years than the Kingdom of Christ, which has been operative for nearly 2,000 years. 4. The book of Revelation teaches that the antichrist's territorial boundaries will only encompass the domain of ten horns—the Revised Roman Empire. While this domination is certainly impressive, it is far from global. 5. Only one verse of Scripture states that the antichrist's authority will be over "all"—Rev. 13:7-8. A casual glance, however, at the use of "all" and "every" in Scripture discloses that only a notable portion is in view—not utter totality (see Josh. 6:21-25; 2 Sam. 6:5, 15; 1 Kings 11:16-17; Dan. 2:37-38; 4:1, 11, 12; Matt. 3:5-6; Luke 2:1-3; etc.).

D. *Their Duration*

Throughout the book of Revelation reference is made to a specific period of forty-two months in which these three series are to transpire (11:2, 3; 12:6, 14; 13:5; cf. Dan. 7:25; 12:7). It is virtually conclusive that these consistent references each refer to the three-and-a-half-year time span which constitutes the last half of Israel's seventieth-week predictions (Dan. 9:24-27).[7]

---

[7]This writer holds that the seventieth week of Daniel's writings began with the baptism of Christ by John, and that He was "cut off" by Crucifixion halfway through this final week. A gap was, therefore, created between Christ's rejection by National Israel and His future redemptive dealings with them. This break in time, however, is *not* a dispensational parenthesis which surrounds the church age, but merely a gap which postpones the earthly phase of the kingdom and permits the preordained Gentile graft sufficient time to bear its appointed fruit (Rom. 11). Note the charts at the close of this discussion.

III. *Distinctions Between the Seal Judgments and the Trumpet and Bowl Judgments*
    A. *The Individual Member Duration*
    The release of the individual judgments in the seal series are distinct from the manner in which the trumpet and bowl judgments are set off. The seals are not opened sequentially or progressively over the entire three-and-a-half-year span, as are the trumpets and bowls. Instead, the seals are either opened in immediate succession or all at once. There are two basic reasons for this conclusion.

    One, there is no designation of time allotted to any of the seals. This, however, is not true of the other judgments. The fifth trumpet, for instance, is said only to last five months (9:5, 10). Two, the interdependent relationship of the seals is in sharp contrast to the independent structure of the trumpets and bowls. The latter are unrelated to each other in their progression, whereas the former are logical and necessary outgrowths of each other. The fourth seal serves as an interesting illustration.

    The seal is described as "death." The reader of Revelation should become aware by this point that a unique recapitulation is developing. What brings about this "death" of the fourth seal? The answer comes from the seal itself—"a sword . . . famine . . . and pestilence and . . . wild beasts" (6:8). Note how this seal summarizes the preceding ones. The "sword" refers back to the second seal; "famine" is the third seal; "death" is seal number four itself; and "wild beasts" may easily refer to the first seal—the antichrist and his cohorts!

    If this recapitulation interpretation is correct, then the meaning and instantaneous chronology of the seals is readily grasped. The rider of the first horse is none

SEAL, TRUMPET, BOWL JUDGMENTS

SATAN'S JUDGMENTS
TIME GRID

Seal 1—Crown is given white horse rider. He goes forth conquering—6:2
Seal 2—Rider of red horse removes peace from earth with a great sword—6:4
Seal 3—Black horse rider holds balance to represent famine—6:5-6
Seal 4—Death rides the pale horse with Hades following. He kills one quarter of the earth with (3) hunger, (2) death and (1) beast—6:8
Seal 5—Vision of saints martyred for the Word of God and their testimony—6:9-11

PREPARATION FOR ARMAGEDDON

Seal 6—Day of His wrath is come—6:12-17
Seal 7—Half-hour silence—8:1

GOD'S JUDGMENTS SEQUENCE GRID

	Trump 1	Trump 2	Trump 3	Trump 4	Trump 5	Trump 6	Trump 7
	Hail and fire with blood cast to EARTH—One-third of earth is burned—8:7	Mountain of fire cast into SEA—turned to BLOOD—8:8-9	Burning star—Wormwood One-third RIVERS and FOUNTAINS affected—8:10-11	One-third of SUN, moon and stars made dark—8:12	Locusts TORMENT men—sun made DARK—9:1-12	Angels loosed from EUPHRATES —great ARMY of two hundred million —9:13-21	The kingdom of world has become the kingdom of the Lord and His Christ 11:14-19

PREPARATION FOR ARMAGEDDON

	Bowl 1	Bowl 2	Bowl 3	Bowl 4	Bowl 5	Bowl 6	Bowl 7
	Poured on EARTH—boils on men having mark of beast—16:2	Poured on SEA—it becomes BLOOD—16:3	Poured on RIVERS and FOUNTAINS—like blood—16:4-7	Poured on SUN—men are scorched—16:8-9	Poured on Beast's throne—DARKNESS and PAIN—16:10-11	Poured on EUPHRATES—way of the KINGS of the East prepared—16:12	It is done! 16:17-21

ARMAGEDDON 198?

other than the "beast" of chapters thirteen and seventeen of Revelation. He wages war and kills thousands, while famine and death inevitably follow.

The fifth seal (that of martyrs) completes the picture of the beast's activities. This seal distinguishes between the death of the saints, who are viewed as beneath God's altar in heaven, and those who die in the previous seal, those who go to Hades.

Let us return again to the sequence in which these judgments are released. It is evident that the trumpet and bowl judgments were designed to be activated in parallel sequence. In other words, once the first trumpet has blown, the judgment instantly following would be the first bowl. When these first judgments had run their course, the second trumpet and bowl would occur, and so forth.

In the Seal, Trumpet and Bowl Chart, it should be noted that the time grid, comprising five seals, will run until the fleeting moments just before Armageddon. The sequence grids, composed of five trumpets and five bowls, will have an identical duration to the five seals. Therefore, as the time grid runs its course, the sequence grid, too, is keeping time respectively.

B. *The Initiator of the Judgments*

The seals represent satanic judgments through the medium of natural or earthly resources, while the trumpets and bowls depict divine judgments through the medium of supernatural resources. The seals (that is, the first five) are not, *per se*, divine judgments. The kingdom and administration of the antichrist is the theme of the five seals. Opposite this are the trumpets and bowls which act as heavenly judgments. It is significant to note too, that while the satanic judgments are zeroed in on the saints (cf. 12:13-17; 13:7), God's

The Great Holocaust

judgments have the beast's kingdom as their target (8:7-8, 10; 9:4, 15; 16:10).

C. *The Number of Satanic and Divine Judgments*

It is doubtlessly no accident that the number of divine judgments (ten) is exactly double the number of satanic judgments (five). In Revelation 18:6 God promised to double the judgments produced by the satanic Babylon system. How marvelously this is seen in God's geometric outline of these calamities.

NOTE: A thorough examination of the following charts will greatly aid the reader in grasping the chronological architecture presented in the above discussion.

THE GREAT TRIBULATION AND SUBSEQUENT PROPHECIES

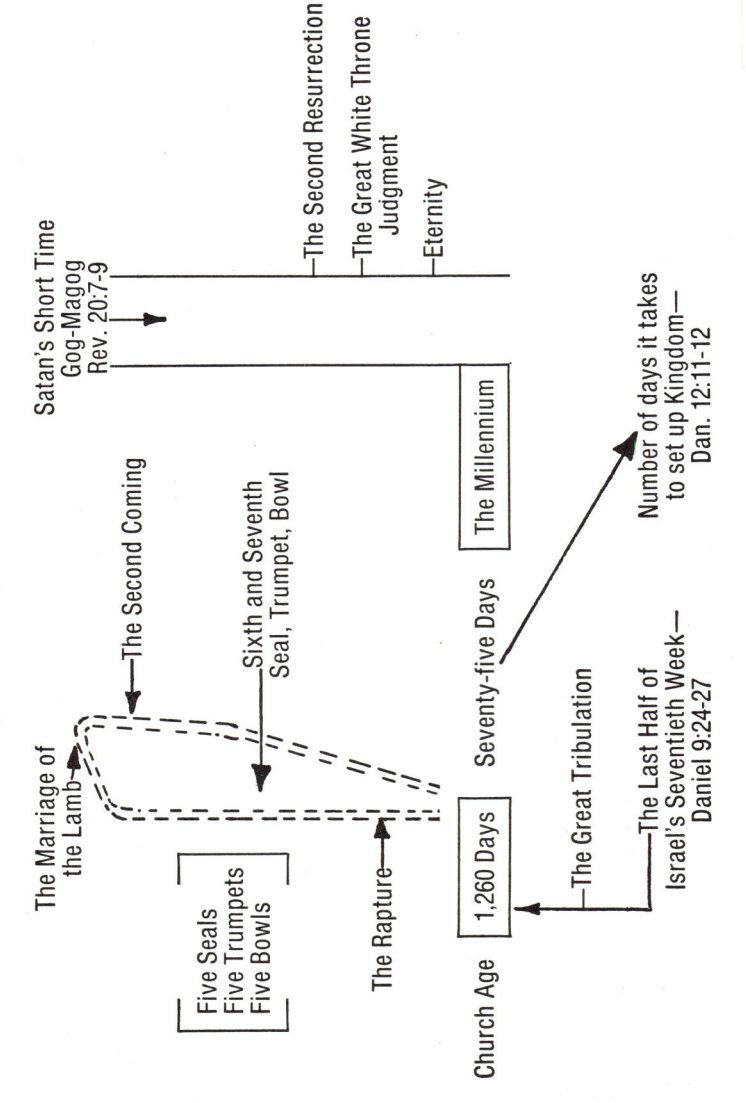

- The Marriage of the Lamb
- The Second Coming
- Sixth and Seventh Seal, Trumpet, Bowl
- Satan's Short Time — Gog-Magog Rev. 20:7-9
- The Second Resurrection
- The Great White Throne Judgment
- Eternity

Five Seals
Five Trumpets
Five Bowls

The Rapture

Church Age | 1,260 Days | Seventy-five Days | The Millennium

The Great Tribulation

The Last Half of Israel's Seventieth Week — Daniel 9:24-27

Number of days it takes to set up Kingdom — Dan. 12:11-12

242

THE CHRONOLOGICAL ARRANGEMENT OF REVELATION 6-22

1. Events Preceding the Great Tribulation
   A. The beast and the ten kingdoms with the harlot—17:1-6, 15, (18?)
2. Events Initiating the Great Tribulation
   A. The beast receives power from the ten kings—17:7-13, 17
   B. Mystery Babylon destroyed—17:16
   C. War in heaven; Satan cast to earth—12:1-17
   D. Beast enters temple and sets up abomination of desolation—11:1-2; 13:1-8
   E. The sealing of the 144,000—7:1-8
   F. Angelic preaching and announcements—14:6-13
3. Events of the Great Tribulation
   A. Introduction and execution of five seals, five trumpets and five bowls—6:1-11; 8:2-9:12; 11:14; 15:1-16:11
   B. The 144,000 are redeemed from earth—14:1-5
   C. The ministry of the two witnesses—11:3-13
   D. Execution of sixth seal, trumpet and bowl—6:12-17; 9:13-21; 16:12
   E. Announcement of Second Coming—10:1-7; 19:1-6
   F. First Resurrection—8:1(?); 14:14-16; 19:7-8; 20:4-6
   G. Armageddon—8:1(?); 11:15-19, 14:17-20; 16:13-16, 17-21; 17:14; 18:1-24; 19:11-21; 20:1-3
4. Events After the Tribulation
   A. Millennium and eternal state—7:9-17; 19:9-10; 21:1-22:5
   B. Satan's little time—20:11-15
   C. Great white throne judgment—20:11-15

INDEX TO THE CHRONOLOGICAL ARRANGEMENT OF REVELATION 6-22

6:1-11=3A	12:1-17=2C	17:15=1A
6:12-17=3B	13:1-18=2D	17:16=2B
7:1-8=2E	14:1-5=3B	17:17=2A
7:9-17=4A	14:6-13=2F	17:18=1A (?)
8:1=3F or 3G	14:14-16=3F	18:1-24=3G
8:2-9:12=3A	14:17-20=3G	19:1-6=3E
9:13-21=3C	15:1-16:11=3A	19:7-8=3F
10:1-7=3E	16:12=3D	19:9-10=4A
10:8-11=?	16:13-16=3G	19:11-21=3G
11:1-2=2D	16:17-21=3G	20:1-3=3G
11:3-13=3C	17:1-6=1A	20:4-6=3F
11:14=3A	17:7-13=2A	20:7-10=4B
11:15-19=3G	17:14=3G	20:11-15=4C
		21:1-22:5=4A

243

Appendix 5
The Rapture

The "blessed hope" of the Christian is that he or she will someday see the "appearing of the glory of our great God and Savior, Christ Jesus" (Titus 2:13). We are "awaiting eagerly the revelation of our Lord Jesus Christ" (1 Cor. 1:7). This is the aspiration of every spiritual saint—to "see His face" (Rev. 22:4).

The purpose of this chapter is to illuminate your understanding of the greatest hope that dwells in the hearts of all Christians—the Rapture. Read its contents carefully—especially since this momentous event may transpire in your own lifetime!

The Rapture Event
1. *Definition:* The term "rapture" is derived from the Latin *rapio* which means "to seize," "to transport" and "to snatch" so as to remove something or someone from one place to another. Although the exact word "rapture" does not appear in the Scriptures, its Greek equivalent is found in 1 Thess. 4:17. Here the word *harpagesometha* (from *harpazo*) is used and appropriately translated "caught up."

The verb *harpazo* appears thirteen times in the New Testament, of which four particular occurrences merit attention. In Acts, "the Spirit of the Lord *snatched* Philip *away*" (8:39); in 2 Cor., Paul was said to be "*caught up* to the third heaven . . . *caught up* into paradise" (12:2, 4); and in Revelation, the male child (Jesus Christ) was "*caught up* to God and to His throne" (12:5). These references make it clear that the rapture is a physical removal of the saints from the earth (see 1 Cor. 15:51-53; Rev. 20:4-6).

THE RAPTURE VISUALIZED

Christ comes with the saints.

Disembodied, but conscious, spirits or souls of saved.

Christ comes for the saints.

Saved

Lost

Saved

Lost

Once the body of a deceased saint reaches Christ, it will be united with its spirit or soul. Living believers, having body and spirit or soul intact, will be instantaneously translated to join the others.

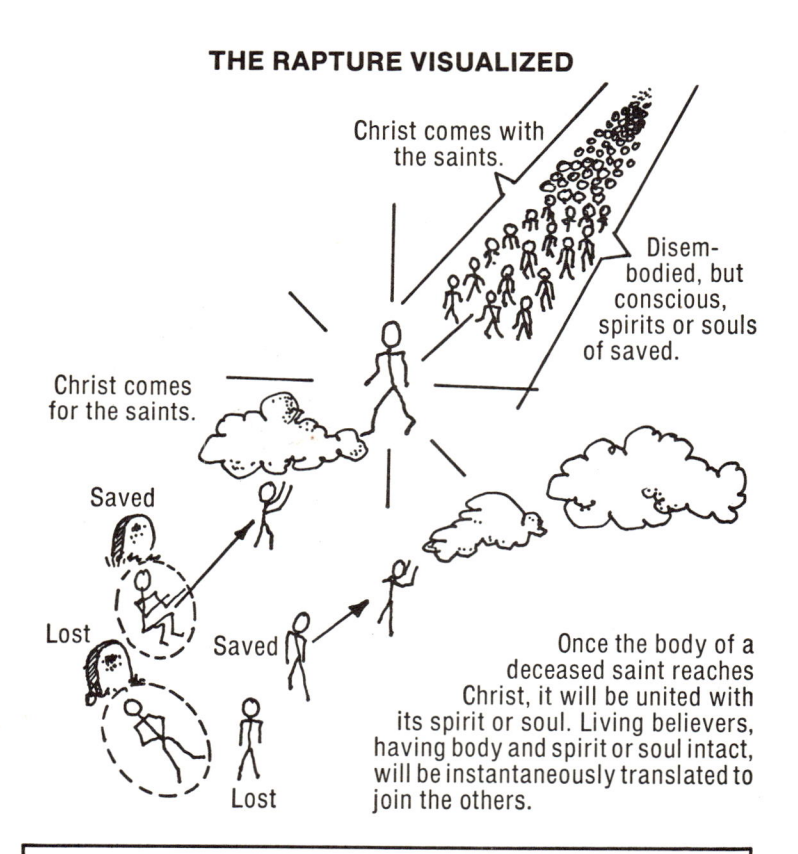

ORDER OF EVENTS:
1. Resurrection of deceased saint's body to unite with his spirit or soul, which God brings with Christ at His coming in the air.
2. Translation of living saints.
3. Marriage of the Lamb.
4. Descent to earth; the Second Coming.

This chart (along with the opening discussion on "The Rapture Event") is taken from the author's work entitled, *The Victor Bible Source Book* (Wheaton, Ill., Victor Books, p. 191-192).

The Rapture

2. *Sequence of Events:* Within the actual descent of Christ and the catching up of the saints, there are five progressive stages of development. The arrangement may be listed as follows:

a. The Lord himself will descend from heaven with a shout, the voice of the archangel and with the trumpet of God.

b. God will bring with Him (Jesus) those (disembodied, but conscious, spirits—2 Cor. 5:1-8; Phil. 1:21-23) who have fallen asleep in Jesus.

c. The dead (that is, the physical bodies of the dead) in Christ shall rise first.

d. Then we who are alive (at Christ's coming) shall be caught up together with them (the bodies of number three).

e. We shall meet the Lord in the air (1 Thess. 4:13-17).

3. *Description of the Raptured Body:* At the time of the Rapture the saints are given their new bodies. Eleven traits are discussed in the Scriptures regarding these new abodes. (We are assuming that the resurrected body of Jesus will be analogous to the believer's new body—1 John 3:2 with Rom. 8:29; 2 Pet. 1:4).

a. They will be able to pass through solid objects—John 20:19-20.

b. They will retain a semblance of the earthly body—John 20:26-28.

c. They will be capable of eating food—John 21:12-14; Rev. 19:9.

d. They will have flesh and bones (obviously different from our present flesh and bones)—Luke 24:39.

e. They will vary in their glory; that is, the extent to which they will shine—Dan. 12:2-3; 1 Cor. 15:40-42a.

f. They will be incorruptible; hence, they cannot sin

ARMAGEDDON 198?

or be affected by disease—1 Cor. 15:42b, 53-54.
  g. They will possess power; therefore, they will never tire or need rest—1 Cor. 15:43; cf. Rev. 22:5.
  h. They will be spiritual bodies—1 Cor. 15:44-49; 2 Cor. 5:1-4.
  i. They will be immortal; they will never die—1 Cor. 15:51-57.
  j. They will not be given in marriage—Matt. 22:30.
  k. They will be given a mind that has no remembrance of earth, but instead, this mind will think God's very thoughts after Him—Isa. 65:17; Rev. 3:12; 22:4. Paul states it in this fashion: "Then I shall know fully just as I also have been fully known"—1 Cor. 13:12!

Difficulties in Chronology

The subject of Christ's return and appearing is most magnificent, but it is regrettably marred with confusion as to the time of His manifestation. Essentially, the debate centers around the relationship of the Rapture to the tribulation period. There are no less than five positions on this critical issue.[1]

1. *Pretribulationalism:* The pretribulationalists view the Second Coming of Christ as a twofold event. The first aspect of His return is secret, and it focuses only upon the rapturing of the Church *before* the period of the Tribulation. This coming is only in the air. The

---

[1] The five views discussed in this chapter all pertain specifically to the premillennial interpretation. The postmillennialists and amillennialists basically hold to an indefinite period of tribulation which is to occur immediately prior to Christ's Second Advent. They identify the Rapture as the single, great resurrection from the dead—which transpires with the Second Coming. These interpreters closely approximate the post- and past-tribulational views.

The Rapture

second phase of His coming, this time to the earth, occurs seven years later and focuses upon Armageddon, multiple judgments, and setting up the millennial kingdom. The following basic arguments are used to support this position:

    a. *Imminence:* The early church believed that not a single intervening event must occur in order for Christ to return and rapture the believer to be with himself (John 14:2-3; Acts 1:11; 1 Cor. 1:7; 15:51-52; Phil. 3:20-21; Col. 3:4; 1 Thess. 1:9-10; 4:16-17; 5:5-9; 1 Tim. 6:14; Titus 2:13; James 5:8-9; Rev. 3:10; 22:17-22).

    b. *Israel Is not the Church:* The Church, according to pretribulationists, is a distinct elect body, separate from Israel and from saints in general. The term "Church" applies to only the saints of this present dispensation—from Pentecost up to the start of Israel's seventieth week. As such, the Church is a "mystery" (or parenthesis in God's economy) not revealed in the Old Testament (Eph. 3:1-7; Rom. 16:25-27; Col. 1:26-29). Therefore, in order for God to deal with Israel in her seventieth week, He must first remove the Church, with whom He now deals.

    c. *Absence of Church in Tribulation:* None of the Old or New Testament passages on the tribulation period mention the Church; hence, she cannot go through this period (Deut. 4:29-30; Jer. 30:4-11; Dan. 9:24-27; 12:1-2; Matt. 24:15-31; 1 Thess. 1:9-10; 5:4-9).

    d. *Removal of Holy Spirit:* The Holy Spirit, as the restrainer of evil in the world, cannot be taken out of the world unless the Church (which the Spirit indwells) is removed at the same time (2 Thess. 2:1-12). Thus, where the Spirit presumably goes, the Church goes too.

    e. *The Departure:* Paul teaches that "the falling away" (that is, "the departure" or the pretribulational

Rapture) must occur first, before the Tribulation (2 Thess. 2:3).

2. *Partial Rapture:* The followers of this particular view hold that only a prepared and expectant section of believers will be raptured *before* the tribulation period, while the remainder will be caught up at the end of Israel's seventieth week (see Luke 21:36; 1 Cor. 15:23; Phil. 3:11, 20; Titus 2:13; 1 Thess. 1:10; 2 Tim. 4:8; Heb. 9:28).

3. *Midtribulationalism:* The proponents of this position hold that Christ will not return for His Church until midway through Israel's seventieth week, between the second and third woes of John's Apocalypse (11:3-14). Like pretribulationalists and partial rapturists, they too, hold that the Second Coming has two distinct phases. Their proofs may be stated as follows:

a. *Last Trumpet:* The last trumpet of Paul and the seventh trumpet of Revelation are identical (1 Cor. 15:52; 1 Thess. 4:16; Rev. 11:15). That this trumpet is blown in the midst of the Tribulation is supposedly clear, due to its location in the Revelation. (Chapter 11 is in the middle of Revelation's twenty-two chapters.)

b. *The Great Tribulation:* This occurs, they say, only in the latter half of Israel's seventieth week (Rev. 11:2-3; 12:6, 14). The first section of the seventieth week is only the "beginning of sorrows," which the Church is said to suffer (Matt. 24:3-12).

c. *Two Witnesses:* The resurrection of the two witnesses (symbols interpreted as being all Old and New Testament saints) is a picture of the Rapture of the Church (Rev. 11:3-13).

d. *Imminence:* The Scriptures do not teach immi-

The Rapture

nence (Mark 16:15; John 21:18-19; Acts 22:21; 2 Thess. 2:3; 2 Tim. 3:1; Rev. 2-3).

4. *Potential Past-Tribulation:* This position asserts the possibility that the Tribulation (a period of trial immediately before the Lord's second advent but distinct from Israel's seventieth week, which is held to be already past) is potentially already completed. This unique view is an attempt to maintain the doctrine of imminence and still hold to a period of tribulation of indefinite duration and indiscernible occurrences.

5. *Posttribulationalism:* This body of interpreters believes that the Second Coming and the Rapture constitute a single event—*after* the tribulation period. They subscribe to the following:

a. *History:* The apostles saw the Rapture and second advent as one unit. Pretribulationalism, and all the other positions, are new doctrines, arising in the last hundred years or so. The oldest, and most honored, position throughout church history has held to this point of view.

b. *Imminence:* The command to watch for Christ's coming could only have relevance for tribulational saints. Hence, the Scriptures do not teach imminence (Matt. 24:32, 42-43, 50; 25:13ff.; Mark 13:28, 33-37; Luke 12:36, 37, 39, 46; 19:11-27; 21:28-36; John 21:18-19; Acts 3:21; 1 Thess. 5:6, 8, 10; Heb. 10:25; James 5:7; 1 Pet. 1:13; 4:7; 2 Pet. 3:12-14; Rev. 16:15).

c. *Church and Israel Are Same:* There is no distinction in the election of Old and New Testament saints. Both share as one in the single body of Christ (Gen. 12:3; Isa. 44:5; 54:1; 60:3-4; Ezek. 47:22; Hos. 1:10; 2:23; Mic. 5:3; Zech. 2:11; John 10:16; Acts 7:38; Rom. 9:6,

24-26; 11:11-24; 1 Cor. 10:16-18; Gal. 3:7, 9, 16, 29; 4:26-28; 6:16; Eph. 2:11-36; Phil. 3:21; James 1:1; 1 Pet. 2:9). Therefore, there is no need to remove the Church so that God may deal with Israel.

    d. *First Resurrection:* The Rapture of the Church and the first resurrection are the same event. Therefore, the resurrection of all Old Testament saints and New Testament saints occurs together (Isa. 24:16-25:9; Dan. 12:1-3; John 6:39, 40, 44-54; 11:24; 1 Cor. 15:21-26; Rev. 14:14-16; 20:4-6).

    e. *Wheat and Tares:* In this parable Jesus taught that the wheat (believers) and tares (unbelievers) must grow together until the end of the age, that is, until the second advent (Matt. 13:24-30, 36-43). There is no pretribulational or partial rapture notion in this passage.

    f. *Great Commission:* Jesus commissioned His disciples (the Church) to go into all the world. He then promised His presence would be with them until the consummation of the age, not just up to the time of the Rapture (Matt. 28:19-20).

    g. *Parousia, Apocalypse and Epiphaneia:* These three interchangeable and overlapping Greek words respectively speak of Christ's "bodily presence," "appearance" and "glorious display." Invariably these terms express a visible and single return of Christ.

Summary: Each of the above positions are held by biblical scholars who love the Lord Jesus Christ and who seek only to properly interpret the Scriptures. Doubtlessly, the intent of each proponent is to inform, comfort and edify the body of Christ. Therefore, regardless of the personal appeal of any one specific interpretation, let each child of God hold his own position with firm convictions but also with an equal

DIAGRAMS OF THE FIVE RAPTURE POSITIONS

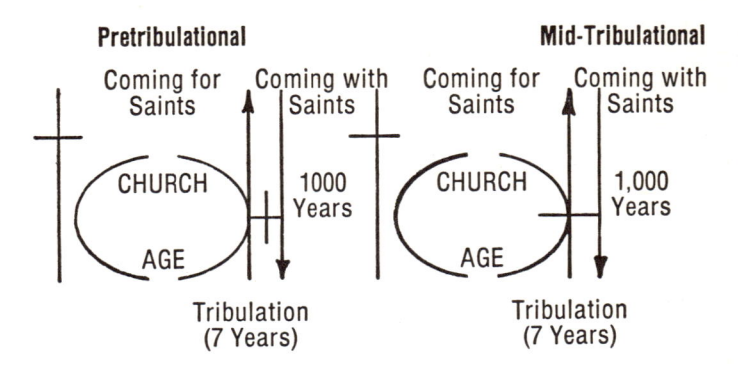

Pretribulational

Coming for Saints | Coming with Saints

CHURCH AGE — 1000 Years

Tribulation (7 Years)

Mid-Tribulational

Coming for Saints | Coming with Saints

CHURCH AGE — 1,000 Years

Tribulation (7 Years)

Post-tribulational

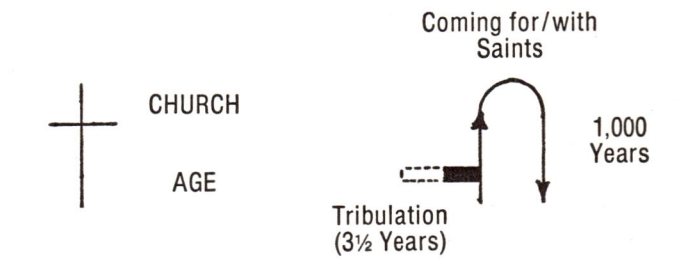

Coming for/with Saints

CHURCH AGE — 1,000 Years

Tribulation (3½ Years)

Partial Rapture

Rapture of Prepared

CHURCH AGE — 1,000 Years

Tribulation (7 Years)

Past-tribulational

Rapture of All Second Coming | First Resurrection Second Coming

CHURCH AGE — 1,000 Years

Tribulation (Indefinite)

This chart was taken from the author's work entitled, The Victor Bible Source Book (Wheaton, Ill., Victor Books, p. 193).

ARMAGEDDON 198?

humility. Christian unity does not depend upon our unanimity to the "proper" succession of eschatological events!

The position of this author is the last one discussed—posttribulationalism. Here are a few more details favoring this position that need our careful eye.

Key Words for the Lord's Coming:
1. *Parousia:* This word is translated in two ways in the Authorized Version—*coming* and *presence*. It is used of men (1 Cor. 16:17; 2 Cor. 7:6-7; 10:10; Phil. 1:26; 2:12), of the antichrist (2 Thess. 2:9), and of Christ (Matt. 24:3, 27, 39; 1 Cor. 15:23; 1 Thess. 2:19; 3:13; 4:15; 5:23; 2 Thess. 2:1, 8; James 5:7-8; 2 Pet. 1:16; 3:4, 12; 1 John 2:28). In every case the word means *bodily presence, arrival, appearance.*

Parousia was a technical word for the visit of a ruler or high official—especially of kings and emperors—to a certain province. How beautifully this matches with the Second Coming of Christ!

Nowhere in biblical literature does this word mean anything other than a visible, bodily appearance. The idea of secretiveness is not to be found in the defining of this word.

2. *Apocalypse:* The Authorized Version translates this word as *lighten* (Luke 2:32), *manifestation* (Rom. 8:19), *appearing* (1 Pet. 1:7), *revealed* (2 Thess. 1:7; 1 Pet. 4:13), *coming* (1 Cor. 1:7) and *revelation* (Rom. 2:5; 16:25; 1 Cor. 14:6, 26; 2 Cor. 12:1, 7; Gal. 1:12, 2:2; Eph. 1:17; 3:3; 1 Pet. 1:13; and Rev. 1:1). This word refers to our Lord's return five times in the New Testament—1 Cor. 1:7; 2 Thess. 1:7; 1 Pet. 1:7, 13; 4:13.

Apocalypse is the combination of two Greek words—*apo*, meaning "off" or "away from," and *kalupsis*,

The Rapture

meaning "to cover, hide, conceal" and "veil." When these two words are put together, the meaning becomes *to reveal, uncover, to be plainly signified* and *to be manifested.*

When Paul says the Corinthian church was "waiting eagerly for the revelation of our Lord Jesus Christ," he means they were actually waiting for His visible manifestation.

Paul uses the same word in telling the Thessalonians that "when the Lord Jesus shall be revealed from heaven with His mighty angels in flaming fire [He will deal out] retribution to those who do not know God and to those who do not obey the gospel of our Lord Jesus" (2 Thess. 1:7-8). Again this is a plain reference to the Second Coming of Christ.

Peter is equally persuasive in presenting the Rapture and the *apocalypse* together. He writes: "You have been distressed by various trials, that the proof of your faith, being more precious than gold which is perishable, even though tested by fire, may be found to result in praise and glory and honor at the revelation [*apocalypse*] of Jesus Christ" (1 Pet. 1:6-7).

"Therefore, gird your minds for action, keep sober in spirit, fix your hope completely on the grace to be brought to you at the revelation [*apocalypse*] of Jesus Christ" (1 Pet. 1:13).

"To the degree that you share the sufferings of Christ, keep on rejoicing; so that also at the revelation of His glory you may rejoice with exultation" (1 Pet. 4:13).

Three times Peter teaches that the Christian's testing will end with the *apocalypse* of Christ. If the use of this word is consistent (between Paul and Peter), then we can safely conclude that the *apocalypse* is another

ARMAGEDDON 198?

word for the Rapture and Second Coming. There is no evidence to support another conclusion.

3. *Epiphaneia:* This word is only used of the Lord's appearing (2 Thess. 2:8; 1 Tim. 6:14; 2 Tim. 1:10; 4:1, 8; Titus 2:13). It means *glorious display, outshining, appearance* and *manifestation.* A most casual glance at these verses will reveal that the Second Coming is always in view. One verse will serve as our illustration.

"And then that lawless one will be revealed whom the Lord will slay with the breath of His mouth and bring to an end by the appearance of His coming" (*epiphaneia*—2 Thess. 2:8).

Summary of the Word Study: It is necessary to understand one crucial point. Each of the above words are interchangeable and overlapping. It is impossible to separate His "coming" (*apocalypse*) from His "bodily presence" (*parousia*) and His "outshining" (*epiphaneia*).

Pretribulationalists are agreed that each of these words is used in reference to the Second Advent. Their contention is, however, that the literal fulfillment of these words will not occur at the Rapture, but only at the Second Coming. Such an interpretation is inconsistent with biblical usage, and serves to present more problems than it solves.

Appendix 6
The Kingdom of God

The central message of the Bible can be stated in four simple words: "the kingdom of God." From beginning to end this is the paramount theme of both testaments. It knows no close rival. Its importance is unsurpassed.

Oddly enough, however, this subject has been terribly abused through neglect. Too few in the church today possess a clear concept of the kingdom of God. Preaching, unfortunately, more often than not, has passed over this indispensable topic. Such an important matter must not be treated lightly.

Here then is a brief capsulization of the chief ideas entailed in the message of the kingdom of God.

The Kingdom Is Explained

The chief idea behind the word "kingdom" is a body of people who share some common bond. The words "of God" identify the nature of that common bond. Put simply, the kingdom of God is comprised of people who submit to God, making Him their King.[1]

From the start of creation the design was fixed. God sought to be man's King. From this position He would direct our lives, bringing to them the intended fulfillment for which they were created. In this relationship

---

[1] The exacting details of the biblical usage for "the kingdom of God" are quite complex. Actually, it refers to the sphere of God's rule, which embraces all of creation (Dan. 4:25, 35; Luke 1:52; Rom. 13:1-2). In our study here, however, we will only explore those areas where the kingdom relates specifically to the believer, the loyal subject in God's kingdom.

ARMAGEDDON 198?

God was to be honored and obeyed, while mankind was to be rewarded and satisfied.

The only snag in the system is man's free will. God's reign is not coercive. He will not compel His subjects to submit to His kingship. That, naturally, left the first couple, Adam and Eve, along with all of their descendants, free to choose if they wanted God to be their King, or if they wanted to rule themselves. The tragic choice is all too evident. Adam and Eve resisted. They went their own way. They, in effect, dethroned God from their lives and set themselves upon this throne instead.

The effects of this original decision remain with us to this very day. Men, women, children and even complete countries have chosen to rule themselves. They want nothing to do with God's kingship or His kingdom. They seek independence and freedom. Unfortunately, however, such persons fail to recognize that an allegiance to Him is the only source for true and lasting liberty!

After the choice of Adam and Eve to rule themselves, God renewed His kingdom offer, though in a different format. They were given another chance, along with their descendants, to join His kingdom. The offer was gracious—free entrance and free provisions, but you must be willing to live by the rules of the King. Nothing could be more fair or just. Still, while a handful accepted the offer, many either doubted its claims or scoffed at its declared consequences.

Today—right now—the kingdom pledges are still in effect. They operate as they have always operated. God offers membership in His kingdom, in which Jesus Christ is the reigning authority, and we either elect to join His nation and live by His rules, or we elect to rule

The Kingdom of God

ourselves and reap the consequences of being an enemy of God's kingdom.

There is no middle ground. We are either inside or outside the kingdom. Either Jesus Christ is our personal King, or we ourselves are the king of our lives. There can be no dual kingship in our hearts. We must choose who will be number one—us or Him.

The Kingdom Is Exposed

Although the exact phrase, "kingdom of God," does not appear in any text of the Old Testament, the concept is central to its day-to-day life and to its eschatology. Often God is seen as King of Israel (Exod. 15:18; Deut. 33:5; Isa. 41:21; 43:15; 44:6; Mal. 1:14), yet the Scriptures speak of a period when He will yet become the King of His people, in an earthly kingship (Isa. 24:23; 33:22; 52:7; Zeph. 3:15; Zech. 14:9). The throne for this reign is David's (2 Sam. 7:5-17; Ps. 89:35-49; Jer. 33:25-26; Zech. 12:8-10), and the one seated upon it is the Son of Man (Dan. 7:13-14). It is this earthly kingdom which Israel anxiously anticipated.

After the close of the book of Malachi in the Old Testament, the prophetic voice of God was silent in Israel for nearly 400 years. Then arose a man who was to initiate the message of the kingdom of God again—he was John the Baptist. Behind him lay the Law and the prophets; before him was the Son of Man. John was a forerunner. He was God's tool for paving the path on which this King would tread (Isa. 40:3; Mal. 3:1; Mark 1:2-3).

John taught that the Messiah, God's King, was alive and ready to establish His kingdom. And when he had baptized Jesus, he boldly announced it was this man who would serve Israel as her King (Matt. 3:1-17; John 1:15-37; 3:22-30).

With the advent of the Son of Man, Israel saw her worries as abruptly ending and her enemies being forever overthrown. It did not, however, happen the way they planned or dreamed. Jesus only continued where John left off—preaching, "The time is fulfilled, and the kingdom of God is at hand; repent and believe in the gospel" (Mark 1:15).

This approach certainly differed from Israel's radical expectations. What did Jesus mean by this unexpected announcement? Why did He preach, rather than merely organize an army and overthrow Israel's enemies? How were the Jews, and we today, to understand Jesus' teaching regarding the kingdom of God?

Let's observe seven matters in Jesus' concept of the kingdom of God:

1. Jesus taught that the kingdom of God was "at hand" (Mark 1:15). The Greek term employed here is in the verbal tense called the consummative perfect, indicating a completed action without reference to culminating results. Therefore, the kingdom of God was present and ready to be set up, *if* Israel would "repent and believe in the gospel." In other words, the establishment of God's kingdom hinged upon obedience to the King. There would only be a kingdom for those who truly repent and follow the message of Jesus.

2. Jesus taught that the kingdom's presence could be proven by His power over Satan (Matt. 12:28; cf. John 12:31; Rev. 12:10). Jesus came as Israel's King for the express purpose of destroying the kingdom and works of the devil (Gen. 3:15; Heb. 2:14; 1 John 3:8), of binding this strong man (Isa. 49:24-25; Matt. 12:29) and of

The Kingdom of God

taking away all his armor (Luke 11:21-22). Stated differently, God's kingdom was to be fundamentally spiritual, touching the hearts of people and uprooting the hold Satan possessed over people. Unfortunately the people hated the Roman tyranny more than Satan's bondage. They were missing the point of God's kingdom.

3. Although the kingdom of God has always been present in the world, spiritually (as noted above), it is still to come to earth in a more direct and physical dimension. This latter phase was to be prayed for (Matt. 6:10), sought (Matt. 6:33) and waited for (Mark 15:43). Jesus taught that this ultimate aspect of the kingdom would be inherited by the poor in spirit (Matt. 5:3; Luke 6:20), by those persecuted for the sake of righteousness (Matt. 5:10), by those who were righteous (Matt. 5:20; cf. 7:21; 21:31), converted (Matt. 18:3) and born again (John 3:3, 5). Although the kingdom of God was more present (or "at hand") than ever before, it still wasn't fully present. This would occur only if Israel would repent of her many sins. Therefore, its fullest manifestation was still to be sought through prayer and holy living.

4. Jesus made it plain that the kingdom of God would be taken away from national Israel and given to a nation (the Church—1 Pet. 2:9) who would produce its appropriate fruit (Matt. 21:33-43; 22:2-14; 23:13; 25:1-13). The time of its removal probably came at the period of Christ's Crucifixion (Dan. 9:26b, 27b). Temporarily, then, national Israel is to be judged and withheld the full offer of the political Davidic Messiah. This suspension will continue until the time of Christ's Second Coming (Zech. 12:10-13:1; Acts 1:6; Rom. 11:1-29). It must also be stated that this momentary cessation of the fuller kingdom offer, however, does

ARMAGEDDON 198?

not exclude them from God's spiritual kingdom offer (that is, salvation). Israel can still accept God's "mystery" kingdom (Acts 2:22f.; 3:12f.; 5:12-14, 17-32; 6:7f.; 9:15; etc).

5. The kingdom which Jesus announced was a "mystery" (Matt. 13:11). That is, Jesus' contemporaries held views about the kingdom that were not in full agreement with the ultimate divine plan. That gave Jesus' teaching the appearance of a mystery. The Jews waited for a political kingdom from God, but Jesus seemed to offer them only a spiritual one (John 18:36-37; cf. Acts 15:14-19; Col. 1:13; 1 Tim. 4:16; 2 Pet. 1:11; Rev. 1:5). The political kingdom would only follow the acceptance of the spiritual kingdom. God is interested in governments, but his primary interest is in people's hearts and eternal destinies. The spiritual is more crucial than the physical. And God determined there would be no earthly kingdom if there were no major acceptance of his spiritual kingdom first. As a result, the kingdom offer was a "mystery" to the closed minds of Israel.

6. Jesus announced that certain ones among His contemporaries would not taste death until they saw the Son of man coming in His kingdom (Matt. 16:28; Mark 9:1; Luke 9:27). This appears to be a dual reference to Christ's transfiguration (Matt. 17:1-8 with 2 Pet. 1:16-18) and to the destruction of Jerusalem in A.D. 70 (Luke 21:5-24). Doubtlessly there were those who questioned the reality or meaning of Jesus' statements regarding His message of the kingdom of God. So, He told them that they themselves would see the proof of His declarations. Before their death they would see His kingship. And so they did, in His Transfiguration and in the judgment of Jerusalem.

The Kingdom of God

7. The "mystery" form of the kingdom of God will come to a climax at the end of the age, in the Son of man's return to judge the nations (Matt. 25:31-46). At this point God's kingdom will become earth-centered and Israel-centered. The political promises and expectations will then be fulfilled with an exacting accuracy (see details of this kingdom stage below).

When all the eschatological dust has settled, it becomes evident that Jesus came to earth, and is returning to earth, for three fundamental reasons, as noted in the following self-explanatory diagram.

The Kingdom Is Enthroned

Finally the earthly phase of the kingdom of God will come. This does not imply that Jesus has not been King of kings prior to this period, for indeed He has been since His Transfiguration (Matt. 28:18; Mark 9:1-13; 2 Pet. 1:15-18; Rev. 1:5; etc.). But His direct and mandatory rule will now be enforced—both visibly and absolutely.

In the garden of Eden we saw the inauguration of this earthly kingdom. But with the entrance of sin, we soon see its removal from the earth. From that time to this, the kingdom of God has been basically spiritual in nature. At the time of Jesus' return, however, God's manner of dealing with people on earth will return to the original garden state. Some day, possibly sooner than we imagine, Jesus will return and set up His earthly kingdom.

Here are the thirteen major facets that constitute this rich future period, commonly called "The Millennium" because of its 1,000-year duration (Rev. 20:1-6; 1 Cor. 15:20-28).

1. For a thousand years Satan and his demons will

WHY JESUS CAME AND IS RETURNING

(1) To Save the World	(2) To Sit on David's Throne	(3) To Establish the Mystery Kingdom
A. Bring salvation—Matt. 1:21; John 3:16-17 B. Bring light to Gentiles—Matt. 12:18-21; Luke 2:32 C. Remove sin—John 1:29. D. Save world—John 5:35 E. Give life as a ransom—Matt. 20:28 F. Give abundant life—John 10:10 G. Destroy Satan's works—Heb. 2:14; 1 John 3:8 H. Fulfill Law and prophets—Matt. 5:17-18	A. Receive David's throne—Luke 1:32, 67-79 B. Be King of Jews—Matt. 2:2, 6 C. Deliver Jerusalem—Luke 2:38 D. Fulfill Law and Prophets—Matt. 5:17-18	A. Present "mystery" kingdom—Matt. 13:1-50; cf. Luke 4:18-19; John 4:42; Eph. 2-3 B. Set up Church—Matt. 16:13-20 C. Fulfill Law and prophets—Matt. 5:17-18; cf. Acts 15:14-19

The Kingdom of God

be bound in the abyss (Isa. 24:21-22; Rev. 20:1-3).

2. Jesus Christ will rule all the earth as King of kings and Lord of lords (Ps. 2:2-8; 67:4; 72:9-11; 82:8; 89:21-25, 27; 96:13; 98:9; 110:1-2; Isa. 2:4; 9:7a; 25:3; 27:5; 45:23-24; 49:7; 51:5; 52:13; 55:4; 66:18; Dan. 2:35, 44-45; 7:9-14, 25-27; Obad. 21; Mic. 4:3; 5:4; 7:15-17; Zech. 14:9; Luke 1:32; 20:43; 22:29; Acts 2:35; 3:21; 1 Cor. 15:24-28; Eph. 1:21; 2 Tim. 4:1; Heb. 1:13; 10:13; Rev. 10:5-7; 11:15-17; 12:5; 19:6-16).

3. All those entering the Millennium will be saved and experience the fulness of the Spirit (Deut. 30:8; Isa. 4:3-4; 32:1-5; Ezek. 36:27-28; Jer. 31:31-34; Joel 2:28-29; Zeph. 3:10-13; Zech. 8:3, 8; 13:1-6; 14:20-21).

4. Children will be born to those inhabiting the earth. They will be like children born today with these two exceptions: First, they will be raised in a perfect environment, permitting them an everlasting longevity, if they choose to follow Christ. Secondly, should they rebel, after the age of 100 years, they will be put to death (Isa. 65:20-23; Jer. 31:29-30; Ezek. 47:22; Rev. 2:26-27).

5. The earth will be filled with the knowledge of God (Isa. 11:9; Hab. 2:14).

6. Israel will serve as the world's capital. All nations refusing to serve her will be punished (Isa. 4:4-6; 60:11-12; Jer. 3:17; 31:35-39; Ezek. 48:35; Joel 3:17; Zeph. 3:15, 17; Zech. 8:3; 14:16-19).

7. Joy and praise will cover the earth (Isa. 12:3-6; 25:8-9; Zeph. 3:14; Jude 24).

8. Peace will fill the earth (Isa. 2:4; 9:5, 7; 11:13; 26:12; 54:14; 60:18; Jer. 23:6; 30:8; 33:16; Hos. 2:18; Joel 2:26-27; 3:17; Zeph. 3:13-20).

9. All sickness will vanish (Isa. 29:17-19; 33:24; 35:5; Jer. 31:8-9; Zeph. 3:19).

ARMAGEDDON 198?

10. Men will work, and their toil will produce a full reward (Isa. 4:2; 61:4; 62:8-9; 65:21-23; Ezek. 34:26-29; Hos. 2:21-22; Joel 3:18; Amos 9:13-14).

11. There will be a temple, and sacrifices (spiritual or praise sacrifices) will be offered in Jerusalem (Ezek. 37:26-28; 40-48; Jer. 33:18, 21, 22; Zech. 14:20-21; Mal. 3:3-4; Rev. 21:1-22:5).

12. It is my opinion that all of the above details spell out the establishment of the "new heaven and earth" (Isa. 65:17; 66:22; 2 Pet. 3:13; Rev. 21:1). Not all Bible students are agreed on the precise timing for the appearance of this new order. Some believe it will appear after the Millennium and the great white throne judgment. Others believe it will appear at the beginning of the Millennium.

Those who hold that the new heaven and earth begin after the Millennium see Rev. 21:1-8 as transpiring after 1,000 years and 21:9-22:5 as millennial. The latter group takes Rev. 21:1-22:5 as referring both to the Millennium and eternity thereafter.

There is little reason to believe that the millennial reign of Christ is to be distinguished from the new heaven and earth. The only difference between the millennial kingdom and the kingdom after the great white throne, will be the removal of all sinners (Rev. 20:11-15), and Jesus' giving the kingdom back to His Father (1 Cor. 15:24-28).

13. At the close of the thousand years, the abyss will be opened. Coming forth from this pit will be Satan and his demons, who go forth to deceive the nations which are in the four corners of the earth (Rev. 20:7-10). Amazingly, an army shall be gathered, the number of which is contrasted to the sand of the sea. This army will then march to Jerusalem and surround the

The Kingdom of God

holy city. Next, God will cause fire to fall from heaven upon this hostile band, and they will all be devoured. This fatal conflict will end all warring, personal or otherwise, for all time!

The purpose of the Millennium is at least twofold: First, it fulfills the prophecies of an earthly kingdom. Second, it proves that people who go to hell will go there because of their own sinful ways and not because the devil made them do it!

The Kingdom Is Exclusive

The judgment of all lost men, from the time of Adam through Gog and Magog, will take place at the great white throne (Rev. 20:11-15). The second resurrection will bring all the guilty to this awesome day of eternal vindication. (It is probable that the fallen angels will be judged here also—Gen. 3:15; Matt. 8:29; 1 Cor. 6:3; 2 Pet. 2:4.)

The location of this judgment will neither be in heaven nor on earth. The unsaved are not qualified for either abode. They will make their home in hell—the second death.

The sole purpose of this judgment is to determine one's level of eternal punishment. The Book of Life will be opened to prove the absence of their names. The books of works will be opened to determine the degrees of their punishments.

The Kingdom Is Everlasting

Who will inherit the earth after the great white throne judgment? The difficulty involved within this question focuses around the subjects of the great white throne judgment. Some writers (especially amillennialists and postmillennialists) see this judgment as

ARMAGEDDON 198?

involving all of mankind, regenerate and unregenerate, since the creation of Adam. Such a position does not distinguish between this judgment and the judgments associated with the Second Coming of Christ (the judgment seat of Christ—for all the saved, and the judgment of the nations and Israel—to see who enters the Millennium). This view presents several insurmountable problems:

1. The rewarding of the saints is always and only identified with Christ's Second Coming (Luke 14:14; 1 Cor. 4:5; Rev. 11:18; 22:12).

2. The judgment seat of Christ is never considered as a judicial bench, but invariably a reward seat for believers (2 Cor. 5:10; cf. 1 Cor. 3:10-15).

3. Matthew distinctly states that "when the Son of Man comes... He will sit on His glorious throne. And all the nations will be gathered before Him; and He will separate them from one another" (Matt. 25:31-32). There is no hint that any telescoping is taking place here. This judgment is clearly *not* before the great white throne judgment, yet its subjects, like those at the great white throne, are cast into the eternal fire (25:41, 46).

4. The subjects of the great white throne judgment are specifically stated as being those who dwell in "death and Hades," the abode of the unrighteous dead (Rev. 20:13; cf. 6:8 with 6:9). For this reason all the participants are cast into the lake of fire (Rev. 20:14). There is no explicit statement that a single saved person will stand at this bar.

5. The location of the great white throne judgment is neither in heaven nor on the earth, for no place was found for them (Rev. 20:11). The judgment of the saints and the nations, however, is clearly upon the earth.

The Kingdom of God

Therefore, it seems safe to say that only the regenerate will enter the Millennium, during which they will bear children in a perfect heaven and earth. The close of this epoch will result in a great rebellion headed by Satan. Following this brief revolt, all the spiritually dead will be resurrected, judged at the great white throne and cast into their appropriate levels of hell.

But what happens to the righteous who entered the Millennium, or to those who were born therein and remained faithful to Christ in the period of rebellion? The solution to this dilemma seems to be as follows: There will always be nations on the earth, over whom the saints will reign "forever" (Rev. 22:5; cf. Isa. 66:22; Matt. 25:34, 46; Rev. 21:24-27; 22:2).

We will be pleased to provide locations of bookstores in your area selling Logos titles.

Call: (201) 754-0745

Ask for bookstore information service